MY PARENTS

ALSO BY ALEKSANDAR HEMON

FICTION

The Making of Zombie Wars
Love and Obstacles
The Lazarus Project
Nowhere Man
The Question of Bruno

NONFICTION

The Book of My Lives

MY PARENTS

ALEKSANDAR HEMON

HAMISH HAMILTON
an imprint of Penguin Canada, a division of Penguin Random House Canada Limited

Canada • USA • UK • Ireland • Australia • New Zealand • India • South Africa • China

Published in Hamish Hamilton hardcover by Penguin Canada, 2019
Simultaneously published in the United States by MCD, Farrar, Straus and Giroux,
120 Broadway, New York 10271

www.penguinrandomhouse.ca

LIBRARY AND ARCHIVES CANADA CATALOGUING IN PUBLICATION

Title: My parents ; This does not belong to you / Aleksandar Hemon.
Other titles: This does not belong to you
Names: Hemon, Aleksandar, 1964- author. | Hemon, Aleksandar, 1964- My parents. |
Hemon, Aleksandar,
1964- This does not belong to you.
Description: Two separate works. | Title from distinctive title pages.
Identifiers: Canadiana (print) 20190044047 | Canadiana (ebook) 20190044055
| ISBN 9780735238381
(hardcover) | ISBN 9780735238398 (PDF)
Subjects: LCSH: Hemon, Aleksandar, 1964-—Family. | CSH: Bosnian Canadians—
Biography | LCSH: Yugoslav
War, 1991-1995—Refugees—Bosnia and Herzegovina—Biography. | LCSH:
Refugees—Canada—Biography. |
LCSH: Sarajevo (Bosnia and Herzegovina)—History—Siege, 1992-1996. | LCSH:
Sarajevo (Bosnia and
Herzegovina)—Biography. | LCGFT: Biographies.
Classification: LCC FC106.B68 Z6 2019 | DDC 971/.004918390092—dc23

Book design by Abby Kagan
Cover design by Terri Nimmo
Cover images courtesy of the author

Printed and bound in Canada

10 9 8 7 6 5 4 3 2 1

Penguin Random House
HAMISH HAMILTON CANADA

MY PARENTS

1

BIOGRAPHIES

The story goes that my mother's grandfather Živko was going back home on his horse-drawn sleigh after a winter night of drinking and gambling, when he ran into a couple of terrifying giants blocking the path. He owned a lot of land, a provisions store, even had servants; he was rich and therefore imperious and arrogant. He determined that the giants would destroy him if he stopped, so he stood up on his sleigh, whipped forth the horses, and rushed at the creatures, who stepped aside to let him through.

His daughter, Ruža, married my grandfather Stjepan Živković, who would never run into a giant and whose family was not rich at all. The marriage was not arranged, which was uncommon in northeast Bosnia* at the time (1921 or so), when marital bliss was inseparable from the goods and properties transacted between the bride's and groom's families. Mama believes that love

* That part of Bosnia is called Semberija and is located right on the border with Serbia, between the Drina and Sava Rivers.

was involved: Ruža's father disowned her for going against his wishes. Ruža and Stjepan would have seven kids; my mother, Andja, born in 1937, was the youngest.

When she was four, Mama's older brother Živan was playing a game with his friends that involved smacking a piece of wood with a stick (*klis*). The piece of wood hit him in the belly; he was full after lunch; his stomach ruptured and he died. The story doesn't quite add up—the piece of wood couldn't have been that heavy—but that was what my mother was told.* When sorrows come, they come not as single spies, but in battalions: right around the time of Živan's death, World War Two entered Yugoslavia by way of the invading Germans. Mama's oldest brother, Bogdan, was nineteen when he joined the partisan resistance movement. Mama remembers that whenever she woke up in the middle of the night during the war years, she'd find Ruža awake, worrying about her eldest son, swaying to and fro on her bed like a Hasid.

The war was complicated in Bosnia, as all its wars have always been, as all wars always are. In addition to the Germans, Tito's partisans had to fight against the royalist Serb forces—the *četnik*s—who openly collaborated with the occupying forces, busying themselves mainly with massacring Muslims. My mother's family is ethnically Serb, and the area where they lived—the village called Brodac near the town of Bijeljina—was solid *četnik* territory. Much of Ruža's family supported the *četnik*s too, by a kind of default that comes with being rich and arrogant. Stjepan, on the other hand, would not have any of that, and not only because his eldest son was a partisan—he was also just a decent man. The *četnik*s would occasionally come by to look for Bog-

* My sister, Kristina, and I would therefore never be allowed to go out and play right after a meal, and had to stay put instead and digest our food.

dan, and when they couldn't find him they'd harass Stjepan. He once hid, in a pile of manure, a box of ammo air-dropped by the Allies in order to deliver it to the partisans. But someone informed the *četnik*s, who beat my grandfather into a pulp, demanding to know where the ammo was. He told them nothing; they took him to a detention camp and would've likely slit his throat if Ruža's family hadn't intervened; he would subsequently be under house arrest for six months. Another time, toward the end of the war, Stjepan gave his only horse to a wounded young partisan on the run. The young partisan promised he would return the horse; he never did, but Stjepan would never regret helping a man in trouble. He must have imagined that someone else, somewhere else, could in the same way decide to help his son.

My uncle Bogdan did manage to survive the war, and was in the unit that fought at the Sremski Front, in the difficult battle that ensured the defeat of the German and collaborator forces and the liberation of Belgrade. As a machine gunner he was always a prime target; he received a bullet in his chest, while two of his assistants were shot dead next to him. A lung had to be removed, and he would never be entirely healthy again. Nor would Ruža ever sleep again, at least not until her death.

Mama was a child when the war ended, but she would never talk about being scared or traumatized by it. Neither did she tell any childhood stories: there were few adventures, she had few animal or human friends, she did not even get into trouble with her siblings. Narratively speaking, Mama did not have a childhood. First she was in the war, the littlest of the kids, and then, with the end of the calamity, a moot but exciting future opened up for her and she had to leave her childhood behind.

In 1948, when she was merely eleven, she moved to attend middle school in Bijeljina, five miles and very far away from her village. She lived in a rented room,* taking a train back home every weekend. She stayed in Bijeljina through her high school years, graduating with good grades in 1957 from—and this is only for the name—Državna realna gimnazija Filip Višnjić.† Then, as ever, she was a devout and conscientious student.

In 1957, she went to college in Belgrade, the capital and the biggest city in Yugoslavia, some eighty miles and a century away from Brodac. She at first resided with three other young women in a dorm room in Studentski grad (Student City). She subsisted on a modest stipend, with little money and few possessions. But she had fun, and still likes to reminisce about the beauty of communal youth, about the ethos of sharing everything—meals, clothes, experience—about the sense that, despite manifest poverty, there was nothing lacking.

There were dances (*igranka*) at the university cafeteria, featuring one Mirko Šouc and his rock 'n' roll band; she would sometimes go to two dances in a single night. U.S. movies played in the theaters, if with several years' delay. Esther Williams reigned;‡ *Three Coins in the Fountain* was a blockbuster, and the song from the movie was enthusiastically sung by the youth, in their, shall we say, limited English. *Kaubojski filmovi* (cowboy films) in general, and John Wayne in particular, were beloved. To this day, Mama—ever prone to passing out before a TV—stays awake for

* Her landlady was Teta Almasa, a single woman who was a devout Communist, kept bees, rode a motorcycle. She remained Mama's friend for the rest of her life, and I remember meeting her: she wore thick glasses, spoke briskly, and was fully devoid of that Bosnian old-lady meekness.

† State Real Gymnasium Filip Višnjić. Filip Višnjić was the Serbian early nineteenth century blind Homeric poet whose repertoire provided the basis for the canon of Serb epic poetry.

‡ Her 1944 aquatic romp, *Bathing Beauty*, distributed in Yugoslavia in the fifties as *Bal na vodi*, was at one point or another seen by practically every student in Belgrade.

Rio Grande or *Rio Bravo* or *Red River*.* Soviet movies could be seen too: *The Cranes Are Flying*,† a post-Stalinist Soviet film about love and war (and rape), would make an entire theater sob in unison. They also watched Yugoslav movies, as the country's cinema was going through one of its golden periods.

The plot of *Ljubav i moda* (*Love and Fashion*),‡ for instance, revolved around the young people organizing a fashion show to fund their gliding club. The movie opens with a tracking shot of a hip young woman riding a Vespa on the streets of Belgrade, not exactly crowded with cars, while a sugary pop song (*šlager*) warns us that a young man might be coming along. Unsurprisingly, she runs into one at a streetlight; in no time he tells her that she should be in the kitchen and not on the Vespa, calling her a "motorized schizo-girl"; she calls him a brute, and love is as imminent as fashion. In the photos from that time, my mother often looks like the girl on the Vespa: the balloon skirt, bobby socks, and a beehive hairdo. Indeed, she remembers watching the shoot for *Ljubav i moda*. When I first saw the movie, I looked for her face in the crowd. The movie features not only young, well-dressed women and men laughing, flying gliders, and addressing one another as "comrade," but also Yugoslav pop stars arbitrarily breaking out into badly lip-synced songs, one of them containing the immortal line: "Because fashion is the whipping cream and love is the ice cream" ("*Jer moda to je šlag, a ljubav sladoled*"). Among those songs was "Devojko mala," which would a generation later be unironically covered by a hip band (VIS Idoli) I loved and listened to.

* John Ford's *Rio Grande* (1950); Howard Hawks's *Red River* (1948) and *Rio Bravo* (1959).

† *Letyat Zhuravli* (1957), directed by Mikhail Kalatozov.

‡ *Ljubav i moda* (1960), directed by Ljubomir Radičević.

Around that time, in the eighties, I had great interest in the music and films from my parents' student days, and their youth appeared to me cool to the point of nostalgia. In contrast, I don't think that Mama ever longed to have lived her parents' lives—by the time of *Love and Fashion*, the gap between the generations was far too wide. My discovery of her cool past allowed for a cultural continuity between us; we could now have a common referential field. I wanted to have lived through such a youth, was envious of the experience of unbridled optimism, joy, love, and fashion. Mama would often marvel at the fact that I listened to the music of her generation, to what she called "our music," but even when I was young, I was never as young as she had once been.

My father wouldn't be who he is without the great Otto von Bismarck. For it was Herr Otto who, after the Russo-Turkish War, orchestrated the 1878 Berlin Congress and the subsequent redistribution of lands among the European empires. It was in Berlin that the defeated Ottoman Empire agreed to cede to the Austro-Hungarian imperial forces the remote province of Bosnia and Herzegovina, which had been in its possession for about four hundred years. The occupation was supposed to be a temporary arrangement, of course, but Herr Otto expected it to last, as did pretty much everyone else involved, including the Habsburgs. Which is why the Crown hurried, as soon as the Austro-Hungarian troops entered Bosnia and Herzegovina, to import from other provinces the subjects who would colonize the new land. After the Young Turks' 1908 coup against the sultan and the subsequent dissolution of the monarchy, the Austro-Hungarians were gifted a perfect excuse to annex Bosnia to their imperial domain and accelerate the colonization. This is where my father's tribe enters the story.

Hauling their meager possessions, including a hive or two of bees and a steel plow, the Hemons migrated from Galicia (now western Ukraine) in 1912, my grandfather Ivan as old as the twentieth century. Just about the same time, my grandmother Mihaljina arrived from Bukovina, the province to the south of Galicia. They all settled near the town of Prnjavor, in northwestern Bosnia, where they were known as the Galicians at the time, since the notion of Ukrainian identity hadn't yet trickled down from the elite intellectual circles who worried about such things. Besides Galicians/Ukrainians, the area around Prnjavor became a home to many colonists: Poles, Bohemians (Czechs), Germans, Italians joined the local mix of Serbs, Croats, and Muslims. A family legend claims that my ancestors came over not only for a swath of arable land, but also for a forest that would be a reliable source of firewood, which gave them a better chance of surviving winters than in Galicia. When the empire was dismembered after World War One, some colonists returned to their newly independent homelands, but most, including the Hemons, stayed in what would become (and eventually perish as) Yugoslavia. Less than a century later, in a census taken a year before the most recent war, there were about five thousand Ukrainian-speaking people in Bosnia and Herzegovina. In one way or another, I was related to a large number of them.

Ivan married Mihaljina in 1925, and they promptly engaged in procreation; my oldest aunt, Marija, was born in 1926. (Now she lives in Edmonton, Canada.) By 1947, my grandmother went through eleven pregnancies, which resulted in one miscarriage and ten children. They all lived on a hill called Vučijak, in a small straw-roofed, dirt-floored, hearth-equipped house, which they shared in the winter with cattle and other domestic animals.

My father, Petar, was the sixth child, born in 1936, just in time for World War Two, which was nasty and complicated around

Prnjavor, where the ethnic mix, complicated even by Bosnian standards, offered myriad opportunities for massacres of civilians and frequent skirmishes among various loosely defined units, including the exotic and murderous *čerkezi*, the captured Red Army soldiers who had switched sides to fight with the Germans. Neither did it help that the border of the Croat fascist puppet state (NDH)* was at the nearby Vijaka River, so that refugees flowed across when the Croat Ustashe units committed their massacres. Armed groups would come by my grandparents' house to requisition food or whatever they could carry away. At least once, Ivan and Mihaljina's family were lined up to be shot, but then were let go at the last moment as someone who knew them pointed out they were meek and benign, unlikely to cause any harm. Even if they hadn't been pardoned, they wouldn't have been all killed, however. My father's older sisters, grown up enough to attract attention, knew to hide; the younger kids knew to slip away. In our part of the world, one reason for large broods of children, in addition to the absence of contraception, was that the more children a family had, the more would survive war, disease, and poverty. In 1943, the Hemons became refugees: they were forced out of their house carrying what goods they could (my father remembers carrying a coffee grinder), not knowing if they'd ever return. They sought refuge with family in the area. When they returned a couple of months later, they found that much of their meager stuff had been pilfered by their neighbors and passing warriors.

When I was a kid, my father told me his war stories, as he still does. Those were the narratives of mischievous children playing

* Nezavisna država Hrvatska. The state was governed by the fascist Ustashe, whose genocidal operations against Serbs, Jews, and Roma, as well as against anti-fascist Croats and Muslims, were particularly brutal and appalled even some Nazis.

with war debris and killing devices. One of my favorites was about how they once threw ammo into a fire and fooled the *čerkezi* into thinking they were being shot at, thereby diverting them from coming to pillage the Hemon homestead. Some of his stories were no doubt embellished, sometimes the war horror was toned down, but there was one whose tragic dimension could never be undone or reduced. When my father was eight and his brother Teodor ten, they found a box of five trip-wire mines, which they shared with three other village boys. The five of them decided to drop the mines into the concrete water reservoir behind the school, because they wanted the explosion to echo. But they couldn't tell the difference between a hand grenade and a mine. They knew that after a grenade was activated you counted to three, but they didn't realize that a mine would explode momentarily. So Teodor pulled the wire and the mine exploded in his hand, blowing it away. In wartime, war is everywhere, devours all space, touching everyone in it, including children. My father remembers the torn veins and tendons hanging from his brother's arm, his face like a crushed strawberry. Uncle Teodor survived, but he lost his eyes. It is quite possible that he pulled the wire first because he was older than my father. The life of the family changed that day, and no one would ever consider or discuss the impossible alternative outcome—that life could become, again, what it had been. But, due to my compulsive writerly deformation, I have considered a different life trajectory: Had the mine not exploded in his hand, maybe Uncle Teodor would've been the first one to leave home for school, perhaps he would've gone on to college. Maybe my father would've stayed at home, never going far from it; maybe he never would've met my mother. This is how history works: arbitrarily and irreversibly.

Thus it was Tata who at the age of eleven left his home and childhood to go to school in Banja Luka, a city some forty miles away from Vučijak. It rained the day he arrived to stay with his mother's cousin; he looked for hours out the window in his room and cried; he went on crying for three days straight. The first time he stepped out to play with the boys from the neighborhood, they beat him up.

Three years later, he transferred to a school in Derventa, only twenty miles away from Vučijak. On weekends, he would bike home to see his family. One winter day, his pedal broke and he pushed the bike through the snow for hours, risking his life not to lose his precious vehicle. In 1952, he went back to Banja Luka for high school, this time staying in a dorm. Those were the hungry years, because a drought devastated crops all over Bosnia. At the dorm, for breakfast the boys would have a piece of bread—one-eighth of a one-kilo loaf*—a cube of jelly, and tea. A boy from Drvar once stole a whole loaf and an entire packet of jelly, for which he was promptly expelled from school.

While school was free, Tata's poor parents had to pay for the cost of his living, so he lived even more modestly than was common. Back at home in the summers, he'd have to work at a collective farm (*zadruga*) to make some money. He kept writing applications for stipends, submitting twenty-five before, in his junior year, he received a positive answer from Elektroprenos, the state energy distribution company. Because they paid him retroactively from the beginning of the school year, he suddenly seemed flush with money, so he spent a big part of it on having a suit made. It was his first one ever, and it shrank with the first rain. He studied like crazy but still found time to play handball at the local club, and to practice kissing with girls. There were hundreds of students in his high school, twenty-two boys in his class; whenever a boy had a stipend approved, he'd buy a pan of

* 4.4 ounces.

baklava to share with his classmates. Tata remained friends with a lot of those boys; he went to the high school reunion in 2016, and only six were present; the rest were displaced, dead, or killed.

He had the highest grade average at graduation, so he was easily admitted to the Electrotechnics College (Elektrotehnički fakultet) at the University of Belgrade. He was back at home when he opened the letter informing him of another, larger college stipend from Elektroprenos. The whole family celebrated; his mother made *steranka*—dough boiled in milk—his favorite dish. But before going to college, he had to go into the army, volunteering for the reserve officers' school so as to serve only a year (as a grunt, he would've served two), reaching the rank of captain. I still remember the brownish uniform he would put on years later before going away for a military exercise, a belt with a strap across the chest and three stars on the epaulets.

Because he saved money from his summer jobs at Elektroprenos while also receiving a monthly stipend, he could afford having fun in Belgrade. He had three roommates in Studentski grad and they went to soccer games, concerts, movies, but Tata nonetheless studied like crazy. He particularly enjoyed movies—in high school he had collected ticket stubs and kept a journal listing all the titles he'd seen.* Like everyone else, he got caught up in the Esther Williams fever; he stood in line to see *High Noon*† and John Wayne flicks. One of his favorite movies was Emilio

* Among the first ones on the list: *This People Will Live* (*Živjeće ovaj narod*; 1947), directed by Nikola Popović. IMDb summary: "The uprising against fascists in West Bosnia starts with enthusiasm, and local folks help partisans in every possible way. A village girl of Serbian ethnicity joins the resistance movement, and falls in love with the partisan commissar Ivan, an ethnic Croat who has been an expert in destroying railway tracks."

† *High Noon* (1952), directed by Fred Zinnemann.

Fernández's 1950 tear-jerker *Un día de vida* (*One Day in Life*),* featuring the traditional Mexican song "Las Mananitas," phenomenally popular in Yugoslavia under the name "Mama Juanita." Tata might still sing it at parties, deploying a poignant vibrato straight from Mexico and the fifties. The movie, now largely forgotten, single-handedly started a Yugoslav Mexican-music scene, whose stars were sombrero-wearing Montenegrins singing in poignant Serbo-Croatian about leaving behind their villages, Juanitas, and mothers for a big city.

My parents met in 1959. My father had a roommate (*cimer*), Nidžo, whose sister Šiša was my mother's roommate. One day Nidžo came by to see his sister, and my father tagged along. The first time Tata saw Mama, she was on the bed studying—her legs Z-shaped, I imagine, her hair fashionably puffed up, with that intelligent reading face of hers. What they talked about, I do not know, but my father was a charmer, and my mother was a joyful young woman, and they went to a dance together. The band must've played Paul Anka, Adriano Celentano, Đorđe Marjanović, the hits from the Sanremo Festival. They soon were dating; they took strolls together, started kissing. My father, typically blunt, told my mother that she didn't know how to kiss, whereas he'd practiced in high school with one Ružica. My mother got upset, and he had to schmooze his way back into her good graces.

Love did not interfere with their studies, however—education was a chance they would never dare to miss, as they were the first ones in their respective families to go to college. My mother would

* The last known copy of the movie is still at Jugoslovenska kinoteka (the Yugoslav Cinema) in Belgrade.

come by his dorm room with two movie tickets to lure him into going out (and possibly making out), but if he had to study, he'd decline and deploy his roommate as a pinch date. Mama had a friend named Boško, who was respectful toward women, and even randomly gave them flowers. My father and Nidžo once cornered the nice Boško and threatened him because his gentlemanliness cast them in a bad light. I suppose Boško backed off, for my father's comparatively uncouth charm continued to operate upon my mother. They kept going out, and eventually, like everyone else, they went to see *Love and Fashion*.

Apart from singing, strumming the guitar, and playing volleyball, my father was constantly telling stories to whoever was willing to listen—he was good at it, and still is. The stories were mainly about his family and their Vučijak neighbors: Branko, Duja, Makivija, Savka Troglavka, who became stock characters. One time he dreamt in installments: for a couple of successive nights his dreams were somehow narratively connected—or at least that's how his story goes. The first morning, he woke up and told his roommates about the dream he'd had, which was interrupted at the most suspensful moment, and then the following night the dream continued, and in the morning he told them what happened next, except that dream also ended without resolution. And then he dreamt again, and after a few days the word about his cliff-hanging dreams spread, and his roommates and many others in the dorm couldn't wait to hear the next dream installment. In Tata's rendition of the story, he eventually woke up in a room full of quiet people shushing one another, waiting for him to reveal the dream's end. He couldn't remember it, so he made it up.

Many of the friendships commenced in those days lasted for decades, only to be extinguished with war and time. Šiša stayed in Belgrade, as did Nidžo, who would die an alcoholic in the early nineties. When my parents visited Belgrade a few years ago, they called Šiša up, and she refused to see them.

For my parents, their student days were merry. In the pictures from those times, they're always beautiful, partying and laughing, surrounded by friends, radiating abandon, the light around them at the wavelength of happiness. When I reached the age my parents were in those pictures, I became a moody young man. At that time, I was reveling angrily in the liberty that comes with an uncertain future; their joy looked to me like a pure excitement about all the brilliant things heading their way.

In the summers, my father worked—part of his Elektroprenos stipend—at an electrical substation near a village (Puračić) in central Bosnia. But in 1961, my parents-to-be decided to go to the coast together for a summer holiday. Mama asked her father if she could go to the coast with Petar, her boyfriend. Stjepan had not met Tata, but he told her: "Why are you asking me? You're smart enough to know what you're doing." Mama stopped over at the substation to pick Tata up on the way to the coast. He had been working twelve-hour shifts daily so that he could earn some free weeks for the holiday. So it was in Puračić, according to my father, that they made love for the first time at the school where they were staying for the night. To the coast they went the following morning; neither of them had ever seen the sea before.

In January 1962, Mama's mother suddenly died at the age of sixty-six from an undiagnosed pneumonia. Devastated by Ruža's death, she managed to graduate in February, and started working in March at the Bijeljina municipal office, which had given her a stipend. This was the worst period of her youth. She kept going to her mother's grave to weep, but could not make herself go see her father—she couldn't bear her mother's absence—and he sent her a message asking her not to forget him. When she finally went to see him, she couldn't utter a word and just kept crying. Tata would come from Belgrade to be with her, and it was around this time, Mama remembers, that they started making love.*

That May, she met the storied Hemon family for the first time. It was for my aunt Maljka's wedding. The party took place at my grandparents' estate—that is, in their muddy yard. My mother wore heels, which kept sinking in the mud. Soon thereafter, in the summer of 1962, Tata went to Germany for a kind of residency (*staž*), which involved working on constructing a substation and power line system. His salary was 2,880 deutsche marks, and Herr Bittner, his boss, was very happy with him, so much so that he offered him a job.

Meanwhile, in Bosnia, my mother was in a bad shape, mourning for her mother, pining for my father. The day Tata was supposed to return, she waited at the bus station for him, but he never arrived. It took a few days for her to receive a postcard telling her that he had gone to see his sister Juljka, who lived in Leicester, England.† She was angry he hadn't told her he was going; she felt left alone. It would not be the last time.

My father declined Herr Bittner's job offer. He was bound by the Elektroprenos stipend, and he missed Mama. When he

* When their first time came up during my interviewing them, Mama was certain that she was right. "Your father," she said, "does not remember anything."

† A long and sad story: After World War Two a large number of Ukrainian Red Army soldiers who were POWs in Germany or elsewhere chose not to return to the Soviet Union. These men looked for Ukrainian brides outside the homeland. A letter was circulated among the Ukrainians in the Prnjavor area from a Ukrainian living in the UK and looking for a wife. It was Aunt Juljka's turn to get married, so a correspondence was commenced with the man, who eventually sent his picture and money for the train ticket. Aunt Juljka went to England, where she lived unhappily until she died in Peterborough, in 2006.

returned to her after Leicester, they slept together; she told him she was afraid that she could get pregnant; if she did, he said, they would get married. A suggestion turned into a proposal; he didn't quite fall on his knee to ask for her hand in marriage, but she did say yes.

They got married on November 11, Armistice Day, in Belgrade, at the Palilula municipality. It was a small wedding, only their friend Žarko as the best man (*kum*) and Šiša as the maid of honor (*kuma*), plus a small group of fellow students. Neither set of parents was present, the only family a cousin who lived nearby. There was no honeymoon. My father immediately returned to working on his bachelor's thesis. My mother went back to Bijeljina.

A picture from the wedding hung over my parents' bed throughout my childhood, boyhood, and youth: in it, they're both smiling; Mama holds a bouquet of flowers; there is a huge, bright circle that for many years I took to be a low light fixture (literally) and a moon (figuratively), but was in fact—if one looked closer—some kind of a coat of arms, featuring Tito's profile in relief.

My father defended his bachelor's thesis with great success. It won a prize (Kolubarska nagrada) given to research work in the field of energy transmission; the plaque hangs framed in my parents' house in Hamilton, Ontario. A job for Elektroprenos was waiting for him in Sarajevo; my mother left her municipal job in Bijeljina. In March 1963, they moved to the city where they would live until the most recent war. When they arrived they had nothing but luggage. They'd never been in Sarajevo before, and it was a wholly unknown place. The first day they stayed in a tiny apartment with Tata's cousin Olgica and her family, including two small children. The following day, suitcase in hand, Tata went to check in at Elektroprenos, and when they asked him where his wife was he pointed at her out the window, sitting just outside on a park bench, her suitcase at her feet.

She soon got a job as an accountant at Energoinvest, the largest state company in Bosnia, where she would work through her retirement. They found a room in Marijin Dvor, with a couple who had two teenage children. The couple—Teta Jozefina and Čika Martin—would be like grandparents to me for the rest of their lives. And that is because they were like parents to my parents, who, other than Olgica, had no family in Sarajevo. When Mama got pregnant, but then discovered that the pregnancy was pathological—conjoined twins—and had to end it, Jozefina helped her get through a difficult mourning period.

Mama did get pregnant again, and I was born on September 9, 1964. In those days, men were not allowed in the delivery room, but even if they were, that day my father was on an out-of-town mission to fix a fallen transmission line. Upon receiving the news on the way back, he got drunk with his friend Duško—this is one of the handful of instances when Tata was inebriated. Mama showed me to him through the window as he stood in the park outside the maternity wing. The story goes that he exclaimed that I looked as ugly as Tshombe.*

One of the perks of socialism was that working people would be given an apartment by the state company that employed them. After two years at Jozefina and Martin's, my parents got a place from Elektroprenos and moved to Čengić vila, a newly built housing development on the outskirts of the city. For a while, they had to take me back every day to see Teta Jozefina and Čika Martin, or I would have a tantrum. Within a couple of years, we moved to a bigger apartment in a new building near the old train station. This was where we would live until the war started in 1992.

* The Katangese warlord responsible for the death of Patrice Lumumba in 1960.

My grandfather Stjepan died in November 1967, and I do not remember him. But there is a picture of Mama in mourning wearing black, as I stand next to her trying to console her. In March 1969, my sister Kristina was born. Tata was in Russia at the time. A year before, he had applied for a fellowship in Moscow, which was approved after Mama got pregnant. He decided to go anyway, and returned when my sister was three months old.

As years went by, my family enjoyed what by local standards would've been a middle-class life: we had a car (first an Austin, then a Ford Escort); we enjoyed summer vacations on the coast; we had a color TV. We also had a weekend cabin (*vikendica*) on Jahorina, a mountain outside Sarajevo; Tata designed and built it with very little help; Mama filled it up with homey detail. Throughout my childhood, we would go to Jahorina nearly every weekend; my sister and I would spend our month-long winter break there, skiing. When we stayed at home, refusing to go with them so that we could have a party, they'd go by themselves. "It's heaven up there," they'd call us to say. They loved the place; that's where they planned to live in their retirement.

In 1980, Tito died. All of Yugoslavia mourned. The footage from a soccer game between a Croatian and Serbian team (Hajduk vs. Crvena zvezda) showed the players embracing and sobbing upon hearing the news; the supporters in the stands sobbed as well. The newspapers featured editorials entitled "Even after Tito—Tito" ("*I poslije Tita—Tito*"), which became a ubiquitous slogan, suggesting that the biggest monument to Tito was Yugoslavia itself. *Oslobođenje*, the daily Sarajevo paper, offered a free picture of Tito, which could subsequently be seen in stores, and windows, and taped to windshields of taxis. For days, only classical music was played on TV and radio. The leaders, kings, and presidents of the world showed up in Belgrade for Tito's funeral; a million people on the streets followed the procession, inconsolable. The country was unified in mourning. But emotions and myths are limited, temporary, and tragically whimsical unifying forces. We didn't know it then, but Tito's death was the beginning of Yugoslavia's demise. It would take eleven years for the country to reach its bloody end.

Just before Tito's death, Tata got a bigger, better job at Energoinvest, and in 1980 the company deployed him to Kinshasa for three years to work on building power systems in Zaire. Mama stayed back in Sarajevo with two adolescents, who were, let me attest, a handful. He'd come back home every six months, bring presents and stories, sometimes smuggled ivory and rolls of snakeskin. The same summer, Mama, Kristina, and I went to visit him in Zaire, where we had the time of our lives.

Tata was in Kinshasa when his mother, Mihaljina, died in the spring of 1982. He had not been able to see her before she died, nor return for her funeral. His father, Ivan, had by that time lost his sight entirely, and was sinking deeper into dementia. Toward the end of his life, Grandpa Ivan would get up from his sofa with great effort and walk in small Parkinsonian steps across the room, convinced that if he kept walking he would eventually reach Ukraine.

After Tata's return from Africa, where he made some money, we moved up a notch or two to what would've been, in the limited socialist stratification, upper middle class: we added a room to our apartment; Kristina and I wore foreign-quality clothes and owned imported LPs; Tata started planning another *vikendica* on Jahorina. The company did business in many countries, mainly in the third world, so my father traveled all over Africa: Libya, Ethiopia, Tanzania, Zaire, etc., but also France, the UK, Germany. Mama would occasionally join him on a trip: they traveled to Paris and Florence together. He was away and abroad a lot, and my sister and I missed him; he would bring back for us cool jeans, chocolate, and LPs. Our life felt more stable, partly because we now had savings that were, in socialist Yugoslavia, substantial, by virtue of being deposited in dollars, thus not subject to rampant inflation. But outside our life, things were not stable, which I enjoyed, because there was a loosening of socialist tenets and censorship, a sense of moving toward liberalization of politics, economy, and public space. You could still get in trouble for saying and thinking things (and I did), but the Yugoslav socialism, its gods and myths, Tito included, were rapidly losing their sacred status. This was confusing to my parents, particularly Mama.

In 1987, just as the tears became visible in the fabric of Yugoslavia, some of our Zaire money was spent on building another *vikendica*, next to the old one. That summer I worked with Tata on it—I got paid, since I had a band at the time and we needed a rhythm machine. His idea was that we could rent out the second cabin to tourists and skiers, make it pay for itself; after he and Mama were gone, my sister and I would inherit a cabin each. It was important to our parents to build something they could leave behind for their children; they imagined that, many years into the future, Kristina and I would bring our families for skiing vacations to the family complex they built for us. One day, as we were working on the second cabin, Tata told me that he could see my friends and me playing cards (*preferans*) in that cabin one day, reminiscing: "We built this when Petar was alive." In other words, in building something to leave for his children, he was building a monument to himself. We did build the cabin; it was rented for a few years. I never played cards in it, and I never will: the cabin burned down in 1992, right at the beginning of the war.

For many years, Yugoslavia was a solid, comfortable country, largely because Tito was smart enough to position himself away from the Soviet Union and its dominance. This made a strong, relatively open Yugoslavia valuable to the West, which expressed its support by way of abundant international loans. Much of that money was spent on building a strong military, capable of defending, if need be, against the East and the West. But the political structures Tito left behind in order to maintain the ethnic and political balance had been inherently weakened by the decades of a single-party, great-leader system. The viability of the country was further undermined when Yugoslavia lost its strategic value with the fall of the Wall and the unraveling of the Soviet empire. When the loans were called in, the economy started falling apart, and the privileged military class—dominated by the Serbs—looked for new leaders.

In 1991, Mama took an early retirement from her job at Energoinvest, where she had worked since my parents arrived in Sarajevo. More consequentially, the first free elections were held in Yugoslavia, the nationalist parties winning in all of its six federal republics. Slovenia and Croatia declared independence, which broke up Yugoslavia and started wars for territory. It soon became clear that the conflict was likely coming to Bosnia. In January 1992, I went to the United States, where I live now. At the end of February, the Bosnian independence referendum was held. Most of the Serbs boycotted it; the rest of the population voted for it overwhelmingly, and Bosnia became independent. The nationalist Serbs pounced, executing a well-prepared military operation, supported by the Milošević government in Belgrade, taking over towns and villages with majority Serb population and cleansing them of the presence of others. In April, there were barricades on the streets of Sarajevo—Tata and Kristina would take a walk together to see them—and the Serbs took up positions in the mountains around the city. Toward the end of the month, there was already regular shooting, and my sister followed her then-boyfriend, who had family in Belgrade. My father wanted to leave and go to the old family house in Vučijak, near Prnjavor, largely because it was the time of the year to tend to his apiary, but Mama resisted—she did not want to leave her home, fearing that she might never come back. They had to spend nights in the building's basement, as their windows were exposed to gunfire and there was already plenty of shooting and shelling; after a while, my father refused to cower and slept in his bed, snoring untroubled by the war noises, while my mother spent nights talking to their neighbors, some of whom were suspicious about my father's absence, unable to believe he was in his bed sleeping. Finally, Tata convinced Mama and they went to the Sarajevo train station, with Mek, our Irish setter, to go to Prnjavor, but the train didn't leave. For a few days, they'd go to the station, the train wouldn't leave, they'd come back. On May 1, on the way back home from the station yet again, Mama declared that she was done trying to leave. The following morning, my father talked her into trying one last time. They took Mek again, and very little else: no warm clothes, no passports, not even their personal IDs. The train left at 12:30 p.m. or so. Later in the afternoon of the same day, May 2, the siege closed around the city and heavy shelling started. The train my parents took was the last one out; no train would leave for many years.

My parents made it to Vučijak, and stayed there for the summer. Tata worked on his bees; Mama tended the garden. The news from Sarajevo—and from everywhere in Bosnia—was terrible. The trucks full of Serb soldiers singing songs promising murder would pass by the family house on their way to the front. The dog got bitten by a tick and almost died. Then Mama's gallbladder got inflamed and extremely painful, so she had to be transported for surgery to Subotica, a city at the Serbian-Hungarian border, where Mama's brother Milisav lived. Soon thereafter my father got out too, and, after Mama recovered, they moved to Novi Sad, where another brother, Dimitrije, had a small apartment in which they could stay.

This was at the time when what was left of Yugoslavia—Serbia and Montenegro—was breaking world records in inflation rates. Not only did my parents have little money (all the savings were lost), but even what they had was becoming more worthless by the minute. Tata found a way to work in Hungary, just across the border, and was away a lot. Kristina was in Belgrade, so Mama spent a lot of time in the tiny apartment with Mek, confiding in him. Once she took him out to a park, where he got into a fight with a Rottweiler; she tried to separate them and the Rottweiler tore her hand apart, so that a surgery was necessary.

Eventually, Mama, Tata, and Kristina applied for Canadian landing visas, and the application was approved. In December 1993, my parents and sister landed in Hamilton, Ontario. They found an apartment on the fifteenth floor of a large building. There was so much nothing in their new place they could not begin to fill it up.

2

HOMELAND

It has become beyond fashionable to hate the late Yugoslavia, or diagnose it retroactively as a kind of Frankensteinian assemblage of mismatched parts whose dissolution was thus inescapable and inevitably bloody. But when a few decades from now some expert historian on a think-tank sinecure looks at the devastation in the United States left in the wake of Trump and his troops, s/he might discover abundant evidence of hundreds of years of hatred and inherent U.S. racism, with all kinds of historical inevitability leading to the catastrophe. S/he would be wrong, just as were those who disparaged Yugoslavia, for in both cases there is a history of conflicting traditions and tendencies, of struggles against the worst of the people's instincts for a better polity and a kinder country. The bad guys won in Yugoslavia and ruined what they could, as soon as they could; the bad guys are presently doing pretty well in the United States. But nothing is inevitable until it happens. There is no such thing as historical destiny. Struggle is all.

Yugoslavia, a country of the south Slavs, was formed as the

Kingdom of Serbs, Croats, and Slovenes, on December 1, 1918, in the immediate aftermath of World War One. Three major empires had just disintegrated after centuries of eventful existence, allowing for the creation of obscure small states whose people experienced the post-imperial chaos as freedom. Among the south Slavs populating the Balkans, the idea of a compound state had had a history and had inspired leaders who believed in the benefits of unity. As an attempt at that unity, the kingdom contended with the complications inherent in a space populated by peoples who were at the same time too similar and too different. In 1929, the kingdom became Yugoslavia, as King Aleksandar (unrelated to me) changed the constitution to become an absolute monarch. In 1934, he was promptly assassinated on a visit in Marseille. The propagandistic story had it that the king's last words were: "Take care of my Yugoslavia." My paternal grandfather, Ivan, traveled to Belgrade to be there for the grandiose funeral. Both of my parents were born as subjects to a teenage King Peter the Second,* who escaped the 1941 German invasion to end up in, of all places, Chicago. There he died, as many of us will.

World War Two was bloody in Yugoslavia, but was there a place in Europe where it wasn't? The Germans found many willing servants among local fascists and nationalists whose main historical modus operandi, like their masters', was genocide—their descendants would be at it again a couple of generations later. But the Communist Party of Yugoslavia, illegal before the war, was versed in resistance and underground networks and sparked, under Josip Broz Tito's leadership, a national resistance movement that outlasted the Germans and "domestic traitors," despite their efforts to extinguish it in waves of unspeakable atrocities.

* Though the country was ruled, as in a grim fairy tale, by the sinister Regent Pavle.

Say what you will about Tito and the postwar regime so centered around his personality that it barely outlived him, but under his leadership the party organized a resistance movement and liberated Yugoslavia. He also managed to keep the country at a safe distance from the Soviet Union, breaking away from Stalin and his absolutist control in 1948. Tito was a clever, if authoritarian, leader, positioning the country between the East and the West in such a way—making it nonaligned—that it could benefit from its distance from and connections with each side.

Tito and the party came out not only as the winners, but also as the historical force that carried Yugoslavia into the twentieth century, rebuilding it after a devastating, brutal war. With the doctrine of brotherhood and unity (*bratstvo i jedinstvo*) to counter the post-genocidal traumas and resentment, the country strove to create a civic identity that overrode ethnicity as the primary identifier. This took some suppression, but in retrospect, it may have been worth it, if only for a little while. The country had a defined utopian goal toward which its citizens could strive; there was optimism, a better future could be conceived of, and my grandparents' generation's hope that their children would have better lives was rapidly fulfilled. For a few decades, the socialist Yugoslavia was a common project everyone could work on. My parents belong to the generation that took crucial part in that work, only to discover that it was all in vain.

True history is always played out on a personal level. It's hard today to comprehend the magnitude of the leap into a better life someone like my mother made in Tito's Yugoslavia. Back in 1948, in the wake of a cataclysm, the new regime instituted gender equality and mandatory and free education, so a peasant Bosnian girl, born in a house with a dirt floor, could go to school for free. Had she been born a generation before, she wouldn't have gone to school. She would've worked the land with her parents until she got married, whereupon she would've popped out children into her middle age, unless she died giving birth or from sepsis after a botched amateur abortion, like one of her father's sisters. Mama's future was entangled with Yugoslavia's, enabling her to leave behind the poverty that had lasted for centuries.

Yugoslavia provided a framework into which my mother fully grew, having departed, at the age of eleven, from her more or less nineteenth century childhood. She built the country as she was building herself. After the war, a practice of "voluntary youth actions" was established, where young people of Yugoslavia volunteered to build roads and railroads as part of "youth brigades" (*omladinske brigade*). In 1960, while in college, Mama was one of the young women and men who spent their summer constructing a road that would connect Belgrade and Niš, part of a larger project of uniting parts of Yugoslavia by way of a highway, known as Autoput Bratstvo i jedinstvo (Highway of Brotherhood and Unity). She would tell her children stories of shovel-inflicted blisters and solidarity and friendship and joy, or so we imagined it, because the truth was they were not always given the hardest tasks. They'd shovel soil and help the professionals, but more than anything they'd sing patriotic songs and chant slogans in praise of hard work: "Comrade Tito, you white violet / all of youth loves you!" ("*Druže Tito, ljubičice bijela / tebe voli omladina cijela!*") and "In the tunnel, in the darkness, / shines a five-point star!" ("*U tunelu usred mraka / sija zvijezda petokraka!*") There would be celebratory bonfires, around which there would be more singing, and probably some comradely making out would take place. For years, she would be proud of the sweat she spilled with the best of the Yugoslav youth to construct the highway, of earning her *udarnik** badge, of taking part in building the country, even if symbolically.

The practice of youth work actions (*omladinske radne akcije*) lasted into the eighties, and she often suggested that I should do it too because I'd always have the experience of taking part in common projects, working with others, and singing with them by the bonfire. I always defiantly refused. For not only did voluntary youth actions become, by the time I was young, a parody of the great ones from my mother's youth, but my teenage politics were indistinguishable from my precocious cynicism. For one thing, I never cared for that kind of shared work-related ecstasy; no blister or sunburns could ever make me proud and joyous; I thought that youth brigades were a form of forced labor whose main goal was indoctrination; I deplored what I called their "primitive patriotism." I committed myself early to a life of contemplative, productive laziness and hated singing along with other people, being one with a collective, even at rock shows. I was what they call an individual. After the war, to our mother's dismay, my sister and I started referring to the Highway of Brotherhood and Unity as the Highway of Youth and Foolishness (Autoput Mladost ludost). But now I envy her; I envy the sense that she was building something larger; I envy the nobility and honor that might come with being part of a civic endeavor.

It was at a youth work action that my mother became a member of the Communist Party, due to her hard work and positive spirit and the *udarnik* badge. Many of her friends and fellow volunteers joined the party too, for it was a cool thing to do. She was

* *Udarnik*, translatable in English as "shock worker," was a highly productive worker, someone who'd show the way, be the vanguard, for the less productive ones.

a devout party member thereafter, and it became part of her personality, as much as a religion might be for a religious person. She believed (and still does) in social justice, generosity, and a fair distribution of wealth. She believed in the system committed to making the country better; Tito and the party were that system. Before World War Two, she liked to say, there had been only seventy-five kilometers of paved road in all of Yugoslavia, while the Highway of Brotherhood and Unity alone was about four hundred kilometers.

Much like any other state, Yugoslavia trained its citizens to be patriots, taught them to be enthusiastically obedient, by way of public rituals. While the kids of the United States had to (and many still do) pledge allegiance to the flag, we had Tito's picture in every classroom. From the very beginnings of Yugoslav socialism, the cultural enforcement of patriotism depended on ideological pageants like the Relay of Youth (Štafeta mladosti), which was important for maintenance of Tito's personality cult: a baton symbolizing best wishes for his birthday would start in Kumrovec, his birthplace, and travel around Yugoslavia carried by the hands of youths, stopping in various towns and cities for a worshipful speech and rally (*slet*), allowing the youths to pledge their allegiance to their leader. On May 25 each year, the baton would be delivered to Tito by a young person deemed to be simultaneously exceptional and typical. The big birthday celebration would take place at a stadium in Belgrade and would feature the youths performing choreographed exercises to show their mettle and commitment. At the culmination of the spectacle, the chosen youth would run up a long flight of stairs and hand over to Tito the blatantly phallic baton and, panting all along, recite a statement of grateful adulation, allegiance, and best wishes from all the peoples and minorities (*narodi i narodnosti*) of Yugoslavia. Tito would sometimes benevolently pet the baton carrier on the head. The whole show was always televised and families around the country watched it like it was the Super Bowl.* We did it too, but as soon as I entered adolescence, I had no compunction about mocking the atmosphere of idiotic uniformity, the ideological clichés and the young muscly men twirling wooden rifles and lifting their female comrades over their heads, while the commentators treated the whole propagandistic display as a spontaneous expression of the youths' love for Tito and as a work of public art. Eventually I lost interest in it altogether, not least because Tito died in 1980, while the relay continued. In the eighties, at the peak of my rebellious years, it was delivered to some bland apparatchik whom I routinely perceived as my exact enemy. In 1987, the official poster for the relay, designed by a sneakily subversive Slovenian art group, turned out to be an exact copy of a Nazi propaganda poster. Within a couple of years, the relay was as dead as Tito; within four, so was Yugoslavia.

Mama was always offended by my dismissiveness of all that propaganda, of the disciplining patriotic rhetoric, by my dismissing the belief in socialism and the loyalty to the party. She'd often resent me for "finding nothing sacred," and took it personally, as an expression of my disrespect for her. A gap opened between us, ideological and generational, resembling in many ways the gap between her and her parents' generation, except that I never (until fairly recently) felt guilty about that discontinuity.

When Tito died, I was sixteen, and gleefully eager to partake in the unraveling of the socialist ideology, mainly because I found it oppressively boring. I was a natural, cacophonous anarchist, my ideological guidelines provided by the guitars of the Clash and the Jam and Gang of Four. By default, and typically, I appreciated everything that annoyed my parents, before I even considered its

* Which is, of course, exactly the same kind of ideological pageant.

actual value. Proudly and rebelliously, I accused my parents' generation in general—and Mama in particular—of failure to live up to the utopian promises and hand me over a future I could find worthy and comfortable. I was committedly oblivious to the fact that they had to work for what I took for granted. As far as they were concerned, however, I was well taken care of and had little to worry about, other than my school. When my mother asked me, "What are you complaining about? You have everything!," I would proudly retort, "I have no future!," thereby alluding, over her socialist head, to a line from the Sex Pistols anti-anthem "God Save the Queen." I recall a long and lengthy argument with my mother, which eventually turned into a shouting match, about a letter written by a group of Yugoslav dissident intellectuals demanding unfettered freedom of speech. I didn't know what exactly was in the letter because it was banned from being published; therefore I read only the editorials that endorsed its banishment. So I insisted on the right to read it and make up my own mind, while she claimed that those dissidents did not have good intentions. I was sixteen, living with my parents, and therefore all about principles, while she insisted she had taught me nothing—"You taught me to use my own head!," I'd scream. "That's as well as you can do!" She was convinced that we clashed often because we were too similar.

It is also true that there were times when she had doubts. In the late sixties, the students of Yugoslavia hit the streets just like their peers all over the world. The socialist Yugoslav government didn't have patience with massive dissent, particularly at a time when "external and internal" enemies were even more active than usual. The party machinery renounced the Yugoslav youths and their bourgeois tendencies, as did the institutions of the state, and the youths got their young asses kicked both rhetorically and actually. Mama, who always liked to announce her principled fondness of the youths (*Ja sam uvijek volila omladinu!*), was so disgusted that she stopped going to party meetings for a year, until Tito came out and strategically acknowledged that some of the student demands had merit. It took a few years before she fully returned to the party's fold, but never again with the same youthful enthusiasm.

With all that, life in Yugoslavia could never be reduced to its ideological practices and public rituals of indoctrination, even if they were essential to the culture. The progress and optimism that marked the decades after World War Two were evident in the creation of the middle class, which consisted of people exactly like my parents who, born in homes with dirt floors, ended up with college degrees and good jobs in big cities. They owned cars and weekend houses, spent summer vacations on the coast, and traveled out of the country without visas. They lived in rent-free apartments provided by state companies where they worked through retirement. They took care of their elderly parents in the countryside, visiting often (but never enough) and returning home with supplies of hearty peasant food, which they stored on their balconies and in the freezer chests bought with low-interest loans. Their children lived with them well into their twenties, even beyond, constantly and shamelessly. They planned to retire somewhere in nature, that is, to their weekend house.

Much as in a "free" country like the United States, Yugoslav culture reflected back to its middle class their everyday practices in the form of narratives cleansed of conflicts and doubts, infused with latent propaganda, and spiced with a lot of good humor, all of which made the system look eternal, natural, and indestructible. The Yugoslav culture—which really meant television and popular music—of the sixties and seventies, up to Tito's death, featured people like my parents, regardless of their ethnic background. They'd turn on the TV and see themselves, played by household-name actors addressing one another as comrades and cracking the same kinds of jokes about women gossiping, men being unable to locate their socks, and their country-bumpkin mothers-in-law coming for a visit, buckets of stinky pickled cabbage in tow.

Yugoslavia was a discursive universe, if you will, wherein the largest object was its freshly minted socialist middle class. In that universe, everything made sense to Mama because she was an indelible part of it, because it grew around an idea she worked hard to make real. She was a citizen of the country she built with her very hands, earning an *udarnik* badge, her Yugoslav identity a consequence of her life decisions, an outcome of her human, historical agency. Homeland was a practice, a daily operation, not a nostalgic one. She did not define homeland by the hundreds of years of unalterable history, but by the efforts and dreams of people just like her, people whose siblings were wounded in the liberation war, who left home at the age of eleven to go to school, who earned blisters at youth work actions, who in college shared their room and food with four friends from exactly the same background, and who were the first ones in their family since the beginning of time to earn a university diploma and buy a television set on which they could watch themselves. Eventually they'd be told by their own children (that is, me) that all of their efforts were in vain because they had been fucking it up from the very beginning.

Mama experienced the breakup of Yugoslavia as a dissolution of her homeland. What was destroyed was the framework within which her life—its very trajectory—had been self-legitimizing, where she never had to explain herself to anybody. But her family homestead had been within the geographical borders of Bosnia since time immemorial; except for the four college years, she never lived outside it until she migrated to Canada. While Yugoslavia was a practice based on an idea, Bosnia and Sarajevo were the actual space where she lived, with smells and neighbors and a particular language. As long as Yugoslavia lasted, Bosnia fit into the idea and practice—it was the part of the country where the values of brotherhood and unity were practiced most sincerely and crucially.* With the demise of Yugoslavia, Bosnia was left unprotected and the complicated multicultural space was severely damaged. Mama had to leave it, and for good.

With her migration to Canada, she lost, figuratively and literally, everything that had constituted her as a person: from property to ideology; from shared public rituals to her bedroom; from the sentimental tchotchkes she'd kept since the beginning of her married life to her chosen citizenship; from the unconsciously familiar smells to the ubiquity of her native language; from the proximity to her friends and siblings to the comfortable feeling that everyone around her had access to the same referential field. Overnight she became a nobody, she often says, a nothing.

In Canada, she spends much of the time in and around the house. The house is modest and adorned with some family pictures, mostly of her children and four granddaughters, and various souvenirs from her former life in the former Yugoslavia: a picture of Tito; a model of a monument to the victims of fascist terror in Kozara, where her brother fought in the liberation war; a monograph about Emerik Blum, the founder and the first director of Energoinvest, where she spent her entire professional life. She doesn't drive, so when she goes out, she accompanies Tata to visit his family, many of whom now live in the vicinity of Toronto. When they get together, the Hemons do their Ukrainian stuff, which is all well and nice, but provides little space for her. In fact, in her true Yugoslav spirit, she deplores all that nation-

* Before independence, Bosnians used to say: "Fuck the country that has no Bosnia!" ("*Jebeš zemlju koja Bosne nema!*")

alist sentimentality, the Ukrainian sort included. Though she appreciates Canada and her life there, the loss of Yugoslavia and Bosnia still casts its long shadow across that frozen land.

My father was fond of Yugoslavia, and still deems it to have been a pretty good country. When he traveled abroad for work, he felt he was representing it; when he traveled within its border, he was at home in all of its parts; he had family and friends all over. One of the standard songs he has always enjoyed singing at parties is about the beauties of the land between the river in Macedonia (the Vardar) and the mountain in Slovenia (Triglav), which is to say Yugoslavia, "birthed by our struggle" and "created by the worker's hand" and for which "a lot of blood was spilled."* He rooted passionately for national sports teams, even if his watching, for instance, the Yugoslav national soccer team usually meant berating the players' unprofessional laziness.

But his relationship with the idea of Yugoslavia was—and is—different from my mother's. For one thing, he didn't spend much time in the youth work actions, because in the summers he worked for Elektroprenos, ever ambitious and eager to learn. Though he was a member of the Communist Party, it was more a matter of a necessary line on his résumé, a condition for his professional advancement, than anything rooted in any kind of ideological thinking or deep beliefs.

On May 4, 1980, the day Tito died, my father and I were watching a Sunday afternoon variety show, mainly to follow soccer scores, when the broadcast was interrupted and the words *Umro je Drug Tito* (*Comrade Tito Has Died*) appeared on the screen. It

* "Jugoslavijo" ("O Yugoslavia!"), an unofficial anthem of the country, particularly after Tito's death.

was 15:05 (or 3:05 p.m.). Tito had been ill and the news was not unexpected. Nevertheless, we were in shock, because we didn't know what to do, as there was no precedent available to us—Tito's Yugoslavia was the only country we knew. I was sixteen, so I looked up to my father, who rose to bow his head before the TV, as though before Tito's bier, his hands overlapped over his groin. I did the same thing, and so we stood there in silence, waiting for the next thing to come, hoping we would receive some instruction from the screen. Eventually a presenter came on to read the official statement, unable to hold back his tears. I thought I should cry too; I felt guilty that I couldn't. Instead, I was thinking about my thinking that I should cry and about my feeling guilty and considering forcing some tears, all of which took me out of the tragic situation to a place from which I could reflect upon the situation, which is why I looked at my father as he stared at the screen. He seemed affected by the news, but also aware of the absurdity of our standing still and silent before a TV.

Each year right up until the war, the sirens all over Sarajevo (and in many other Yugoslav cities) would wail on May 4, exactly at 15:05, to mark the moment Tito (officially) died. People on the streets would freeze, trams would stop, drivers would get out of their cars and stand at respectful attention in the middle of the street until the wailing stopped. Each year, I made sure I didn't find myself on the street lest I would have to keep still in an absurd gesture of obedience to a ghost. But I'd always look out the window to watch the moment when time temporarily ceased to flow. It was always an eerie sight, like an image from a B-movie where an alien force immobilizes all life on Earth. Each time, I'd recall that bonding in awkwardness with my father, our improvising within a historical instant. For that was the first time it appeared to me that there was a germ of ambivalence about Tito and Yugoslavia on his part. He never acknowledged it or mentioned any of it, which is to say this could well be my projection—my father may well have been as much of a Yugoslav patriot as anyone.

A homeland cannot be consituted without nostalgia, without retroactively establishing a past utopia. In nationalist/patriotic imagination, nostalgia helps construct a perfect land of the past, pure and exclusively "ours" until it was contaminated by traitors and foreigners. Nationalist nostalgia is thus the source for insidious fantasies without which any Make X-land Great Again ideology is impossible, providing excuses for genocidal operations needed to restore the imaginary original purity. A private, personal nostalgia, however, always depends on the senses. No less of a fantasy, it is nonetheless privately constructed around the personal memories of sensory experiences: smells, tastes, visions, sounds, life in all its quotidian sensual detail. The personal homeland is the place where everything was more intensely experienced once upon a time and now seems unquestionably authentic, which is why its primary location is usually childhood or youth.

That is why Tata's true homeland is Vučijak, the first home he ever left and could never return to. In my father's Vučijak everything tasted better than anywhere else—not only the apples (wormy at best, plagued with some kind of fruit-shriveling fungus at worst), but also the water (mud-flavored, home to unspeakable microorganisms), not to mention the *steranka* cooked with milk freshly extracted from one of the cows enjoying their Edenic situation. The authenticating hyperreality of nostalgic past found home in my father's endless Vučijak stories, the remembered intensity fueling his passionate, compelling narration. The running joke in our family is that Vučijak is the center of the universe, complete with an attendant mythology.

Vučijak is therefore a place fully constructed in Tata's mind and far more real than the actual place. Wherever he went around the world, including Canada, he spent much of his head time being in Vučijak, talking about it, comparing everything to the standards once established there; he never mythologized Sarajevo, where he lived for most of his adult life, to a comparable extent. Yet at no point in his life did he ever consider or even mention the possibility of returning to Vučijak, where after my grandparents' deaths he even inherited some land. The whole nostalgic operation is contingent precisely on his absence from Vučijak since his childhood. A perfect homeland is never available; otherwise the ideal might run into an indelible and ugly reality. Nationalists resolve this tension by way of exclusionary reshaping and violence; they strive to make the actual country fit their fantasies, for which genocide is often required. My father just tells stories with a lot of nostalgic embellishments.

The value of Vučijak is also contingent upon the fact that it was the only land the Hemons could ever call their own, literally and metaphorically. When my grandparents moved as children to Bosnia, the idea of Ukraine as homeland was, to say the least, feeble, at the level of rudimentary nationalist abstraction. They came from Galicia, a territory where nations and religions mixed in ways that—after the great ethnic cleansing of World War Two—are now neither remembered nor comprehensible. My grandmother's father, for instance, was Polish-speaking. (Many Ukrainian words I learned from my grandmother turned out to be Polish, which I discovered upon my first visit to Ukraine.) I remember seeing a picture of my grandmother's family in which her mother and sister wore traditional Ukrainian dresses, while her father wore a suit and her brothers wore those peaked Polish caps.

Thus was the Ukrainian homeland exclusively a cultural practice, an abstraction created by and therefore present in the songs and stories and language, all of which were shared and reproduced in Vučijak, or wherever they may have ended up after the Big War Bang scattered them all over the universe. No one in my family went to Ukraine more than a couple of times in their life, and for a week or so each time, even though we still have family there. The abstract Ukrainian homeland was therefore never even comparable to the original, because the original was never available.

To properly describe my father's identity and the related conception of homeland, I have to invoke an image of concentric circles: my family practiced their Ukrainianness on the hill of Vučijak, which was in the area near Prnjavor, which was in Bosnia, which was in Yugoslavia; Ukraine remained unavailable, except as the place of origin. After Yugoslavia fell apart and Bosnia was wounded and divided, after the migration, Ukrainianness became precious; seemingly paradoxically, Vučijak also increased its value.

In Canada, the Hemons were exposed to and helped by Ukrainian Ukrainians, who have a very strong presence in Canada, but the price was contracting a certain troubling amount of nationalist rhetoric, mythology, and politics. My father regularly watches the Ukrainian-language channel, and enters discussions with the native Ukrainians about the political situation in Ukraine, even though he has been there only once, and briefly, since its independence. In his weekly choir practices, he sings with his brothers songs in which patriotic Ukrainians give their lives for their homeland, but they themselves have no interest whatsoever in visiting that homeland, let alone "returning there." And his knowledge of Ukrainian history was mainly acquired by way of hearsay and reading obsolete books, which do not even rise to the level of nationalist propaganda, since they might have been written in 1917 or so. In Canada, Ukraine is a nationalist homeland, which for Tata has no connection with any kind of personal reality or sensory experience, an abstraction squared.

At the same time, one of the defining markers in the nostalgic universe that revolves around Vučijak is that all that Tata learned about being Ukrainian he learned there. He learned from his parents and cousins and neighbors, all of whom were concrete in their bodies and practices, and are now deposited in endless story cycles. The home of the Ukrainian homeland is Vučijak, which, like the rest of Tata's life (apart from the four years in college) has always been in Bosnia. Which is to say that singing Ukrainian songs in Canada brings back the hill in Bosnia called Vučijak.

All of his identities are interconnected and interdependent. This is the kind of thing that a history of migration in our family allows for: an irreducible and incredibly rich identity rooted in concentric homelands. But that rich complexity has a steep price: our family has left behind a trail of homelands, no longer available except by way of memory, music, and storytelling. Our history is the history of unassuageable longing for the home that could never be had.

3

CATASTROPHE

My father likes to talk to people, ask them questions, tell them stories and hear theirs. Sometimes when I read, or watch TV, or just silently stare into space, he sits next to me and orders: "Talk!" I bristle, but then I yield and, of course, end up talking. It's not just that he cannot stand silence, nor is it that he cannot bear the thought that people might have nothing to say to each other. It's also his voracious curiosity, undampened by his age—everyone, he assumes, has some story to tell, not least his professionally storytelling son. My father expects other people to engage with the world, which has somehow delegated him to probe you, and conduct a conversation. Silence is the death of storytelling, and thus of love.

In 2007, my wife, Teri, and I and our newborn daughter, Ella, went to visit her parents in Florida for Christmas, and my parents came along from Canada. Teri and I had married in Paris earlier that year, which was when my parents had encountered hers and gotten splendidly along with them. Now, in Pensacola Beach, my parents spent time with Teri's extended family, which frequently gets together and features untold numbers of aunts, uncles, and cousins, including the friends of the family who have been over time absorbed into the kinship. My parents quickly saw that the essential structure and practices of an African-American family were very much like those of our Bosnian one, and they liked that quite a bit. One thing was somewhat lacking, however—Teri's family didn't do as much of what my family always did (and does still): they didn't spend a lot of time telling stories. Their history, for whatever reason, was not entirely available by way of collective, public narration.

Thus, as we walked one balmy day along the splendid white-sand beach toward Fort Pickens, where the great Geronimo had died imprisoned by the freedom-loving United States, as seabirds coasted over our heads below clouds scarce and meringue, my father said to my wife: "Teri, tell me about your family. What bad happened?"

Teri was gracious, but could not fully satisfy his curiosity. Apart from the general and everlasting calamity of U.S. racism—applicable to an entire population—there were few particular historical and family disasters she could tell him about. My father found that perplexing, even a bit disappointing—for if nothing bad had happened, it was hard to imagine how any stories could be forthcoming. If nothing bad happened, what do we have to talk about? If nothing bad happened, what was it that happened? What is the story of nothing happening?

Teri knew, of course, that my parents had failed to experience the siege of Sarajevo and ended up as refugees in Canada. She knew well that bad things had happened in the history of the Hemons, the baddest and the most recent one being the war in Bosnia. But my father's question was one of those moments when I felt compelled to explain my parents to my good wife, to establish and introduce the theoretical foundations of their thought system, to instruct her—and anyone willing to submit and listen—on the ways in which trauma alters the very structure of the world and reality.

For I instantly understood why my father would ask a question like that, I recognized his compulsion. The "what bad happened" was a shorthand (or longhand) for catastrophe. He asked her to lead him into the history of her family by way of outlining the ruptures that defined it, for that's how he would tell the story of our family: the wars, the injuries, the displacements, the losses, the struggles, the moments of danger and despair. There could be no history without catastrophe; to outline a history, one had to narrate its disasters; to formulate one's position in the world, one had to define oneself in relation to the experienced catastrophes. And that which could not be narrated could not be comprehended. A family—a world, a life—without a catastrophe could not be conceptualized, because it was an impossible proposition. If catastrophe is the dramatic event that initiates the resolution of the plot,* then its absence suggests a possibility that the tragic plot will never be resolved. A catastrophe, in other words, might be a trap, but it also allows for a narrative escape. If you were lucky enough to have survived the catastrophic plot twist, you get to tell the story—you *must* tell the story.

I'm of a staunch belief that anything that can be said and thought in one language can be thought and said in another. The words might have a different value or interpretative aura, but there is always more than enough overlapping not to dismiss the process of translation, which is essential not only to the project of

* *Encyclopædia Britannica*: "Catastrophe, the final action that completes the unravelling of the plot in a play, especially in tragedy. Catastrophe is a synonym of denouement. The term is sometimes applied to a similar action in a novel or a story."

literature, but to the project of humanity as well. Yet it can be exceedingly difficult, particularly if the meaning of a word/concept is inscribed in the body.

There is thus the Bosnian word *katastrofa*, which, most obviously, comes from the same Greek word* as its English counterpart "catastrophe." But in Bosnian—or at least in the language my family uses—*katastrofa* seems to have a substantially different value and applicability than "catastrophe" has in U.S. English. The Hemons use it all the time, deploying it in the contexts that would be less appropriate in English. My mother would, for instance, reprimand my father by saying, *Ti si, ćale, katastrofa!* (Translatable as: *You, Pop, are a catastrophe!*) because he left a trail of dirty socks all the way to the bedroom. Or my father, in his report on a pipe bursting in their house wall, would use *katastrofa* to refer to the necessity of digging through said wall to find the source of the leak. My sister, who lives in London, would describe as *katastrofa* the leaden January skies depressingly looming over England and her head. And I could apply *katastrofa* to, say, the inability of Liverpool FC to defend set pieces, or to the realization that I'm in the bathroom without toilet paper and the nearest roll is at least a hallway away. One of the few Bosnian words Teri understands is *katastrofa*, mainly by way of hearing me bemoan various unfortunate turns of events, including a traffic jam on the way to pick up our kids from school and, not infrequently, the balance in our bank account.

None of this indicates that we don't take the possibility of catastrophe seriously. On the contrary, the ease with which the word *katastrofa* is applied is related to its very ubiquity. Rather than existing exclusively in magnanimous, tragic dimensions, *katastrofa*

* *Katastrophe* (καταστροφή), meaning *overturning.*

is everywhere, its particles always shimmering all around us like shrapnel on a sunny day.

I was once visiting my parents in Canada, and at some point drove them to visit some of my numerous family in and around Hamilton. My mother was in the backseat, and as I followed a curve in the road, her gaze fell upon a bridge being constructed over what would become the Red Hill Valley Parkway. The bridge was unfinished, reaching halfway across the valley and, in the fifteen seconds or so needed to make it around the curve, we saw its exposed armature, its sharp edges looming over the void of the valley. In those fifteen seconds, however, Mama managed to say: "Look at that bridge. It looks pretty weak to me. That bridge will surely collapse."

I was, to say the least, taken aback, so much so that I began driving a bit carelessly while commencing an argument with Mama about the fact that never in recent Canadian history had a newly built bridge suddenly collapsed.* I insisted that she tell me how in the world could she make such a claim, but I was doing it so aggressively that she clammed up and would not further discuss the bridge and the certainty of its future demise. In the fifteen seconds the half bridge had been exposed to her gaze within the benign Canadian landscape she managed to identify an impending disaster. Her catastrophic perception as well as her ability to instantly formulate it were finely tuned to the particular frequencies of *katastrofa*, her very reality shaped by it.

And it was something my sister and I grew up with. Mama was prone to not only warning us about danger but describing an imagined gruesome consequence: "Don't run around with that pencil, you'll stab yourself in the eye." Or: "Leave the scissors

* In 1958, Vancouver's Second Narrows Bridge collapsed, killing nineteen and injuring seventy-nine people.

alone, you'll cut off your fingers." We were annoyed by it—and still are, if she warns her granddaughters in the same manner—and took it too often to be a mode of thinking that can simply be willfully corrected. It was only recently that I realized that way back, when she was a kid, her brother was innocently playing *klis*, his mother perhaps warning him, "Be careful with those sticks!" only for her worst nightmare to come true.

I remember reading somewhere about an experiment in which film footage of a modern farm was shown to a group of aboriginal subjects* who had never seen anything like it, and who were then asked to list things they saw—and they all said: chickens. The people running the experiment looked at the footage, couldn't see any chickens, showed the footage again to the aboriginal group, and they all, again, said: chickens. This time, the footage was slowed down, and the experiment-runners discovered the chicken. It was present on the edges of the shot in fewer than twenty frames before it walked out, which is to say it was visible for less than a second. The obvious conclusion would be that human perception is always primarily attuned to what is already known and familiar, a kind of perceptual confirmation bias.† Which is to say that *katastrofa* is my mother's chicken.

My parents are self-taught experts on *katastrofa*, against their will, despite their desires; the most recent war was without doubt the greatest occasion for self-education. My mother hadn't expected

* This may have been an inadvertent fantasy, as I couldn't find any reference to the experiment. It might also be an example of subjective validation, a cognitive bias by which a person will consider a piece of information to be correct if it has any personal meaning to them.

† Wikipedia: "The tendency to search for, interpret, favor, and recall information in a way that confirms one's preexisting beliefs or hypotheses."

the war to come, so it crashed into her life like a meteorite, and with much the same disorienting effect. She still remembers her shock: the shell explosions, the curfew, the dissolution of her routines, her inability to fit the fact of war into the structure of the reality within which she operated. I remind her now and then that she had said, when I called her from Chicago in the spring of 1992, "It's going to stop soon, they're already shooting less than yesterday," and she acknowledges her naïveté. But she in turn reminds me that everything they had worked for was erased overnight by war, not only rendering it all retroactively meaningless, but also irreversibly destabilizing the very possibility of any structural permanence in their subsequent life. After the experience of war, she couldn't sustain her belief in the inertia of reality—in the force that makes things continue as they are. Her mind now rejects the possibility of another war, but at the same time the unnatural rupture she had experienced makes any kind of stability suspect. Back before the war, she, like many, was protected by the unimaginability of the unimaginable—a comfortable, if false, assumption that what cannot be imagined cannot happen, or even be happening.* Presently, she would still, if she could, hide behind the unimaginable, but what had been unimaginable has already happened and is therefore always imaginable, and thus has that screen been shredded. To her, being old or sick is not a *katastrofa*—for that is, she says, natural—so she's not afraid of it. It's not that she fears war either; what she fears is that something will destroy the newly acquired (very Canadian) stability, that something might undo that particular reality.

My father was also traumatized by the war, but what he experienced as a *katastrofa*—a very personal one, he says—was primarily the rupture in the continuity of human nature. Before

* This is known as normalcy bias, a belief people enter when facing a disaster.

the war, he could believe in the stable goodness (or not-goodness) of people: they were who they were and you knew who they were; you avoided the bad ones, appreciated the good ones. What catastrophically shocked him was the abrupt transformation he saw among some of his friends and acquaintances from neighbors into haters, from good to bad, from decent people into killers—that was the unimaginable for him, that *overturning* of human nature. When I ask him if he spends time expecting another *katastrofa*, as yet unimaginable, he says, "We're old. There might be a *katastrofa*, but we won't be around for it, so we don't care."

My sister, Kristina, who has switched career paths in her forties to become a psychotherapist, appears clear-eyed about the whole thing. "*Katastrofa* is the imaginary (and sometimes real) actualization of the worst possible outcome of a given situation," she wrote to me. "The situation could vary from a missed bus or burnt lunch to death and war." She went on: "*Katastrofa* is the state of expectation of the worst, as well as preparation for avoidance, for the struggle against it, or for the managing of the outcome. That state is sometimes conscious, but it is permanently subconscious." She also thinks—and I agree—that there is some cultural determination to this perpetual expectation. My father recalls his father firmly believing that it was impossible to live for fifty years without experiencing war—Deda Ivan himself had experienced two world ones. And both my sister and I remember the slogan, attributed to Tito himself and repeated to all the children and citizens of Yugoslavia for decades before the war: "We must live as though peace will last for a hundred years, and be ready as though war will start tomorrow." One day, the war did start tomorrow, ending the peace that had lasted for the record forty-six years. If scientists are right in claiming that trauma can have epigenetic consequences, creating genes that can then be passed to descendants, then *katastrofa* is inscribed in our cells.

I once asked my parents what the opposite of *katastrofa* would be. "Normal life," they said, in unison. To them, normal life is a self-evident category—it's a life that is normal. After I pressed them, they expounded: it requires stability, always dependent on the constancy and continuity of the state and government, which allows for raising, educating, and empowering children, as well as for an overall sense of progress. Normal life, my father clarified, also has nuances, and it's improved* with things like beekeeping, singing, children, skiing, sports, etc. I realized that for them normal life was in fact the very life they had before the war, what they had lost. Normal life is therefore simultaneously a nostalgic and a utopian project, both irretrievable and unachievable.

Normal life is delimited and defined by catastrophe: it's the life unruptured, the life before *katastrofa* made it unavailable and, at the same time, visible. And, inversely, *katastrofa* is whatever ruptures life, what makes its stability, its necessary biological and emotional inertia, impossible. Much as catastrophe in tragedy necessitates the resolution of the plot, *katastrofa* necessitates a narrative of normal life, which we can perceive only through the catastrophic screen dividing our life into the before and the after.

But compulsively imagining *katastrofa* has another important function. Because trauma is always a rupture of normalizing continuity established by routines, because it always violates the ontological inertia that establishes "reality" as real—that which is must continue to be—it is always previously unimaginable. The worst possible *katastrofa* is the one we could never imagine. Ergo, each imagined *katastrofa* protects us from its full impact; it is the weakened virus that might inoculate us against the real thing. Imagining all the bad things that could happen reduces the number of the really bad things that could actually happen, limiting

* The exact translation of the word he used—*uljepšan*—would be "beautified."

them only to what is unimaginable. The imaginable *katastrofa*—imaginable because imagined—is always already absorbed into the as-yet-unruptured domain of reality; it has already taken up its place in the narrative armature of life experience. Or, more simply, it fits right into the stories we tell ourselves to make sense of the world. The price of this self-soothing is terrible, even if it is well worth it: all of our reality, and hence all of our narration, is organized around catastrophe.

But there is another way to ease the anxieties related to the ever-oncoming catastrophe, and that is to look into the future by way of a weather forecast. I still don't fully understand my parents' obsession with the weather forecast, but it was never not present. We used to eat together at the time of the afternoon news program, listening to the radio as if to an oracle when the weatherman came on at exactly 4:25. In Canada, my parents' favorite channel features not only weekly projections, but also offers information (or informed guesses) as to the weather and temperatures in the morning, afternoon, evening, and night, complete with little icons with the sun or a cloud or slanted raindrops. They often act scandalized at the prognosis ("Oh, my God, it is going to rain in the afternoon!"), as though an afternoon rain following a sunny morning violated some basic rules of the world's proper behavior. But the forecast allows them to engage with the future and the possibility of catastrophe inherent in the idea of the future, in small manageable doses. Obsessing over the future weather is a kind of homeopathy for their traumatized souls.

One more thing: I wasn't entirely truthful when I said that I don't fully understand their obsession, because I have it too. Presently, on my not-so-smart phone, I have a couple of weather apps, which allow me to see not only the forecast for the day and the week, but also the statistical probability of precipitation, and also UV indices, wind speed, and humidity levels. I don't care about the weather, really, as I do very little that depends on it. All I care about is the future, because all I worry about is catastrophe.

Which leads me to another confession: my mind is linguistically obsessive, ever relentlessly and involuntarily generating wordplays and verbal distortions, which frequently find their way into my narratives. There must be a diagnosis covering that kind of constant chatter inside my head, some medical term referring to the fact that, every day of my normal life, I talk aloud to myself in Bosnian, usually in the voice of a Sarajevo street thug—cursing, threatening, insulting, mainly myself (or, rather, that weak part of myself that is not a Sarajevo thug). Well, that language-obsessed mind has spontaneously come up with the name of Sergei Katastrofenko—an imaginary Slav, likely Ukrainian—who has been flickering for a while as a possibility of a character, or a joke, or a catastrophe. The name Sergei Katastrofenko often bounces around my head as I scan the world for my collapsing bridges and other chicken nuggets of disaster, even as he hasn't quite acquired a full voice, let alone a body. But if he ever acquires it—and when that happens, I know I'll be losing my mind—he'll become a perfect embodiment of *katastrofa*, of the idea that no reality, nor the narrative of it, is possible without random catastrophic events.

4

OTHER LIVING CREATURES

Part of the Hemon family lore is that the Ukrainians imported beekeeping to northwest Bosnia. Before their arrival, the natives kept bees in mud-and-straw hives; in order to extract honey they'd kill the swarm with smoke and destroy the hive. In contrast, the Ukrainians brought an apiculture featuring wooden hives and frames and methodologies of harvesting honey that not only kept the bees alive but helped them thrive. There is also a family story in which my great-grandfather Teodor had dysentery just as World War One was ending. As the end was approaching, he demanded to be taken to his bees. He sat by the hives and wept, saying goodbye to them. The following day he died.

Naturally, my grandfather Ivan became a beekeeper himself; indeed, he was one of the founders of the Apicultural Society in Prnjavor. Throughout my childhood, whenever I went to visit my grandparents, there was a bee willing to sting me. But there was also the ubiquity of honey, of the most fragrant kind. There was also my grandfather's shack, where the beekeeping equipment and tools were kept, redolent of wood, honey, and wax. The only place where I can nowadays encounter that smell is in the Barn, my father's workshop, where he stores his beekeeping stuff.

My father helped his father with his bees whenever he could, learning from him. But we lived in Sarajevo, and Tata traveled a lot, so that he established his apiary only after Deda Ivan went blind and was incapacitated. It fell to my father to continue the beekeeping, and he would spend weekends, sometimes weeks, working in a small apiary at my grandparents' homestead. The purpose and goal of his beekeeping wasn't just the honey, but also a connection with and an extension of the family tradition. It allowed him to enter a managed mental zone, a headspace centered around a total focus, where the only sound was buzzing and all you could perceive was the highly choreographed, logical world of the hardworking bees. My father has always been high-strung, but beekeeping did not reward tension and stress—the apiary was a domain of peace.

Even when I was at an age that made me disinclined to talk or listen to my parents, I enjoyed Tata's expounding on the science and philosophy of beekeeping. Nothing related to bees and honey was ever bad, everything was always fascinating. Honey could never get spoiled, he claimed, because of its antibacterial properties, and because the impurities float to the surface, where you can just skim them off. As far as he was concerned, the better the honey, the more solid it becomes when crystallized—the best honey would be rock-solid, yet it could be easily liquefied with a steady application of warmth. The honey buried with the pharaohs in their pyramids was therefore still edible, and probably delicious. Propolis, which the bees use to seal and disinfect their hives, could heal anything. Royal jelly, which the bees use to nurture the larvae that would become the queen, was the healthiest substance in the world. A secret of healthy life was at least a spoonful of honey a day. We used to make fun of our parents and their parental insistence (i.e., nagging) by claiming that they believed that all one needed to raise children properly were two regularly issued orders: "You should be studying" (*Bolje bi ti bilo da učiš*), which was Mama's favorite, and "Take a little bit of honey" (*Uzmi malo meda*), which was what Tata would say whenever any of us was under the weather, or was just craving something sweet. The former covered the mind, the latter the body, and the combination of the two covered everything.

After he was diagnosed with prostate cancer in 2005, Tata concocted a mixture of propolis and royal jelly and ingested it copiously, though there was not even a shred of evidence that it could have any effect on the cancerous growth—what had healing properties, if anything, was the belief in the inherent goodness of the concoction. And he could rhapsodize on the beauty of the bees' organization and discipline: they dance to show other bees where a new field in bloom was; they move in a particular way around the queen bee—and he would pull out of a hive the frame that was home to a queen and locate her by reading the bees' movement. When I looked at the frame, all I saw was a chaotic mess of potentially dangerous insects; what he saw was a highly harmonious community, an orderly society. The world of bees was for him the one realm where everything was always good, the way it had always been and was always supposed to be, where it all made sense.

It has long been accepted among our family that the immediate reason for my parents' leaving Sarajevo on May 2, 1992, was that the apiary in Vučijak needed to be attended to. The spring works of beekeeping were overdue; the hives had to be prepared for the summer so that the bees could thrive. Throughout that first war summer, the bees thrived indeed, since my father had nothing else to do but care for them, what with the war suspending all non-survival activities in my parents' lives, and his need for inhabiting a logical, organized society massively increased. Honey was my parents' only source of income, and they could not quite appreciate the historical irony of selling honey to the passing Serb troops on their way to fight for the cause that undid their/our life. When my mother got sick and had to be transferred to Subotica for a surgery in 1992, Tata stayed behind for a bit, not least to prepare the bees for the upcoming winter. He expected to come back the following spring, as he had many springs before. But he never would.

In 1992, I lived in Chicago's Ukrainian Village, working for minimum wage and hopping between cheap apartments. I was obsessed with mail (as I still am), since that was the main means of communication with my family—there was no Internet then, and phone calls were prohibitively expensive. So obsessed, in fact, that even if I'd filed the change-of-address form upon moving from an apartment, I'd still feel a compulsion to go and check with my previous landlord to see if some mail had been delivered. One day in early 1993, I stopped by my previous apartment, where the landlady—a mean Ukrainian widow—told me there had been no mail for me. I did not believe her and checked, on a hunch, the garbage container behind the building. At the bottom, among leaking plastic and dog-poop bags, I discovered a bundle of letters for me, among which there was a letter from my father, stinky and stained with garbage juice.

In that letter, my father wrote about the news that he'd received about his bees. The letter came from Hungary, where he worked at the time, but it was written from a very sorrowful place: he'd heard that his apiary was destroyed. Earlier that winter, he wrote, someone kicked the hives down off their stands and broke them open to steal the frames with honey left as food for bees, pouring the hibernating swarms out on the snow, where they froze to death. I can't find the letter, as it is in some box in the storage room, so I can't quote him exactly, but I clearly remember his writing—as I remember my tears while reading—that for him the destruction of the bees was worse than having left Sarajevo and losing everything in the war. What kind of people, he asked, would kill bees for no reason? The annihilation was not just of the apiary, but of the entire family tradition, of our presence in Vučijak, of his life there. Beyond that frozen swarm was nothing but a void. And the void followed him to Canada, where there was winter and nothing else—no family, no friends, no home, no work, no bees.

But in the early spring of 1994, just a few months after landing in Canada, Tata miraculously identified a beekeeper at a mall parking lot: the man's pickup truck was packed with empty hives. Tata accosted him and introduced himself as a fellow beekeeper. They had an informed conversation in a mixture of languages; the man was of Hungarian extraction; he gave Tata his contact info, invited him to come and look at his apiary; he told him about an upcoming meeting of the beekeepers' association in Hamilton.

Being a beekeeper is not unlike being a member of a worldwide sect complete with its own transnational language and mythology. It turned out that the Hungarian was married to a woman from the former Yugoslavia, so he could speak a little bit of Serbo-Croatian too. Tata was soon assisting the man in his apiary, engaging with him in theoretical discussions on the morphology of the queen bee. He attended beekeeper association meetings, where he met other beekeepers. With the help of his fellow beekeepers, he met a fruit producer who had on his farm a declining apiary, with no beekeeper to take care of it. Fruit producers often keep bees on their farms for the purposes of pollination and yield increase, so Tata was offered the apiary for nothing other than a promise that he would make it flourish and provide the fruit producer with a few jars of honey for personal use.

Eagerly, Tata did the necessary work and restored the apiary. At that time, Mama and he lived in a large apartment building, where they worked as superintendents (even though he had a job at a factory as well), so that he was able to establish a workshop in the basement where he could construct hives and frames. Once, as a few of his strong hives were getting close to swarming* and he could not go to the farm to check on them, he installed them on top of the building across the street. It was facing a cemetery, a prime feeding territory for bees with all the flowers and trees, and therefore the building's roof was a perfect place to stimulate swarming. The trouble was that neither my mother, who would have been apoplectic, nor the super of the building across the street knew what Tata was up to. I can't remember now whether I was present or whether I fully imagined it as he was telling me, but when he packed the building's elevator with hives full of bees to take them up to the roof, a tenant joined him for the ride. The tenant, possibly too Canadian to ask, kept staring warily at the hives, unnerved by the mysterious buzzing from the wooden

* If there is abundant food, the bees in a hive thrive and multiply, which leads them to start feeding a regular egg with royal jelly, thereby epigenetically creating another queen bee. When the new queen bee hatches, the old one takes part of the bees—a swarm—out of the hive. For an hour or two, the old queen bee hangs from some promontory point near the old hive, with all the other bees clinging to her. An alert beekeeper, having expected the swarming, shakes the swarm off into an empty hive and adds it to his apiary. If the beekeeper fails to catch the swarm, it will simply fly away in search of some new home, never to return.

boxes; my father kept mum. I envisioned a scenario in which, somehow, the bees escaped and attacked the neighbor, and my father lost his job, or even his immigration status, etc. But I also knew that he was the master of his apicultural domain and knew what he was doing. The bees swarmed on the building's roof, and he returned them to their home apiary without incident.

After my parents bought their current house in 2000, the bulk of Tata's apiary was moved to a clearing in the woods behind his workshop. He retired from the factory, and his main activity and sole purpose in life has become beekeeping. At the peak of the season, he might have forty or fifty hives, which require an enormous amount of work. But he extracts up to a ton and a half of honey and sells it to family, friends, and acquaintances. More important, between May and October, there is something to do every day.

He designed a label he sticks on the jars full of his merchandise. It features a bee that looks like a yellow jacket, and the words HEMON'S HONEY. At the bottom of the label, the words PURE NATURAL HONEY are proudly brandished. There is also a little paragraph for those simple customers who think that honey goes bad when it crystallizes:

> The natural form of honey is a crystal. It liquifies by warming in hot water (to 50 degrees C) where it holds all its natural characteristics.

Honey notwithstanding, the crucial part of the whole endeavor is just keeping the bees alive, as they are ceaselessly under the assaults of pesticides, parasites, and the unpredictable, cruel Canadian weather. In the winter, Tata worries about the long stretches of cold that prevent the bees from getting out of the hives to empty themselves, which they can do on a relatively warm day. It is not uncommon that half of his hives die by the spring; every summer he doubles the number, only to lose a half again the following winter. He fights varroa, the pernicious parasite that decimates bees, smoking the hives with the appropriate medicine. Then there are weak bee communities, those sad queenless hives, which need to be merged with the strong ones. And when the bees thrive they swarm, so that for much of the summer he is on watch lest swarms escape, never to be found again. More than once, he strategically ordered new, stronger queens from Australia. He had to stop raccoons from destroying empty hives. He devised a tool to collect a swarm hanging high on a tree: a basket attached to a long stick, with a hook to shake the branch. He designed a kind of table with a window on top to melt wax off the honeyless frames. He smuggled in a rotor from Bosnia (it was cheaper) and built a machine to open up the frames before honey extraction by way of a centrifuge, which he also built. The everlasting project of beekeeping requires constantly finding solutions and making decisions. Beekeeping is a mode of constant struggle, a matter of steady concern and involvement, something that keeps him away from the void by keeping him busy. After he was diagnosed with prostate cancer, he spent a few weeks working fifteen hours a day. The work, he said, helped him not think about cancer.

All people are created equal, but Tata vastly prefers those who show interest in the marvelous world of bees. He has cornered innocent bystanders at various parties, after they have innocuously stated their fondness for honey or expressed interest in how it's made. I've seen bafflement and amazement on the faces of the captive audience as Tata delivered in his limited English an unrelenting monologue on the theory and practice of beekeeping. Conversely, he has low tolerance for those who do not sufficiently appreciate the wonders of apiculture. A friend of mine once casually told him: "I don't consume as much honey as I should." To which Tata responded: "Well, that's your problem."

I went with him a couple of times to a Ukrainian Independence Day festival, which takes place every August near Toronto. There he sets up a table and lines it with labeled jars of Hemon's Honey, plus small containers of propolis solution. The customers are predominantly Ukrainian, so he speaks Ukrainian with them, in a dialect that is not only of a fly-in-amber variety, since it is what was spoken in Galicia a century before, but also features Bosnian words. There are only two kinds of honey he offers, dark and light (though the label identifies them inexplicably as WHITE/GOLD), the color depending on where the bees predominantly collected the pollen. When the prospective customers inquire about the selection, he'll point at the dark honey and identify it as *forest*, while the light kind is *field*. But for some, probably nostalgic, reason, Ukrainians are particularly fond of buckwheat honey. When a customer asks whether he has buckwheat honey, he'll dismiss their naïveté, delivering an unsolicited lecture: buckwheat honey is not that good to begin with; moreover, there isn't much buckwheat in Canada, and it's genetically modified anyway; the customer will back off. When a woman asked to try some of his honey, he said: "Why do you have to try? It's honey."

Though I have tried to mitigate his grumpiness by being solicitous and smiling, neither of which comes naturally to me, I understand that to him honey and beekeeping have a self-evident value and meaning others cannot perceive in just the same way. His *apilife*, the harmonious, logical domain of bees where he has full agency, is an alternative to his actual life, the chaos of history, where his agency is normally reduced to survivalist improvisation. Though I have little interest in the actual work of beekeeping, as I've never cared about doing manual work, I fully endorse its ideological value, its rich field of meaning. I can identify with my father's striving to find and protect a domain in which he can practice agency with dignity and some form of sovereignty. What beekeeping is to him, literature is to me.

Mama has always been prone to stating the obvious, but with added ethical weight. I have a distinct memory of her raising her hand, her index finger pointed upward, to declare conclusively that bees were good because they were very useful in their collecting honey from flowers; they deserved respect because they worked all the time. Her endorsement was in response to her children's making fun of their father's beekeeping. We were surprised by her response, as she never quite understood or accepted Tata's obsession with bees, which she primarily saw as just one of his many excuses to get out of the house. One of the reasons for her shortage of understanding, I think, is that bees only come en masse—they cannot be individualized and therefore cannot be anthropomorphized, nor have personalities. She, in another words, can't talk to them.

Mama anthropomorphizes animals primarily by addressing them as if they could understand what she is saying to them. On Jahorina, she often talked to the local skinny squirrels as if they were tiny babies; she talks the same way to the Canadian squirrels living in her backyard. She also speaks to feral Canadian cats, which she feeds, as they frequent the homestead, attracted by the abundance of squirrels. Sometimes, particularly in the winter, she lets those cats into the house, where they lounge about near the woodstove; she might deliver a monologue to the content cats explaining why they enjoy the warmth of fire so much.

Back when I was a boy, I constantly dreamt of having a pet, as all non-psychopath kids do. I was indoctrinated by the anthropomorphic cuteness of Disney characters, adept at forming a special bond of loyalty and understanding with their humans. I brought home sick pigeons, stray cats, and rain-soaked puppies, where they'd foul the furniture, sleep on the pillows, and shit on the carpet, none of which stopped me from begging Mama and Tata to let me keep them. I never got close to converting them, but Mama was the weaker link, as she'd talk guiltily to the puppy or the cat before making me kick them out on the street to struggle for survival.

Finally, in my twenties, I brought home a Siamese kitten, named him Stipica. Mama offered the feeblest resistance, and in no time she warmed up to him. The name* helped a lot, as she could baby-talk to him while he purred curled up next to her. When Stipica contracted peritonitis and subsequently died,† she was heartbroken, so much so that she preemptively vetoed any future pets.

But my sister and I, of course, paid no heed to her veto. On the way back from Jahorina, my sister picked up a stray white-and-black cat we christened Čedo, a name that to us sounded like a peasant one and therefore fitting her origins. Mama objected, again, as did Tata, but they were summarily ignored. Soon Mama was talking to Čedo in the high-pitched voice she normally used with children.

Čedo lasted longer than Stipica, and was a very smart cat. "She understands everything!" Mama would announce, after Čedo would bat at her calves asking to be fed. We'd let Čedo out on the street, and later call her from the balcony, by way of making a

* A diminutive of Stipe, a common Dalmatian name.

† His last action on this earth was climbing into my electric-guitar case to pee. This has no relevance except as a random memory.

hissing sound Tata, Kristina, and I used to locate each other in a crowd, and she would emerge from the bushes or from under a car. Čedo never lost her stray-cat edge, particularly enjoying the wrestling matches with my hand, which she would scratch to the point of bleeding. When I once mock-angrily said, "Čedo, you animal!," Mama protested, "Don't you talk to her that way!"

We'd find Čedo purring on Tata's chest as he stroked her head until he saw us, whereupon he'd shoo the cat away. Having a pet was an urban, bourgeois affectation and went against the peasant ethics of utility, where animals are fed and taken care of only if they have a functional role to serve—no one kept cows for their big, beautiful eyes, or dogs because they fetched. When we visited Vučijak and brought Čedo along, Tata would go out of his way to show to his family that he didn't care about the useless creature, sometimes even kicking at the cat, to Mama's consternation. But when he discovered a mouse in one of his beehives, he installed Čedo near his apiary and ordered her to hunt for the pest. Čedo spent much of the day squinting in the sun and doing absolutely nothing. When she eventually got up and caught the mouse, she legitimately and irreversibly earned Tata's affection.

Čedo also died, run over by a car outside our Sarajevo apartment building, and Mama was heartbroken again. Before we could even bring up getting another pet, Mama told us with absolute certainty that she would not let any other living creature into the house, because she couldn't stand mourning all over again.

Nonetheless, in the summer of 1991, within a year of my mother's most stringent pet prohibition, my sister brought home a gorgeous Irish setter we named Mek. Mama's resistance crumbled pretty much instantly, and the dog was absorbed into the family with no qualms. The following year, Mek would be with my parents on the last train out of Sarajevo. He spent the summer of 1992 with them in Vučijak, and then lived with Mama in the tiny apartment in Novi Sad.* He was her only companion throughout that time; she talked to him as to a close friend, and he, she is convinced, understood everything. When my parents worked out a way to migrate to Canada, Mek sensed the forthcoming departure, and would follow her everywhere around the apartment or lie at her feet if she sat down, because he feared that they might leave without him. Tata tried to persuade her to leave the dog behind, but she insisted that she was going nowhere without Mek. Her brother also tried to present a case for not taking him, but she just wept until he gave up. To her, Mek was not only family, but the one and only link to her previous life, his innocent love the only thing she could carry on to her new life.

So Mek arrived in Canada and shared my parents' immigrant life until he died at the age of sixteen. Mama cooked for him, worried about his arthritis, brushed and stroked him, talking all along. Tata spoke to him too. One of Mek's favorite things was Tata's whispering into his ear. His eyes would widen and he'd readjust his posture in reaction to something Tata would say, so much so that Mama would exclaim: "He understands everything!" What Mek did indeed unconditionally understand was their love for him.

After he died in 2006, Mama was in deep mourning, because Mek was family. There are still framed pictures of Mek all over their house; to this day Mama is likely to burst into tears when remembering him and all that they went through together. Tata scattered his ashes in his apiary, where, next to the chair where Tata likes to sit, listen to the bees, and contemplate eternity, there is a little wooden plaque reading MEK 2006.

* For the full story of Mek, see the chapter "Dog Lives" in *The Book of My Lives*.

After Mek, my sister and I finally took Mama's veto on new pets seriously. We no longer lived with our parents, while the mourning for Mek and all that he stood for (the loss of home, homeland, family, past, etc.) was far too big for us to counter. When Tata was at work, in the factory or with the bees, Mama had no one to confide in. At last, Nataša, my cousin Ivan's wife, bought a parakeet for Mama's birthday, so that she would have someone to talk to. Mama named it Mika, baby-talking to her daily, enjoying the bird's chatter, until it died. Mika was her final pet. But she still regularly chats with the backyard squirrels and feral cats, and watches nature shows on TV.

Mama finds love of animals as natural as love of children. Somehow, they contain goodness, some quality untainted, and untaintable, by the world. Animals also provide opportunities for her exercising generosity and kindness; they're props for her care and charity; they're the equipment for her empathy workouts. One of Mama's recurring, constant needs is to give something to someone. Giving to people is not as easy as it seems—who can know what they really want or need, while some might not even deserve it. But animals, like children, have nothing, so they need everything, which allows her to keep giving.

Since they've lived in Canada, Mama's favorite TV show is *Inspector Rex*, featuring a German shepherd so intelligent that he would track suspects, open doors, or spot drugs or corpses, thereby solving tough criminal cases. He understands everything, like a human. Except, Mama would add, animals are better than humans.

5

SPACE

When I write about my parents I'm compelled to claim that their displacement is the central event of their lives, what split everything into the before and the after. Everything after the rupture took place in a damaged, incomplete time—some of it was forever lost, and forever it shall so remain. Upon their arrival in Hamilton, they at first lived in a two-bedroom rental apartment on the fifteenth floor of a nondescript building, paid for by the Ontario government. Until they furnished the apartment with donated secondhand furniture, there was nothing in it. They took English classes with other refugees and immigrants, acquiring words for things they lost, didn't have, or couldn't understand. The very scarcity of possessions reminded them that they were foreigners living in someone else's space, relatively comfortable as it might have been, and that their home space was now in the before, forever beyond their reach.

Back in Bosnia, my family possessed property; we had spaces we called our own. Not only did we live in an apartment that was pretty big by the standards of socialist housing, but we also had the Jahorina cabins. My parents loved the mountain; nearly every weekend, they were there, with or without their children. They insisted it was nature (always good for you) that drew them to Jahorina, but the primary value of the cabins was that Mama and Tata could keep busy. They are the kind of people who are always doing something, ever in the middle of a number of short- and long-term projects, the kind of people who believe they'll die the day they have nothing to do. Thus Mama cleaned and organized the cabins, pickled vegetables, roasted peppers on an outdoor grill my father built, etc. Meanwhile, Tata had a workshop in the cabin basement; he'd build a nailless table; he'd restore an old chair, extending its life span indefinitely; he'd construct shelves for our Sarajevo apartment; he'd design and develop the who-knows-whats of handymen, which his unhandy son could never truly comprehend, let alone appreciate. Upon the return from Jahorina on Sunday, Mama would often complain that Tata was in the basement the whole time, except to eat and sleep. To Tata, that meant the weekend had been well spent.

Now I understand that on the mountain as well as in Sarajevo, they were perpetually invested in constructing their lives, in continuously defining and refining the space in which their lives unfolded. In a country marked by many generations of abysmal poverty, where socialism was the ideology of the day, there was little money to get the goodies; there were in fact few goodies to get. The quality of life had to be built from scratch—construction was more important than consumption. The vague, distant goal of my parents' lifetime project was to enjoy a modest retirement living on Jahorina, a theme park of their hard work, where everything around them would speak of their time in the world.

With their displacement, they lost all that. At the beginning of their life in Hamilton they had to find work and learn the basic ways of being in North America, with no family, friends, or neighbors, confronting the illogical vagaries of the English language, plus ubiquitous cars and malls, and long, dreary winters devoid of mountains.

After a while, though, things started to look up a bit. First, more family arrived: two of my father's brothers with their broods, some cousins, and even some friends. Now they could get together to reminisce about their previous life and pool their knowledge of and kvetch about the weird ways in which Canadians conducted their lives. Moreover, my parents got hired as superintendents in a forty-apartment building, which included a modest salary plus rent-free lodging. Mama cleaned, collected rent, kept things in order, and chitchatted with tenants as she used to with her Sarajevo neighbors, her disassembled English notwithstanding, while Tata did repairs in the building and took care of the garbage, all the while working in a factory at a job well below his engineer qualifications but just above his English skills.

Most important, the vast basement of the building was big enough for my father to carve out some space and set up a workshop. He not only constructed hives and frames there, but also restored the pieces of furniture the wasteful Canadians commonly dumped in the garbage he was in charge of managing. He even experimented with drying meat in the basement: he hung some pork, lightly smoked elsewhere, near a window with a ventilator. It was edible, but far from impressive, or even enjoyable, although he insisted it was as good as any dried meat.

The meat-drying debacle, however, pointed to one of the crucial issues related to my family's displacement. They, as many immigrants do, identified themselves by way of the food they ate—food was one of the few conduits of continuity between the before and the after. Among my family in Canada and their friends, much time was spent debating dietary and other differences between "them" (Canadians) and "us" (people from Bosnia and the former Yugoslavia): "Their" bacon was soggy; "they" didn't know how to make sausage; "their" sour cream was not thick enough; "they" didn't eat things we ate; "they" were fat and incapable of truly enjoying life because "they" worried about getting fat all the time.

My father would occasionally return from a simple mission of fetching milk with a couple of lamb heads he discovered in the remote corners of the supermarket. He'd demand that my mother boil them, which she outright refused to do. Much of the lamb heads' beyond-dog-food-factory afterlife was spent in the fridge, their eyes bulging in morbid surprise whenever it was opened. Tata would finally deal with Mama's boycott by boiling the heads himself and then sit defiantly at the table to pick lamb brains with the tip of a knife. As my mother scoffed, he relished not only the alleged taste, but also the fact that lamb heads, given the pleasure they provided, were ridiculously cheap in Canada.

Because my parents had worked hard for everything that they would eventually lose, they were tormented by Canadian wastefulness. To them, and to Tata in particular, there were always so many uses for things nobody seemed to want. Once, the real estate company that employed them decided to replace a large number of old refrigerators in the building, their warranty life span ending. My father was thus instructed to remove the fridges from the apartments and leave them by the garbage shed, where they'd be picked up and taken away to a dump. He could not get over all those good, perfectly functioning fridges ending up in a scrap heap—to his poverty-conditioned mind the waste was unimaginable. He talked to everyone he knew in Hamilton, beginning with his family, to ask if they needed another fridge; he called me in Chicago, only to be disappointed that I had no need for extra refrigeration. Mama, a pathologically honest person, was beside herself over his trying to give away someone else's property. She begged me to interfere, but I couldn't help, as I was not, I hasten to admit, up to the task of dealing with the difficult ethical conundrum the situation presented: Does waste still rightfully belong to someone who wasted it?

The fridge overabundance, however, offered a possible solution to the smoked meat problem. At a family get-together, my father and his brothers spontaneously brainstormed: suppose they take two of those old fridges, rip out the plastic lining, put them on top of each other, drill a hole in between and another one on top, attach an improvised tin chimney, then stick the chimney out the basement window—thus they could smoke meat in the basement! My mother was desperate, and complained to me that their obsession with smoking meat blinded them to the laws and civilized customs of Canada. There was nothing I could do. Fortunately, the project was canceled when they discovered a farm outside Hamilton owned by a Slovenian, where they could personally select their animal before it was slaughtered and smoked.

The irreducible problem with living in an apartment building was that my parents were always in someone else's space, so when they had a chance to buy a house, they grabbed it with their callused hands. The house was in a cul-de-sac and modest, with a small backyard and a structure that the real estate agent referred to as the Barn. It was, in fact, a workshop, which one of the previous owners—an Austrian-born engineer—built for himself. In no time, the family joke became that my father bought the Barn and the house came with it. Mama likes to say, not joking, that Tata lives in the Barn and comes to the house only to eat and sleep.

For some immigrants, property is what they own, what gives them legitimacy, their piece of the foreign land, which becomes home by virtue of it legally belonging to them. But for my parents, the house, the Barn, and the piece of land they acquired were but half-empty shells to be filled out with their projects, spaces for their agency. A deed was not enough to make those spaces their own—like the early settlers, they needed to reshape them to fit who they were.

Over the years they've lived there, they've undertaken a number of projects that transformed the space into a domain for their self-(re)actualization. My father added a chimney to the house, which required his carrying bricks up the ladder to the roof, my mother fretting that he might fall and crack his spine. The chimney allowed them to place a wood-burning stove in the basement, so that when I call in the winter to check in, their report often features a quaint fire crackling in the stove as Canadian snow is falling outside. They also unloaded, with my uncle's help, a truckload of soil in the corner of their backyard so as to establish a vegetable garden, where every summer they grow tomatoes, peppers, onions, cucumbers, chard, and pole beans.

The list of additions and improvements to the original property is long and impressive, while the Barn has become the veritable headquarters of all the (re)building projects. This was where Tata built an outdoor table and benches so that in the summer they can lounge in deep shade and proudly consume their meals entirely (the requisite meat notwithstanding) from the *natural* produce they've harvested in their own garden. Most important, the Barn is where Tata's many beekeeping handiworks take place: where he makes his hives and frames, extracts honey, keeps a shelf (which he built himself) entirely dedicated to the propolis reserves.

Maintaining the compound somehow requires a wall of screwdrivers; boxes of nails and screws of all sizes; electric tools he buys behind Mama's back, or with the Home Depot gift certificates I give him for Christmas; plastic buckets and jars for honey; old sweaters and overalls he wears to work, which he refuses to let Mama wash lest they disintegrate; a refrigerator containing pots, which have been there for so long that they contain mysterious ecosystems; various objects collected for no obvious purpose other than avoiding wastefulness—say, a tray full of dull knives, etc. There is also a wood-burning stove, a cord phone he picks up when I call, an ancient stereo that allows him to hum along with CDs of choral music or listen to the immigrant programs in the many languages he can understand (Bosnian, Serbian, Croatian, Ukrainian, Polish, Russian) and the many he cannot. Clusters of plastic bags hang off the nails in the crossbeams, weighted with stuff (hinges, nozzles, bolts, sandpaper) that might become useful for some undetermined future project.

And then there is one wall that in its random, perplexing combination of fragments looks like an art installation: a magazine cover with a picture of Jane Fonda and the headline "Me Jane" and, below it, "Fonda finds serenity in movie biz jungle"; an incredibly tangled extension cord hanging on a nail; a 2007 calendar from the Louvre featuring *Mona Lisa* inside a picture frame too big for it, with another empty frame on top; a road map of Europe, a begrimed mirror obscuring Scandinavia; a couple of stopped clocks showing different times, one of them partially covering Fonda's face; a single bulb, thumbtacked in its packaging right above the mirror; and an unused timer above that. In late December one can find a pumpkin or two festering on the floor.

Other than his reconditioning projects and the honey in plastic buckets and jars, nothing that enters the Barn ever leaves it—it is a waste-free space. Some native-born stranger versed in reality-TV diagnoses would see it as a place of hoarding, but everything in it makes perfect sense not only to my father, but to me as well: the inside of the Barn is the inside of my father's head, the clutter an actualization of his mind, the overpopulated territory of his personal sovereignty.

There is more: Behind that "Me Jane" wall there is an additional room he built to house a circular saw, above which smoked meat hangs to dry, as the smokehouse, immediately beyond the Barn, tends to be overcrowded. With the smokehouse, which he built brick by brick, the meat-smoking issue was resolved: chunks of bacon, hocks, loins, and sometimes salmon hang inside. Next to the smokehouse is a brick oven—which he, yes, also built, in order to roast meat using the traditional Bosnian *sač* method.*

And then there is a wood storage area under a roof that Tata, of course, improvised himself. If you walk under that roof, between tall stacks of firewood needed for the stoves, smokehouse, and brick oven, you come upon another shack that contains more stuff. I'm not sure what's in it, but whatever it is, it must be very valuable, as in that Zen parable in which a master responds to the question "What is the most valuable thing in the world?" by saying, "A dead cat's head—because you can put no value on it."

If the Barn is my father's mind, the apiary is his soul. Depending on the year and the season, there are between twenty and forty hives in a small clearing facing east just beyond the clutter complex. In the summer, it is abuzz with the bees getting out to do their work, a sight and sound so pleasing that Tata has placed a chair (recovered from garbage) just above the hives so that he can sit in his throne and enjoy his domain. If my father ever experiences transcendence, this is where it happens, an instant before the hum of working bees causes him to doze off.

The sovereignty of the domain is precarious, however, ever in need of protection. Although every year my parents return to Sarajevo for a couple of months at the end of the (usually long)

* A conical cast-iron lid topped with ashes and embers covers a pan where the meat and potatoes are slowly baked.

winter, they are reluctant to leave their territory in the summer. They worry about the heat scorching the garden, about bee swarms escaping without supervision, about burglars, about any number of unforeseeable things. Once upon a time they left their home and never came back, finding themselves displaced. Protecting and maintaining the place they have in Canada has become their primary, overarching project.

And they're willing to fight for it. Apart from the struggle against the brazen birds picking cherries, which my father counterattacked by placing a ventilator under the tree so as to scare them away (with middling success), the greatest and the longest of the battles has been against raccoons. One summer, not so long ago, a family of raccoons living in the woods out back discovered the joys of my father's apiary. They came upon some empty hives and figured out a way to lift the tops, pull out the frames, and then scrape and lick off honey residue. My father would find his hives toppled over, frames and tops strewn around, many of them damaged, reminiscent of the demise of his apiary back home in Bosnia. Drawn into the domain by the smell and taste of honey, the raccoons also stole vegetables from the garden, chased away feral cats to eat the food my mother provided for them, and were most certainly eyeing the treasure in the smokehouse.

Following one particularly egregious raid, Tata put the hives back where they belonged and replaced the frames and tops; he nailed one corner of the top to each hive, so that you (being human) would have to lift the top slightly, then swing it to the side to get to the frames. It took no time for the inhuman raccoons to figure out how to overcome that obstacle, and the battle intensified. He'd call me to rail about the raccoons, those devious, evil animals, and declare his determination to end their incursions by ending their lives. At family get-togethers, spontaneous brainstorms were now devoted to means of raccoon entrapment and subsequent liquidation.

One day, I called and the first thing my mother said was: "Your father is losing his mind about those raccoons. I don't know what to do. You've got to talk to him." She'd just watched a local news story about a man who killed a raccoon with a shotgun, an action apparently illegal in the city of Hamilton, where only Animal Control was to handle wildlife. "Your father does nothing but plot how to kill those raccoons." Apart from being a habitual animal lover, she was concerned that my father could in fact be arrested: the TV showed the raccoon-killer entering a police car handcuffed. Sometimes, I'd have them both on the phone—Tata in the Barn, Mama in the kitchen—and they'd argue, essentially, over jurisdiction: he claimed his right to kill the raccoons, as they were trespassing on his domain; she insisted on the fact that they lived in Canada, where laws must be obeyed, and not in the Balkans, where anything goes.

Eventually my father devised a trap that allowed him to capture four baby raccoons, but not their mother. He imprisoned the baby raccoons in a deep barrel, on top of which he placed a heavy piece of flat wood. He was confident there was no way they could get out. He expected the mother raccoon to come look for her babies and fall into the same trap. He patrolled his domain diligently, hoping to catch her before she figured out a way to escape, then exterminate the whole pest family. On one of his patrols, he discovered that the piece of wood had been pushed off the barrel and that three of the baby raccoons in the barrel managed to escape, only one remaining. Apparently, they'd climbed on one another's shoulders, making a baby raccoon ladder of sorts, lifted the lid, and gotten away. They left behind a volunteer, probably the youngest one, to deal with my father's fury. He realized he'd made a tactical mistake in not killing them right away and thus lost the battle. To his credit, he acknowledged his defeat and released the last baby raccoon.* But that could've also been so that he could righteously turn his anger on my mother and her softhearted animal-loving—it was because of her nagging, he insisted, that he hadn't executed the baby raccoons. They'd argue on the phone with me with such intensity that they wouldn't hear me hang up. When they calmed down and we talked again, I urged Tata to call Animal Control, telling him they would take care of it. Eventually he did, and they came to set some traps. It was always the most obvious and diplomatic solution, but Tata's obsession was related to his jurisdiction principle: his domain was his responsibility.

Alas, nothing lasts forever, except for raccoons. One day, he looked out the bathroom window and saw a raccoon sitting on the table in the shaded area behind the house where my parents like to hang out in the summer. The raccoon was calmly picking grapes off the vine growing on the lattice providing the shade and putting them in its mouth. Once again, my father was outraged, even if he never actually ate those grapes; their main value was that they reminded him of the grapes they had in Vučijak, where they also provided shade for the outdoor table. He devised a way to protect the fruit by building a frame for a wire cage around them. I was in Hamilton at the time of construction, and listened patiently as he ranted against the raccoons yet again. He showed me a roll of chicken wire he would use for the cage and said: "This wire is twenty dollars. Twenty dollars can buy a lot of grapes. But it's not about the grapes. It's about the principle."

Unlike the raccoons, I'm in awe of my parents and their prin-

* Which for all we know could now well be the Supreme Ruler of Hamilton wildlife.

ciples. The lazy, condescending clichés available in the North American mainstream culture present immigrants, at best, as innocent arrivals to the baffling new land; or, at worst, as human-shaped racoons set on stealing everything from the natives. In the condescending native imagination, immigrants are swallowed and digested by the host culture and its practices, which are presumably so recondite as to make the new immigrants akin to children; in the racist imagination, they cannot even begin to understand how "we" live. What all of those platitudes fail to acknowledge is the resourceful transformative power of immigrants, even of those who, like my parents, arrive in their mid-fifties with a scant knowledge of English. My parents did what the early North American settlers had done once upon a time: they transformed the space they found themselves in. My parents didn't decimate any indigenous people, but they did have to deal with bureaucracy and papers, with finding jobs and getting fired, with the language deficiency conducive to humiliation, all the while constructing a space that could be indelibly their own.

The domain that my parents have built for themselves is possessed of perfect human sovereignty. In it they do and create things that allow them to be themselves, to fashion who they are; this is where they have agency, a bubble outside of which they are reduced to passivity inflicted by history. Their house, the Barn, and the backyard are the places where they're not refugees. Time they could not regain, but space they could, and so they did.

6

FOOD

When Kristina and I were little, our parents left for work around 7:00 a.m. They'd never have breakfast (*doručak*) before going to work, or even coffee. Mama would rush us through a simple fortifying meal, featuring sugar mixed in egg yolk, or a piece of bread with honey, jam, or lard sprinkled with paprika. Later, when we were older, she'd leave stuff for us on the table. Then, one day, we fed ourselves, eventually daring to skip breakfast at home altogether.

The family meal of the day, which we called lunch (*ručak*), took place around four o'clock, after Mama and Tata returned from work, unless Kristina and I had school in the afternoon. This was the time when we sat down to eat together as a family. Mama would prepare the meal the night before, or we would have to reheat leftovers. The meal was usually substantial: soup, main dish, often a thick stew of some sort, all of it enhanced with a lot of bread. Meal preparation could start a day or two before, with Mama asking for our suggestions/requests, or just deciding based on what she had in the pantry and freezer. Our requests were frequently ignored, as they were either too complicated or we were shameless in our soliciting for money to spend on *ćevapčići*.* As with all kids around the world, outside food was always more attractive.

Ručak was a meal with an established protocol. We could not read at the table or watch television. We were expected to brief our parents on our day before we dug into our food, report on our schoolwork.† We had to try a little bit of everything offered, and finish what was on our plates, for if there was too much left, Mama, having cooked late into the previous night, would feel wronged. Either way, we would eventually have to consume the leftovers, as there were always leftovers. The protocolar family bonding would be conducted against the background of the afternoon radio news, which our parents half listened to while showing requisite interest in our school experiences and thoughts. Whatever was wrung out of our recalcitrant selves had to be terminated at 4:25, which was when the weather forecast was on. The radio had to be turned up, no one was to speak. When in our adolescence my sister and I began to question all authority knee-jerkily, we regularly objected to the sacredness of the afternoon weather forecast, contending defiantly that the meteorologists‡ either had no idea what they

* The Bosnian national kebab, made of a mixture of ground beef and lamb.

† "How was school?"

"Fine."

"What did you do in school?"

"Nothing."

"Do you have homework?"

"No."

‡ Whose names, Čedo Orlović and Vuko Zečević, shall always be remembered by all the Sarajevans of our generation.

were talking about or were outright lying. At least once we experienced the gloriously gleeful moment when we could behold a blizzard outside just as the forecaster was promising us a fine and sunny day.

After our parents' post-lunch napping, there could be coffee and cake. The dinner (*večera*) was often just a snack, or whatever could be individually foraged from the fridge. For this meal we did not sit down to dine as a family; indeed, Kristina and I were permitted to read or even watch television while eating. And when we reached full and reckless adolescence, we would go out for the evening without eating, leaving our parents to doze in front of the TV and wait for the last forecast of the day, which seldom arrived before their dreams.

One consequence of having such a schedule was that food management had an element of time management. We did not eat lunch when we were hungry, but when it was time to eat. Our days were organized around food; meals were planned and scheduled. This was rooted in the hardworking peasant experience of our grandparents and the generations before them. They could not leave the field to have a snack—they ate before the sun was up, when the sun was high, when the sun went down, and they ate stuff with caloric value so as to fuel the hard work until the next meal. To this day, when I visit my parents in Canada, my mother announces the night before, and then the morning of, what she plans to prepare or reheat for lunch. Nowadays, when my parents' lunchtime is 2:30, my father, having finished in his workshop, appears in the kitchen between 2:25 and 2:29 to lift the lids, rummage for a spoon, and taste whatever might be in the large pot. A meal could be postponed until the work is done, but it could never be forgotten. The notion of forgetting to eat is utterly inconceivable to my parents, or, for that matter, to me. I am convinced that, since the time when our ancestors took their knuckles off the ground to walk unsteadily in pursuit of better nutrition, no Hemon has ever forgotten to eat.

Because food is so entangled with work, it can never be a matter of mere leisure. Even if we were on our way to the coast for a vacation, we would rarely stop at a roadside inn where famous spit-roasted lamb or grilled trout was served. When we did, it was a big deal, and it happened, at best, once a year, thus becoming a highlight of our trip. It was far more likely, however, that Tata would insist we push through to avoid the heat and replenish ourselves with the stuff Mama prepared and loaded in a golden tin container. That golden tin container, a rectangular cornucopia, is one of my childhood fetishes. I remember it with utmost precision and can revolve it slowly in my mind for a memoiristic examination of the smallest detail. Boiled eggs, green peppers, yellow cheese, sausage, and bread; all acquired in that container a flavor I can recollect now, and, with it, the sheer cliffs of the Neretva Valley, the green glimmer on the river, the smell of the karst vegetation as it warms up under the relentless sun.

Nevertheless, food is a matter of pleasure, precisely because it is so entangled with work. For one thing, eating when hungry, particularly if the hunger has been earned by toil, is deeply pleasurable. The ethos is communal—work is shared and exchanged—and always includes a reward: an occasional feast that brings people together for an exuberant celebration of completion. My grandmother once had forty-seven people over for lunch, all family except for a couple of neighbors.

Mama and Tata's social life (and therefore their children's) regularly featured a bunch of their friends getting together for a lot of food and drinking and singing and laughing. Sometimes, the friends would come over to our place; at other times, we'd all go to someone else's. The occasion would be something to celebrate (a birthday, New Year), but it could also be arbitrary, merely fulfilling a regular need to be together with other people. Either way, the table would be loaded with dishes, all of them prepared by the woman of the house: the *meza* (cold cuts, boiled eggs, cheese, pickles), filo-dough pies (cheese, spinach), soup, *sarma* (pickled cabbage rolls), meat (roasted), potatoes, salads, bread, and then at least two kinds of dessert (cake, cookies). There was always far more than necessary, which would compel the hosts to insist that everyone put more on their plates (*Ma, uzmi!*), while rejecting the spurious claims that another bite would lead to an abdominal explosion. So the guests would take more, and the feast would go on for a while, everyone talking and shouting over one another, joking and teasing, often singing, all in a state of high agitation and plain joy. Nobody would ever call that whole endeavor *dinner*—the activity revolved around food, but could never be reduced to it. In Bosnian, the verb that describes such an activity is *sjediti*, which means to sit, as the whole operation consists of sitting around the table, eating, drinking, and being together for the purposes of well-earned pleasure. If I want to invoke an image of my parents being unconditionally happy (not an easy task), I envision them with their friends at table, roaring with laughter between bites of the delicious fare and sips of slivovitz or grappa.

This could last for an entire weekend: sometimes we'd go to Boračko jezero, a modest mountain lake resort where Elektroprenos had a retreat building (*odmaralište*), to join my parents' friends and their families for May 1, the socialist Labor Day. The inextricable part of the fun and joy there was the presence of others, and the spirit of abandon reigned from morn to midnight and beyond. But the central, inescapable bonding ritual was spit-roasting a lamb that would then be shared by all. There, as everywhere we lived, food was meant to be shared, which is why it is never permissible to eat while someone else is watching and not eating. Food is other people. We hate eating alone, just as we hate being alone.

There are no records or memories of my parents ever going out on a dinner date, before or after they got married. I don't remember them ever getting dressed and leaving us for a restaurant where they would enjoy delicate non-homemade dishes, imbibe expensive alcohol, and gaze lovingly into each other's eyes. They never felt the need to enjoy food and each other's company in a public space, talking over their fancy dishes about something they could not address in a different situation. For one thing, unless there was a need to resolve a pressing family-logistics issue, neither of them ever pauses between bites long enough to conduct a conversation. While Mama might try to chitchat over the meal with her mouth full (for which she always scolded us as children), Tata doesn't talk at all. As far as he's concerned, the primary goal of having a meal is to finish it, preferably by wiping out everything on the plate, and then going about his business.

There really was no restaurant culture in the Sarajevo of our previous life. The restaurants were either expensive or not good, most commonly both. The best of them catered to the worldly locals who liked to seek inebriated abandon in the dubious bohemian pleasures my work-obsessed parents would never dream of indulging. There were a couple of restaurants that appeared frilly enough to signify privilege, the places where foreign delegations would be feted by the big shots after a day of unproductive negotiations, by and large because the establishment was thoroughly bugged by the security service. These were out of our league, eavesdropping notwithstanding. The kind of fancy restaurant

Mama and Tata would even consider taking us to, however, couldn't have been much more than a pizzeria, and that only if my sister and I lobbied for it, although I cannot recall a single time we ate pizza as a family. I can, however, remember several instances of our going to that particular kind of state-owned joint where cranky bow-tied waiters in stained overalls brandished napkins over their forearms and grunted at us, where tablecloths only implied their original whiteness, where gray aluminum ashtrays housed odious ghosts of past cigarettes. There we'd treat ourselves to fried veal brains and a small cabbage salad on the side.

Not even in Canada did my parents acquire a habit of going out for a meal. While Hamilton is not quite a culinary mecca, the primary reason for this reluctance is that visiting a restaurant means my parents would have to leave their zone of hard-won nutritional comfort to encounter a world of food unlikely to meet their strict requirements. Spending money on a meal in unknown gastronomic territory, and all that in English, while Mama's cooking is axiomatically the best in the world and their several fridges are full of reliable food, including the already proven leftovers, would just be foolish and irresponsible. In my family, eating is not meant to be an exploration, nor an expansion of cultural experience. Part of the food pleasure is in meeting set expectations, while its indelible utility is in providing energy for labor, and therefore for survival. Food is an existential necessity, an irreplaceable element in the structure of daily life, and it should never be fucked around with in some expensive place that also happens to be devoid of friends and family.

The only Hamilton place where the two of them might venture for a meal is the Mandarin, a Chinese restaurant featuring mounds of fried things and stewed stuff, plus very un-Chinese multilayered cake with industrial-strength frosting. The attraction to the Mandarin is largely a consequence of its all-you-can-eat wonder buffet, wherein the utopian concept of cheap and endless abundance, dreamt of by generations of Slavic peasantry, is finally fulfilled.

When my parents were growing up, there was little food, never mind bottomless buffets. As adults, they reached a level of comfort when they had enough; and then there was even more, so they took out a loan to buy a freezer in order to stock up. Their poor-people food ethos, where nothing should ever be wasted, aligned perfectly with the fact that unchecked consumption was not available in socialism, everyone getting according to their needs and all that. An aspect of ethical food management was thus always striving to avoid waste, which might be a problem when one is confronting a Chinese buffet, where all that is left uneaten might end up as garbage. I've seen my father at the Mandarin pile on so much food, then soak it with an ungodly combination of sauces on offer, that I'd fear he might have a heart attack; he would eat all of it, then go for seconds and thirds. Moreover, a need to exploit the buffet and its low price to the max is a crucial part of enjoying it. There is also the pertinent fact that it is not certain, nor can it ever be, that a moment as abundant and enjoyable as this one—what with inexhaustible supplies of fried rice and spring rolls and dumplings and chicken wings—could be counted on to happen again. Eating more, beyond being full,* means extending this safe and pleasurable moment, for the next one is never guaranteed; you eat now, for who knows what's around the bend? The food intake is proportional to the uncertainty of the

* The English idiom "being full" doesn't work in Bosnian. The equivalent Bosnian word *sit* describes not a sense of fullness, but an absence of hunger. There is also a proverb: *Sit gladnom ne vjeruje*. The full one doesn't trust the hungry one. The proverb doesn't work in English because "full" and "hungry" don't belong to the same semantic zone.

future. This is, by the way, how I gained forty pounds upon arriving in the United States.

Food can never be enjoyed unto itself; it's never just a sensory experience, let alone a matter of sophisticated taste. Its meaning is always dependent on the outcomes of potentially catastrophic situations, its value always assigned in the context of particular lives and histories. Taste as such has no purchase, for it is impossible to divorce the experience of eating from the constant practice of survival—even if one eats to enjoy life, one has to stay alive first, which requires far more than merely entertaining the senses. The restaurant critics who pretend that their expert epicurean taste entitles them to evaluate food are nothing but fools who think that something as basic as eating could be objectively appraised. My parents have never been in one of those Michelin-star-craving restaurants where thimblefuls of artistically arranged healthy ingredients are served on a satellite dish, but I know for a fact that the mere sight of something like that would appear insultingly ridiculous to them. Tata's favorite dish is *steranka*, which his mother made for him when he was a kid. It's dough boiled in milk. For my mother, eating the heel of a fresh loaf of good bread is a three-star experience.

Once or twice I took my parents to a white-tablecloth restaurant within my financial reach, insisting that they must enjoy the experience. Instead, they were confused by the long, convoluted descriptions of the dishes, suspicious of the server's solicitude, and pessimistic about the nutritional value of the pretty arrangement. "We'll be hungry in an hour," Mama would pronounce, inescapably projecting into the unstable future. In a stable, leisure-oriented world, being hungry in an hour would mean that you would simply eat in an hour. But as far as my parents are concerned, no one knows what might happen in an hour—at the very least, they might be working on something that would not allow them to stop, since hunger would only impede them from getting it done.

"This is fine, but Mama's *sarma** is so much better," my father might say, facing a bafflingly small chunk of meat on top of a stump of undercooked vegetables. He would leave nothing on his plate while complaining about everything.† That is because *sarma* is not only calorically rewarding but has also been confirmed as legitimate by virtue of always being made in the same exact way. *Sarma* is ontologically stable—that is, they know what it is and what it means. The bizarre thing about the very concept of the restaurant, so obvious as to be invisible, is that it's a place where strangers serve strange food to strangers, knowing absolutely nothing about what they like, about what they think, about who they are, about what their life history is. Restaurant food is impersonal, uncommunal, consumed in the isolation of public space. In my parents' culinary universe, pleasure and perfection are achieved by generations of fine-tuning, adjusting it all to personal preferences. Mama cooks what has been cooked by all the other women in Bosnia; Tata asks her to make his favorite dishes in the way he likes them, and she does them so. What restaurant can provide that kind of service? This creates a

* Pickled cabbage rolls.

† My parents received a $300 voucher for a chichi restaurant as a gift for their semicentennial wedding anniversary. The restaurant was in the Niagara wine country, and my sister went with them, as they wouldn't have gone otherwise. She reported that Tata grumbled the whole time, compulsively calculating what they could've bought with that money—they could've fed themselves for two weeks, if not for a whole month. His disapprobation was so relentless that it spoiled the meal, thereby confirming the axiomatic premise that eating out at fancy restaurants is no good.

mutual psychological collaboration between them, an addictive and symbiotic food-centered operation wherein Tata gathers (shopping) and produces (smoked meat, honey) the supplies for Mama to transform into food.*

In my family, food is part of a complex system of knowledge that has its own hierarchy of value, wherein meat and bread are at the top. Meat is appreciated in all its variations: cuts, smoked meat, sausage, spit-roasted. It has inherent value because, in the peasant past, it never came from a butcher or a supermarket, but from living creatures whose numbers measured wealth, who might have had names and spent winters in the house with the family.

When she was growing up, my mother's family lived on fertile land and never had to worry about having something to eat, but they would still risk their lives to save piglets from a flood. My father's family had meat once a week (Saturday) when he was a kid, twice a week in good seasons. Throughout my childhood, and indeed life in Bosnia, the Hemons would slaughter a pig sometime in November and spend days preparing the meat. Naturally, there was a communal, ritualistic aspect to it all. The pig would somehow always know what was coming and would for hours squeal in horrible distress, well before the pigsty door would open for the last time. The men who knew what to do would kill it, quickly and ruthlessly. It would be hanged on a rack to fully drain of blood; then it would be scalded and cut open, its guts

* Similarly, Baba Mihaljina used to load Deda Ivan's plate with whatever was for lunch, plus bonus leftovers, and set it on the chair that was his table; he would eat everything, and then ask: "Mihaljina, am I still hungry?" If she said yes, he would get more; if she said no, he'd lean back against the wall and pass out.

ripped out. The oldest male member would have the exclusive right and duty to cut off the testicles so they could be pan-fried for him.* Then the pork would be transformed into foods that would last through the winter: bacon, sausage, headcheese, cuts, *čvarci* (rinds), things without a name in English. The entire pig was used, nothing thrown away, except the shit that my aunts would squeeze out of the intestines so they could be used to make sausage.

All this is to say that the value of meat was also proportional to the work it took to put it on the table. This is why vegetables have always been considered inferior. Though tending the garden takes some work, vegetables just grow, and when you want to eat them you just cut them or add them to the meat—vegetables contained no drama, they could not be given names, nor could they ever become a measure of wealth and property. Vegetables are thus tolerated for being inherently a side dish, not quite real food. Though vegetarians might be respected (if ever encountered), they are hard to understand—the choice not to eat meat implies levels of comfort and privilege few of us have ever managed to reach. My family cannot quite fathom it: Why eat only broccoli when you can eat any meat you want?

Bread, on the other hand, is practically sacred. In Bosnian, there is an idiom applicable to a saintly good person: "as good as bread."† Though it does take land and hard work to produce wheat and grind it into flour that will become dough to be kneaded and baked into bread, its symbolic value has less to do with all the effort than with the fact that it's the poor people's most basic staple—if you have bread, you have food, and if you have food, you live. Bread, in other words, equals life. My father's favorite

* I was happy to be decades down the list.

† *Dobar k'o hljeb.*

expression for work is "earning a crust of bread,"* while my mother (and everyone I know) harbors a deep respect for bread. She used to admonish us for not leaving it on its flat side but upside down, as that is somehow disrespectful. Nor is bread ever thrown away. My grandmother and aunts made a dish from old bread called *popara*: they steamed the stale bread and added lard to cover up the strong undertones of mold. I make French toast for my kids after I pick out the moldy bits from an old loaf. My ex-wife used to tell people I forced her to excavate a piece of bread from the garbage and eat it.†

Spoony food—soups, stews, or whatever requires spoon deployment to be consumed—is also high in my parents' nutritional hierarchy. This is also rooted in the peasant past. For one thing, spoony food is inclusive, as you're inclined to dump all kinds of different stuff into it. The Hemon borscht—an ideal spoony dish—as it's been prepared by my mother, by my aunts, by my grandmother and generations of women before her (and also me), is as inclusive as can be, requiring all the available vegetables to be thrown into the pot, plus at least two kinds of meat,‡ until the very spoon with which it is slurped is a horn of plenty.

A perfect meal features soup, bread, sometimes savory pie, meat, some extra starch (potato), and salad; dessert is optional, but it should be at least available later, with coffee. A spread like this does not cover a healthy-nutrition range but an ideological one—the food-production experience manifests itself in the hierarchy, which expresses a value system. There could be other hierarchies, but my parents have a hard time reading those val-

* *Zaraditi koricu hljeba.*

† In truth, I merely pointed out that it was in the garbage, and made a strong moral case against bread ever being wasted.

‡ Except, for some reason, fowl.

ues. Sushi is incomprehensible to them. Why not fry the fish? And even if you did, you'd be hungry in an hour. The fancy food discourse—the sophistication, the wine-matching, the exotic ingredients, the obscurity of the work put into it, the idea that enjoying an artfully prepared dish must not be related to hunger—makes no sense whatsoever.

And then there is the salad conundrum: a vegetable salad, necessary though it may be, is but a humble side dish, a mere chaser for the heft of bread, meat, and potatoes, or some hearty stew, or, even, rarely, fish.* Unless something terrible happened, no one in my family has ever eaten only salad for a meal. Similarly, to eat a salad at the beginning of a meal is a major violation of the proper order and natural food hierarchy, which demands that the main meal of the day be opened with a spoon.

A few years ago, I had dinner with my parents at a bistro in Washington, D.C. Sharing the round table with my sister, her husband, and some friends, I could tell that our parents were getting nervous. First, Mama announced somewhat apologetically that she was not hungry at all, which I knew was because she was overwhelmed by the English menu made worse by all its Frenchie affectations (*hors d'oeuvres*, *foie gras*). She would like something simple, she said—which, of course, could mean any number of things. Tata, on the other hand, would never begin to suggest that he would reduce his food intake out of discomfort—if anything, discomfort requires more intake. Thus, with clamorous determination, he declared, "I will have soup!" as if we were all on the edges on our seats waiting for his decision. But an issue arose when he also wanted a salad: both were offered as starters, whereas

* Fish was the kind of food you might be interested in on a seaside vacation, where normal life operations are temporarily suspended and where you could theoretically eat again in an hour.

he wanted to eat his salad with the main dish. How, then, could that be resolved? The issue, of course, was indicative of the ways in which (North) America worked for him, and not just in relation to food—nothing quite makes sense, while being, even more tryingly, completely oblivious to its senselessness. Sensibly, I suggested that he order both, then eat the soup and keep the salad so as to consume it with his main dish. Mama ordered some fish, justifying her choice to the indifferent, if befuddled, young waiter by saying she was not that hungry. When anxious, Tata comes off as grumpy, a state compounded by low blood sugar: when it was his turn to order his food from the waiter, he practically barked at him trying to explain he wanted both soup and salad, but would keep the salad for later. I could tell the waiter didn't understand, and when I tried to explain (thereby coming off as condescending to my father), he became even more confused. We managed to make sure that both soup and salad were coming and at the same time, but the whole incident pointed at the fact with which we have always lived: eating is far too important to ever be stress-free. I watched Tata's stress announce itself in his jumping knee, in his arms crossed at his chest, in his inability to focus on the conversation taking place at the table. As soon as the soup and salad were placed before him, Tata ceased all eye contact and communication. First, he slurped his way to the bottom of the soup bowl, keeping his lettuce-and-tomato salad close. When a busboy picked up his soup bowl and then reached for the untouched salad—assuming he was done with it—Tata's hand reflexively flew to protect it at such speed that the busboy pulled his hand away as if from the snapping jaws of a shark. To alleviate the busboy's panic, I explained that my father would like to keep the salad. Then steak frites were served, the salad was finally activated, and everything was consumed in the proper order—a bite of steak, a frite, a forkful of salad, repeat, never letting go of the utensils, never stopping his knee from jumping, never saying a word, until there was nothing left but a few tear-like drops of vinaigrette in the salad bowl. Then he had vanilla ice cream.

"How was it?" I asked.

"Was good," he said.

In my parents' ethical universe, a portion of which could always be found in their fridge, leftovers play an important role. To throw food away is a sin against the generations of poverty. This is also why special value is ascribed to the last and smallest edible particles: to the meat around the joint bone, to the heel of bread, or to the burnt potato sticking to the bottom of the roasting pan. I'd been brought up to believe that these were particularly tasty, only to undergo an epiphany a few years ago, realizing in a single painful moment that it was all poor people's bullshit, nothing but peasant propaganda, ensuring that even the tiniest, unpleasant morsels are eaten and nothing is ever thrown away.

Hence my parents' fridge is always full: apart from what is needed daily (dairy, meat, wilted vegetables), there is the stuff that awaits its final consumption: half a sausage that may be weeks old; eggs scrambled once upon a time but presently nurturing their own little colonies of living organisms; the week-old soup in a little pot covered with a saucer, which my mother will retrieve a moment before it goes bad to reheat it for my father. My parents can't throw away food, just as I can't kill a living thing—something deep inside us, some cellular moral law, prohibits such an act. Not so long ago, I undertook a heroic effort to clean my parents' main fridge. Two swollen garbage bags later, the fridge still appeared full, as though possessed by some magic wherein the more you take out, the fuller it gets.

Nothing was ever thrown away in our house.* At any given time, at least half of the food in our fridge was leftovers, distributed into small pots and bowls and a rare plastic container. The leftovers would never be served to guests; it was our duty to dispose of them as a family, while the most resilient remnants were to be exterminated by Tata. For some reason, one of the fatherly duties—and I fulfill it myself in my family, which is entirely oblivious to the theoretical foundations of my sacrifice—is to dispose of leftovers. "*Ćale* [Pop]," Mama would say, "do finish that *sarma* from two weeks ago," and he would duly oblige, falsely asserting that *sarma* is actually better the older it gets.

This food hoarding—if that's what it is—is not necessarily related to my parents' personal memories of hunger. Mama does not remember ever being hungry or worrying about food. Tata was only hungry after leaving his parents' home to go to the boarding school, where there never was enough food for an adolescent boy, but that lasted only until he got his first stipend. In other words, they never, not even during the wars they lived through, experienced systemic deprivation that would constitute an existential threat. Their food anxieties are rooted in a shared history in which subsistence could never be guaranteed, where living was always survival, and where food abundance was ever temporary, at least by virtue of being seasonal, entirely dependent on hard work and weather and luck. My mother once spotted my father piling jam on a piece of bread and asked: "Why do you need to put on so much?" He responded: "In memory of a boy from Drvar I knew in high school, who was so hungry he stole a loaf of bread and a packet of jam. They found out and expelled him."

* Except the fancy French cheeses Tata brought back from his trips abroad, which would, untouched because unknown, fester into a clump of plague-smelling rot.

And even if my parents rose out of poverty to become socialist middle class, they learned that the structure of comfort they had spent their lives building offered no protection from history, which would, in the early nineties, come crashing down on their heads. Whatever food anxieties may have lessened with middle-class stability were doubly reactivated with the war, which totally validated the survivalist food ethics they had been so familiar with.

The value of leftovers is also rooted in a particular domestic economy and the gendered division of labor. Since time immemorial until, at best, my parents' generation, women were the ones expected to manage food, in addition to rearing children and all the other domestic duties. Baba Mihaljina spent her life between the kitchen and attending to the livestock and various small children, first hers, then her children's. Deda Ivan would work in the field, and then come to the house for a meal—bread, borscht, pierogi, *steranka*—she would prepare from scratch. She would save everything that was not eaten—and this also before they had a fridge—to serve it again until it was all gone. Leftovers equaled time and labor that she could put into other chores or, rarely, rest.

Toward the end of her life, Baba Mihaljina was diagnosed with colon cancer. It was taken out; she was given six months to live, and was sent home to die. She stayed around for a couple of years, partly—I'm convinced—because she felt that if she died there would be no one to take care of my grandfather, who by that time was blind and plunging into the dark realms of undiagnosed dementia. I remember her standing at the woodstove, holding up a full colostomy bag at her side, stirring a pot of soup, dabbing the sweat above her lip with the corners of her headscarf.

Her food was a conduit that transmitted love. Peasant women worked too hard and too much to find time to cuddle and play with the kids; instead, they'd make their favorite dishes. This is another source for the ethical value of food—it carries love. Back in the day, upon Tata's return from some long trip of his, Mama would make a zucchini pie (*tikvenjača)*, thus expressing whatever happiness she might have felt for having him home. These days, when she comes to visit me, she insists on making something she believes I like and crave. Sadly, my diet and taste buds have changed, so there is less and less of her comfort food I long for. She gets hurt when I reject something she prepared for me, and I have to concede and allow her to actualize her love in the form of apples stuffed with walnuts and poached in honey. So for days after her departure, as I devour *tufahije*, my caloric intake triples.

When my grandmother died from colon cancer, my father was working in Africa. He received the news while staying at the Kinshasa Intercontinental, and could not get back in time for her funeral. Alone and devastated, he spent nights pacing in his impersonal hotel room, obsessively recollecting something that had happened in Bosnia some twenty or so years before: He dropped by his parents' because he was nearby for work; he surprised his mother and she was so happy to see him that she decided to make his favorite pie. At incredible speed, she peeled and shredded the apples and made the dough and stretched it thin and rolled it up with the apple, cinnamon, and sugar mixture inside, put it in the oven to bake for forty minutes or so. But he was young and impatient and could not wait and, even though she begged him to stay for the pie, he left before it was done. Twenty years later, in the Kinshasa hotel room, he beat his chest and ripped his hair out for not staying, longing hopelessly for that untasted apple pie, for that moment that could never be retrieved nor relived.

For Kristina and me, "apple pie" has become a code term for

a situation where our negligence toward our parents is likely to result in some devastating future regret. "I won't be coming to see them for Christmas," I would say. She would only say, "Apple pie," and I would be coming to see them for Christmas.

A few years ago, my father went to see a doctor who diagnosed him with high blood pressure and instructed him to cut red meat out of his diet. A week or so later, I called to see how things were going, and Tata picked up the phone.

"What are you doing?" I asked.

"I'm eating bacon," he said with no compunction whatsoever.

I immediately started yelling:

"Didn't the doctor tell you not to eat red meat, and now you're eating bacon?"

"It's not red, the bacon," he said. "It's all white."

For my parents, one of the symptoms of my having become "American" is my new fussiness in relation to food—I seem to pay too much finicky attention to my diet. When I go to visit them, I berate them for eating bacon, force them to eat fish ("We'll be hungry in an hour"), and steam vegetables instead of roasting them. For some dubious future health benefit, I deny them—as I do myself—the food they've always eaten and enjoyed. To my mind, I practice as much dietary recklessness as the next Bosnian, but what my parents see is not so much a radical change in nutritional content as it is a shift in attitude.

The U.S. approach to eating is characterized by the fundamentally puritan notion of self-denial as a means of improvement—to be healthy, one has to eliminate tempting, enjoyable foods from one's diet. The process complies with the basic puritan operation of rejecting—indeed transcending—pleasure in order to become a better person. Many people in the United States see value in denying desire and controlling the body, which could earn them the reward of a better, healthier, and, ultimately, more moral life. This explains a number of self-disciplining U.S. obsessions: meaningless knee-destroying marathons, gluten-free nutrition, 0% milk, kale, yoga, etc. This is where the wretchedness of traditional U.S. cuisine comes from,* as does the overreaction of compulsive eating and obesity. The basic choice is between puritan discipline of self-denial and total, unchecked, addictive indulgence—in either direction, there is little but joylessness.

In the world and history we come from, malnutrition has been the source for many maladies and killed far more people than eating bacon ever could. To my parents, seeking health by way of self-deprivation makes no sense whatsoever. Food has always equaled survival, which is to say that the more food is available and the better it is, the greater the chance of survival. Throughout my childhood, my mother would insist that "health enters through the mouth."†

Moreover, food is joy. It is joy because it contains pleasures earned by work; it is joy because it can be shared with other people; it is joy because it is life, and life is a really good and healthy thing, incomparably better than any spiritual endeavor contingent upon morally rewarding self-mortification. The systemic extermination of joy in the United States is not only unethical but also plain stupid. There is no reasonable argument that could be made against the pleasures of bacon, let alone the bacon my father cut and smoked himself. Only after I berated my parents a few times (and I might do it again) for their overenjoyment of food did I realize

* It is significant that the most exuberant and celebratory meal of the year features turkey, squash, and cranberry sauce, the blandest dishes imaginable.

† *Zdravlje na usta ulazi.*

that, compared with them, I did indeed become American and thus, to some extent, puritan.*

The value and meaning of food is always necessarily altered, just like everything else, by displacement. For one thing, "our" food is either unavailable or scarce in the new place—at least it was at the beginning. Therefore, it becomes a mark of loss, which makes it essential for all nostalgic discourse. For years after their arrival, my mother would deliver analytical soliloquies on, say, the ineffable, yet substantial, differences between "our" sour cream and the Canadian ("their") kind. The authenticity of "our" food exactly matches the authenticity of our life in the past. Conversely, the inauthenticity of our life in displacement can be tasted in "their" food. In Mama's discourse, "our" sour cream is a stable category, possessing unchanging qualities correlating to the unchanging, authentic principles that guided our previous life—the principles that were violated and, indeed, destroyed by the war and subsequent displacement. "Our" food, in other words, stands for the authentic life we used to live, which is no longer available except as a model for this new, *elsewhere* life. It is therefore important that food-related practices from the previous life be reconstructed in the new context. The food, if made properly, might be where authenticity is partially restored despite the displacement. While that authenticity was available in the previous life, it requires tremendous effort to rebuild it in the new one, where the torturous possibility that nothing could ever be the way it used to be is continuously present, like a big nose on a face.

This idea is best expressed in a story I heard in Sarajevo from

* "Puritanism," H. L. Mencken wrote, "is the haunting fear that someone, somewhere, may be happy."

someone who had heard it from someone else, who, in turn, knew the person who knew the person to whom all this happened. In short, the story is as true as can be, even if I fact-checked none of it, because it accumulated relevant experiences and value while passing through other people.

So: A Bosnian refugee—let's call him Zaim—ends up in some small town in England. Life is tough, there are few friends, the family is far away, the longing for Bosnia is painful. Zaim develops a craving for spit-roasted lamb, the most universally revered food in Bosnia. He wants to do it the way it's supposed to be done—stick a whole lamb on a spit and then slowly revolve it for hours over fire and embers, sipping beer and talking to people, until it's finished. Though piecemeal lamb is available in English butcher shops, a whole one is not. Spit-roasting a whole lamb is quite a different proposition from roasting a leg in the kitchen oven; for one thing, with the leg of lamb, the ritualistic, communal aspect is absent. There is one place, however, where Zaim could get a whole, live lamb: a pet store. Zaim purchases a cute little lamb at a pet store, and it even has a cute little name; wholly unfazed by the cuteness, he slaughters the lamb and spit-roasts it. But this is England, where pet welfare is far more important than the longings of a carnivorous refugee. A municipal representative knocks on Zaim's door to visit the little lamb and check on its well-being. "Lamb go away," Zaim says in his bad English, but the visitor does not understand. "Lamb go away," he says: the lamb escaped.

Whether the pet welfare official believed him enough to summon a municipal posse that could search English meadows for the lost little lamb, I do not know. But the story continues in the United States, where Zaim is re-displaced, landing in some town rife with malls and megamarkets. There is everything there, except, of course, a whole lamb, which he cannot find even at

PetSmart. In his profound craving for spit-roasted lamb, Zaim purchases all the pieces needed to assemble a whole lamb: the head, the neck, the breast, the shoulders, the chops, the ribs, the legs. When he collects all the necessary parts, he staples them together. So there it is: a monstrous lamb, which man and history rent asunder but is now put back together by a determined Bosnian, who, beer in hand, proudly and slowly revolves his ovine Frankenstein over the fire. Despite the heroic effort, it still doesn't taste the same.

After more than twenty years in displacement, my parents have assembled a life, nutritional and otherwise, that aimed to be a restorative replica of the previous one, but is in fact a Frankensteinian assemblage of elements old and new. They eat everything they would've been eating if they had stayed in Bosnia, even if it can be hard work to get all the stuff. They depend on their ingenuity as well as on several stores catering to people from the former Yugoslavia.* But the meaning of it all has changed in displacement. Whereas what they ate in Bosnia was typical, an important part of the totality of shared experience, in Canada it makes them appear of a different, exotic world. Their nutritional philosophy is not what connects them to their surroundings, but what sets them apart. They make their food to taste of home, but it inescapably ends up having the taste of displacement.

* They regularly resupply at a store called Punjab, as the owner is a Punjabi who adapted his inventory to a reliably nostalgic Slavic clientele, learning the language along the way.

7

MUSIC

As far as I know, there are no songs that could be sung about the Congress of Berlin, but it was thanks to von Bismarck's Prussian pushiness that I found myself in a schoolyard in Prnjavor one summer day in 1990, where an audience gathered to celebrate the centennial of the Ukrainians' arrival in Bosnia and Herzegovina. A Polish-Ukrainian choir, Zhuravlyi (the Cranes), was to perform as part of the celebration, and they were loitering before call time. They looked conspicuously tall and improbably handsome, brandishing their Cossack mustaches, high boots, and white Ukrainian shirts with patterned collars, flirting with the weak-kneed local maidens. The Cranes were a pretty big deal: On a very big bus they came to this small Bosnian town all the way from Poland in order to help us recall the migration of our foreparents. After the grand centennial celebration, the Cranes would tour all over the not-yet-former Yugoslavia, including Sarajevo, where my then-girlfriend and I heard them singing Rachmaninoff's *All-Night Vigil* at the cathedral. I was unduly proud, as though I genetically belonged in the Cranes' flock, and she was duly impressed; I do believe that afterward we had sex. In Prnjavor, however, the Cranes sang much different tunes, though just as impressively. Sitting in the front row, I was as eager as everyone else for them to unleash their testosterone-laden voices.

But before they did, we had to listen to the opening acts, including the vocal octet Vučijak, which exclusively featured men from my family: Tata and his brothers, Štefan, Bogdan, and Teodor; my cousins Ivan and Vlado; plus Kosta, the husband of my cousin Slavica, visiting from Belfort, France. The ascent of the vocal octet onto the stage is one of the most intense memories I have from my previous life. They climbed the steps to the stage. Kosta led my blind uncle Teodor, who nearly fell as he tripped over the last step. They lined up before the microphones, bumping into one another like discombobulated cattle, wearing the same traditional Ukrainian shirts as the Cranes, except theirs were considerably less glamorous, what with being stretched at the belly, while their Cossack pants appeared baggy enough to conceal an adult diaper. They glanced at one another to communicate a need for a synchronized opening note; their hands rolled up into fists as if to prevent sweat from nervously dripping off their palms; they nodded and burst into song, their voices somewhat uncertain, no doubt due to stage fright—they had never performed before such a large, *international* audience.

The clearest detail in that memory is of the moment when Tata's hand, theretofore an anxious fist, unrolled just as the octet reached the point in their first song when they realized they could no longer fuck it up. They unleashed their voices, their ease and confidence rising, not least because the audience started clapping to the rhythm. On they went, belting away the greatest hits of the Ukrainian diaspora: "Rospriahaite Hloptsy Konyi," "Chom Ty Ne Prishov," "Ivanku Ta Y Ivanku," "Poviyav Viter Stepoviy," and so on. At the end of the performance, the audience promptly stood up to applaud and provide an ovation. As far as the octet was concerned, they never quite sat back down. It was a triumph, one of those instances in family history that is often remembered and misremembered, and at great length too. Yet even the greatest and sharpest memories contain a hole—no one can quite remember who the eighth member of the octet was. It is possible, in fact, that it was a septet.

The audience also included a delegation from Rukh, the Ukrainian nationalist movement that had emerged in western Ukraine during the perestroika years. They wore their proudly Ukrainian shirts and clapped with great excitement, cheering the singers on. The Rukh delegates must've come to Bosnia to seek out and meet the long-forgotten and neglected diaspora, which by virtue of its absence from the oppressed homeland had presumably remained pristine and uncontaminated by Soviet ideology. I suspected that for them the songs my family sang had a fly-in-amber quality, that they might have heard them as perfect records of a time gone, of an innocent and pure culture nearly extinct. They were surely affected by the quaintly obsolescent Ukrainian dialect the singers so confidently used, unspoiled by the sovietization of the language, even if infested by ukrainianized Bosnian words. For the Rukh people the octet (or septet) must've encapsulated a national essence, thus remaining an abstraction, a symbol useful for their nationalist refashioning.

To me, on the other hand, they were my flesh and blood, as concrete as any bodies can ever be, as real as the sweat dripping off their foreheads. Before I saw the octet/septet onstage, I'd admired and loved their singing, but with a measure of condescension, finding their musical enthusiasm lovably exotic with its connect-to-the-roots romanticism. I was a city boy, born in Sarajevo, not in the countryside; I did not speak Ukrainian; and I regularly listened to the kind of music my father summarily dismissed as *struganje*—scraping.* But I swelled with pride as the octet/septet sang, and more important, I was overwhelmed with love: I loved them for their voices, for their courage and anxiety, for their un-Crane-like awkwardness, for their faith in the song and its protections, in the knowledge that, as long as they kept singing, everything might turn out all right.

Back in those days, I freelanced for a Sarajevo radio station, and therefore came up with the idea of doing an audio reportage about the centennial celebration. So I'd brought along a Uher, a radio reporter's portable reel-to-reel tape recorder, and a stack of tapes, to record interviews with my family and the other Prnjavor Ukrainians recollecting the mythical original settlement. What I would do most of the time, however, was record the octet/septet's pre-performance rehearsal in order to play it back to them so they could correct their harmonies and adjust their tempos. Occasionally Uncle Teodor, unimpressed by the presence of the professional equipment, perhaps because he couldn't see it, would arbitrarily assume the authority of a conductor and admonish one of the singers for falling behind or missing a note, and then someone else would snap back at him for talking instead of singing, and the vocal harmony would quickly disintegrate into discordant bickering, and then another take was required and I would rewind the tape to start from the beginning. In the end, I fully taped only two songs, but even in those recordings Uncle Teodor's encouragement could be heard—"Pick it up!" he would say. "That's it!" I may have recorded parts of their stage performance too, possibly the background noise, the din of the audience, maybe some applause, the cheers of the Rukh delegation. Honestly, I

* The word he used was, in fact, rather correct: around that time I was into Swans, Sonic Youth, and Einstürzende Neubauten.

don't remember, and those tapes were never cut into any kind of reportage. They eventually disappeared during the war, like most of my other recordings. Contrary to the common misconception in our foolishly digital society, technology is perishable, while even weak, incorrect, or incomplete memories persist, because they live in and are passed around through bodies. All the more so if the bodies can sing too.

Throughout my childhood, and youth, and life, the Hemons sang. I have no doubt they'll continue singing in the great beyond, as they have at weddings and memorial services, in the church and in the field, or wherever there have been enough of them—which really means more than zero—present in the same space. They sing like they breathe, their need irrepressible and not contingent upon any kind of external stimuli. Alcohol, for example, has rarely been involved, the serotonin high always achieved by way of music. Indeed, Tata insists that alcohol, a common, crucial ingredient in standard-issue Slavic nostalgia, should have nothing to do with it, for it would not be the soul (*duša*) singing in a drunk person, but the booze (*rakija*). My family's love of music is rooted in the culture of poverty common among the Slavs: singing together was the easiest, cheapest, and most comforting entertainment while working the land for survival or while being killed in a war.

My grandparents endured much of their life without electricity and running water, let alone television or any kind of electronic entertainment. So they sang, with their six daughters and four sons, in various combinations, on various occasions. They sang with their neighbors or with the musician stopping by on the way to a dance (*igranka*). They sang sitting in a circle while ripping husks off ears of corn for storage or threading wool, the common peasant tasks. They sang *kolyade*—carols—at Christmastime. They sang teasing songs during that part of the wedding when all the guests approach the groom and bride to give them money in exchange for a piece of cake. They sang tilling fields, raking hay, picking plums out of deep grass and thornbushes to make slivovitz. They just sang.

And in the new land, they learned new songs. Prnjavor and the surrounding area used to be known as Little Europe, since the empire added colonists from all over to the standard Bosnian mix. Which is to say that diverse songs were passed around and shared among the peoples in the area—music, like language, cannot be kept within the stuffy confines of what is known as identity. One of my grandfather's favorite songs, which he would sing to himself while working, no doubt with his Galician accent, was "Tamburalo momče u tamburu" a classic *sevdalinka*, sung originally by Bosnian Muslims, whom he casually referred to as the Turks, which was (and still is) a derogatory term. My adolescent father once fell in love with a Croat girl solely, he still insists, because of the beautiful way she sang Macedonian songs. He's still very fond of Macedonian songs and thinks they are similar to Ukrainian ones in that they're all about "leaving for the world" (*odlazak u svijet*), or, if you wish, about displacement. "The people who don't love music, the tone-deaf people, are damaged," Tata says. "I feel sorry for such people."

Never has my family sung exclusively Ukrainian songs, yet those were the only kind they felt a need to keep alive—the perpetual singing was a way to remember and never lose what they contained. As far as Tata is concerned, singing (*pjesma*) is in the Ukrainian blood; suffice it to say that a common family name among Bosnian Ukrainians is Muzeka—music. And I do remember being awestruck in 2003 by a spontaneous choir of Ukrainians at the Rynok, the main square in Lviv, consisting of old men and ladies, young people and children, who gathered in the afternoon to sing, sometimes for hours. I knew many of their songs, and instantly recognized the same kind of deep devotion I knew from my family. In all my travels, it was only in Galicia that I saw that kind of heartfelt grassroots singing. I am not prone to identifying with groups of strangers—let alone to nationalism or patriotism—but listening to the singers at the Rynok, I couldn't help thinking: *These are my people.*

It is likely that singing acquires a greater value in diaspora, and there is no shortage of diasporic experiences among Ukrainians and Bosnians. The songs my family sings invoke mythological memories of life before the original displacement. The longing for what has been long inaccessible could in singing detach itself from its original object and enfold entire new realities, while using melancholy minor scales. My father's singing face looks nothing like his non-singing self; he becomes someone in a different key, someone I have no access to, unless, perhaps, I sing with him, which I seldom do. "Singing makes everything easier to bear," Tata says. "There is an unburdening in the soul." It is therefore not uncommon that people in my family tear up while singing. "It is possible to cry and sing at the same time," Tata says, as if anyone who knows him would think otherwise. "How can you stop the tears," he asked me not so long ago, "when you hear these lines?"—and he recited, with a trembling voice:

> If you knew, Mother, how poor and unlucky I am
> You would send me a sparrow with some bread,
> And a tit bird with some salt.

Apart from all the animals summoned to ease poverty, displacement, and pain, the cast of characters in the Ukrainian songs in the standard Hemon repertoire is fairly limited: Cossack/soldier, maiden, horse, mother, or any combination thereof, except maybe a solo horse. Many songs contain Cossacks flirting with or seducing girls carrying buckets of water, yet somehow never helping the girls with their burden. Others are about a soldier dying on the battlefield, his mother mourning him, his girl longing and/or crying for him, his metaphorical resurrection fueled by his love of freedom. In those songs, water has special significance; there is plenty of war and steppe, the Cossacks ride their horses, play the bandura, die, and dig said water wells, not necessarily in that order. The maiden is frequently Halya—the name of one of my aunts (dead) and of another cousin (Edmonton, Canada). The trees, particularly the sturdy oak, tend to have symbolic value, as do wheat and buckwheat, while the *kalyna*—cranberry—is practically holy. These songs come not only from the far-off homeland, but also from an entirely different century and attendant economy, now obsolete even in my family. The songs were originally sung by rural, oral people whose minds were mythological, untroubled by modernity. There are no cities in them, no governments, no cars or airplanes, no running water. They frequently feature equestrian Cossack landscapes thoroughly devoid of horseflies or shit, never mind sheep or cows. Neither is there any record of endless toil required for mere survival, nor of any illness that cannot be cured by love, be it for freedom or for Halya. The songs operate at a level of abstraction: my father and his brothers have seldom ridden horses or had any interest in them, probably because even when my grandparents owned one it was used for plowing and tilling; they have never played the bandura; they would get lost or bored in the actual steppe; they don't particularly care about the *kalyna*, let alone the cranberry plant, not even when it's in bloom.* While the dying soldiers in the songs commonly extol the values of courage, freedom, and Ukraine, few Hemons have been eager to give their lives for any

* They can dig a good well, though.

country, let alone Ukraine, where we have only distant family, the descendants of those who had not migrated. The musical vessels of nostalgia in the repertoire—some patriotic, some not quite—invoke the kind of feelings that orbit the lived experience, and cannot therefore be simply described or defined; they can only be (re)imagined as a refracted utopian past. In my family, whose history of ignoble wars and displacements contains no heroes or horses, we prefer vocalizing songs to discussing feelings.

The biggest concentration of Hemons anywhere in the world, Bosnia and Ukraine included, is in the greater Toronto area. There are more than a hundred of them, sorted out in four generations, including many young ones whose names, or even parents, I cannot begin to remember. More than twenty-five years ago, when my parents landed in Ontario at the height of the Bosnian War, the closest family was in Edmonton, where my cousin Halya and her family had disembarked in the late eighties. Little by little, the other Hemons landed in Hamilton—first Bogdan, and then Štefan, with their families.* Teodor's son Ivan† came with his family to Canada by way of Croatia, carrying two notebooks of lyrics and chords for hundreds of songs: the blue one contained Ukrainian songs, the yellow one songs sung all across the former Yugoslavia.

Uncle Teodor's family had lived in Banja Luka, some thirty miles down the road from Prnjavor. As the biggest city in the region with the greatest number of Bosnian Ukrainians, it was home to the Culture and Arts Association Taras Shevchenko

* The fourth brother, Teodor, who had been injured by a mine when he was ten, was disqualified from immigration by his disability. He stayed in Bosnia, where a few years ago he died of a heart attack.

† *Not* the one who was in the octet/septet in 1990. That cousin is a different one.

(Kulturno-umjetničko društvo Taras Ševčenko), whose mission was to preserve and cherish Ukrainian culture, which mainly meant song and dance. For decades, Uncle Teodor and his wife, Štefica,* sang in the association's choir, their daughter, Ana, danced in their dance troupe, while Ivan played the accordion in the orchestra, which was how he learned, memorized, and wrote down an enormous number of Ukrainian songs. He was also part of a band that played at parties and weddings, not just for Ukrainians but for others too; he could play what was popular in Bosnia and Yugoslavia. The two notebooks he brought to Canada were compendiums not only of the songs my family had always sung, but of many they hadn't—and now they could, and would, God knows, until their last fucking note, and then beyond.

The migration to Canada thus marked the beginning of the Hemons' musical renaissance. The trauma of war and displacement was fresh and overwhelming at first, so I don't remember them singing much then, certainly not with their customary intensity and abandon. By 1994, however, they were back into it; since a critical mass of family had migrated, their nostalgia and hurt pressed for expression, while their need for some shared joy became acute. A system was spontaneously established where regular get-togethers became an essential part of everyone's life itinerary. The Christmas season involved a busy schedule: on Christmas Eve everyone went to my cousin Ivan's, on Christmas Day to my parents'; then for New Year's they'd rent a hall with other former Yugoslav Ukrainians; on January 6 they'd go to my cousin Pedja's for Orthodox Christmas Eve, and then the next day to my uncle Bogdan's for Orthodox Christmas, and then a couple of days later to my uncle Štefan's for his name day; then on January 13 they would celebrate the arrival of the Orthodox

* She died as I was writing this.

New Year, and for the Orthodox New Year's Day they'd get together to eat up the leftovers. They'd thus be singing their way through eight parties in three weeks. Whenever I called my parents to wish them a happy New Year, my father would thank me in a hoarse voice, while my mother complained that she was exhausted and they were only halfway through the season. The rest of the year was perhaps less hectic, but there would still be plenty of weddings, christening parties, picnics, or non-required get-togethers, where they could sing for hours on end.

Much of my Ontario-based family attended the party my parents threw in their backyard after Ella, my first daughter, was born, so the singing went on all day long. The variable lineup, which included my father, Ivan, Bogdan, Štefan, and some cousins, never stopped singing for a moment, even if individual singers would take a break to eat, drink, or relieve themselves. As vast as their repertoire was, they covered it at least a couple of times, and eventually had to go for the lesser-sung items in the notebooks—the rarities and B-sides, so to speak. They'd huddle over the blue or the yellow notebook, their heads touching; their glasses smudged with sweat and meat grease, they'd miss certain lines and would hum and howl to cover it up, figuring out as they went along the song they claimed they knew perfectly well. And they kept at it. Children played soccer in the backyard, got tired, ate, cried, fell asleep in their parents' arms, woke up to play soccer again, all to the relentless soundtrack of the expanded Hemon repertoire. At some point all conversation ceased, for it was too difficult to speak over the belting voices, which was why I got miffed and insisted they end it. I understand now that the ceaseless song was but an expression of joy, if stretched over a very, very long time. To be fair, they did try to wind it down after six hours or so, but then Stan the neighbor stopped by. Stan the neighbor was actually Stanislaw, a Pole, which is to say that his Slavic nostalgia had fully kicked in as he listened from across the street to the Hemons' backyard oratorio. He'd comforted himself with a shot of vodka, and then another one, and soon he wandered over all teary-eyed to gaze at them longingly across the fence, whereupon they sat him down, offered him another drink, and then indulged him with the highlights of their repertoire, which required another two hours.

Over time, the Hemons' singing acquired a bit of fame among the Ontario Ukrainians. For one thing, my family have never been shy about singing at other people's parties. Someone must have heard them and passed on the word, for Tata, Štefan, and Bogdan were recruited to sing for the Orion Men's Choir. This was a different game: they sang with thirty other men; they were required to attend rehearsals regularly, and to submit to the conductor's authority, learning to read music; the choristers are divided into four voices; they're often accompanied by an orchestra, while Ukrainian and civilian songs are ambitiously arranged; performances* take place in large venues; they're sometimes joined by a women's choir. Proper choral singing does not quite accommodate the Hemons' proclivity to belt it out at the top of their lungs as if the nearest audience were a couple of hills over, a style developed in their native Vučijak, but they've managed to adjust. They've toured with the choir, traveling as far as New Jersey and New York,† and they've recorded in a professional studio, where the sound engineer edited their singing, producing a kind of technological magic that appealed to my ever-engineering father. When he heard the recording for the first time, he got goose bumps.

* "Showcasing liturgical, contemporary, traditional folk, and patriotic music," according to the choir's official website.

† My father hated New York because it was "too crowded."

It must've been the choral experience of singing outside the context of backyards and weddings that encouraged the Hemons to undertake an endeavor that would've been inconcievable to my ancestors, who had sung their worries away in a kitchen lit only by the stove fire. In the summer of 2015, the Hemons self-released a CD entitled *Hemons: Traditional Ukrainian Folk Songs*, their first (and possibly last) recording. The liner notes do not explain the absence of the definite article in the ensemble's name, but the artists are proudly listed:

> Stefan: Tenor I
> Petar: Tenor II
> Bogdan: Baritone
> Ivan: Accordion & Tenor I
> Gregor: Guitar
> Taras: Sound Engineer

For this project, a third generation of Hemons was added: Ivan's young sons Taras and Gregor (Canadian-born). The CD was sold for twenty Canadian dollars, with all of the proceeds going to a "poor student's [*sic*] fund," that is, to college-age family members in need of financial help. My mother was put in charge of collecting the funds. As of the last audit, there was about $1,350 Canadian in the account, to be disbursed to the young students in the tribe.

On the CD, the Hemons deliver what they've sung at every family gathering since I can remember hearing sounds. There is the perennial "Rospriahaite Hloptsy Konyi," in which the Cossack boys (*hloptsy*) unbridle their horses, and then one of them digs a well (what else?) and flirts with a maiden named Marusya, who is in turn jealous because the well-digger has chatted up another girl. And then there is "Tam, Pid Lvivskim Zamkom," addressing the fact that Ukrainians have never won a war by way of depositing a dead young partisan, blond curls and all, under an oak tree just beneath the Lviv castle; there he lies dead as his mother informs the heartbroken audience that he was the youngest of her five sons, and that his father also died in a war; she wishes that the war hadn't been fought, as a mother would, but then there's that pricey thing called freedom. Another young soldier is dead in "Poviyav Viter Stepoviy," and another mother cries for him, this time aided by a maiden. There are a few more songs where the stories of tragic heroism might conceal plain sadness, and then there are inklings of joy, or at least some non-funereal flowers, as in "Nese Halya Vodu," in which the indomitable Halya fetches water, while one Ivanko trails her like a periwinkle (*barvinok*).

The song list is so familiar to me that some of the numbers I often hear in my dreams. It's the soundtrack for the part of the Hemon subconscious that houses our history. The liner notes suggest as much:

> The Hemon family left Ukraine in the early twentieth century, bringing with them the rich language, the delicious cuisine and the discipline of beekeeping to their new homeland. However, it is their love and memory of the beautiful songs of Ukraine that holds *[sic]* the strongest connection to their past, a love that has grown with them and has come to form a vital part of what it means to be Hemon. Through song the Hemons honor their past, enjoy the present, look to the future, but most importantly celebrate their strength, unity and love as a family.

"The discipline of beekeeping" slays me, while "a love that . . . has come to form a vital part of what it means to be Hemon" buries me. Much of my life, I've been trying to figure out what it means to be Hemon—or, as English grammar would have it, *a*

Hemon. It's perhaps significant that the liner notes mention only the initial departure, while there is not a word about not one, but two arrivals in "their new homeland." The primary, unacknowledged source of inspiration for the music must be related to the fact that no one in my family dies in the country where he or she was born. Like the mythological Cossacks on their horses, we sing while passing from one place to another.

The *Hemons* CD notes also offer "special thanks to our wives for their love and support." One of those wives would obviously be my mother, who provided support by preparing the food that sustained the Hemons in the studio. The Hemons' gratitude notwithstanding, my mother has had a complicated relationship with their singing. She enjoys music, likes to sing herself, but she does not speak Ukrainian and not infrequently feels neglected due to my father's vocal obsession. It was her idea, in fact, to sell the CDs for the poor student's fund, so that there would be some actual use and purpose to all that singing.

As students in Belgrade, my parents sang a lot together, spending much of their non-studying time partying. In the pictures from that era their joyful abandon is visible, complete with their ecstatic faces centered around a guitar. The preferred music from their student days was rock 'n' roll, not only because it was conquering the world at the time, but also because they were leaving behind their peasant roots to become educated urban dwellers. Perhaps that's why they're so fond of the particular genre of former Yugoslav songs known as *starogradske*, which could be translated as "old urban." These songs and their derivatives tap into the late nineteenth century bohemian, bourgeois nostalgia, where love is always unrequited, men drink to forget a woman or their wasted youth, commonly both. Similar to the Bosnian *sevdalinka*, which is infused with *sevdah*—a pleasant feeling of losing oneself to the hopelessness of love, to time passing, to life and the defeats it inflicts—the *starogradska* song generates *dert*, a kind of ecstasy where nothing matters but this moment loaded with tears, wine, song, love. My parents thus sang *starogradske* and *sevdalinke* whenever temporary abandonment was available and permitted, which means on occasions like New Year's Eve or an evening with select friends. The abandon was never defeatist, the intended feeling always rooted in the joy of being with the people dear to their heart. If in my mind's eye I want to see Mama being happy, I imagine her singing among her friends—and there she is with her high-pitched voice, squinting as if to see better into her own soul, throwing up her arms as if discarding all her worries (and there have always been many), sometimes embracing a person next to her to make them turn up the volume. Nowadays, when the Hemons sing *starogradske* she might join in, but she usually sings with a subdued voice, as if doing it only because she cannot refrain. The song list for my parents' relationship is thus different from the Hemon one. So it was from this song list that my father drew for his performance marking my parents' fiftieth wedding anniversary.

The anniversary party took place in a Hamilton church-basement hall, which necessitated, to the consternation of my atheist mother, that a priest sprinkle holy water around and lead the guests in prayer. He also made her kiss the cross, which she did, and which, we would be told later, left a foul taste in her mouth. Following the consecration, my two nieces and my older daughter, accompanied by Felix, my brother-in-law, sang "Que Sera, Sera," and some congratulatory speeches were delivered. And then Tata stepped in front of the microphone and announced that he would now tell the story of their first meeting, marriage, and their fifty years of shared life, and he would do all that by way of song. The motto of his presentation: "The song sustained us, to her we're grateful." ("*Pjesma nas je održala, njojzi hvala.*") There was no musical accompaniment; he was alone, armed with a one-page script in his hand. First came the story of how his roommate, Nidžo, introduced him to Andja. When he saw her, Tata said, she looked like an angel—whereupon he broke into a song about an angel-like woman. He addressed the fact that he'd traveled for work too much in the course of their marriage, leaving Mama alone to wrangle the life and kids, with a song entitled "Forgive Me That I Stole Your Love" ("Oprosti što sam tvoju ljubav krao"). The song includes the lines: "And I was happy with another woman somewhere / And you waited for me"—but no one present would've considered the possibility that he'd actually done any of that. Still, at some point he posed a rhetorical question: "What is the secret of a successful marriage?" He responded in the same breath: "Constancy. I was bad at the beginning, I was bad for fifty years, and I am bad now." His being "bad," I knew, was not a joke, nor him being sarcastic. What it meant was that he felt guilty for not being supportive, for not being present when Mama needed him, for not quite understanding what fueled her resentments, and for not being able to be rid of that burden of guilt. Toward the end of the performance, he related how, on the eve of the war, in April 1992, someone called to tell them that our cabin in Jahorina had been broken into, and he went up there to check and fix the damage. But then he had a hard time getting back home, because the Serbian ring around the city was already in place and they would not let him get through. So he went off the road and followed a path through the woods, and the woods were still full of snow—as in the song, he said, "The Snow Fell on Trees in Bloom" ("Snijeg pade na behar na voće"), which he then promptly belted out for the appreciative audience.

And thus he sang and talked solo for nearly an hour. It was

an unforgettable performance of what can be accurately identified as a monomusical. Throughout it I was alternately suppressing diluvial tears and chuckling on the verge of uproarious laughter. After the show was over, I asked for his script, as I knew immediately I would write about what had happened. I put the script away for future use and now, of course, can't find it—it is in some file somewhere with all the other things I must never forget. My mother enjoyed his performance too, but with some ambivalence—on top of the annoying priest and cross-kissing, she must have felt that the musical rendition of their marital history was somewhat one-sided. Her songs would've been different, but she didn't get to sing them.

Not so long ago, my parents were visiting me in Chicago. On their way back, they listened to a CD of songs from the former Yugoslavia. When the classic Macedonian song "Biljana platno belaše" ("Biljana Whitened the Cotton") came on, they spontaneously started singing, since they both love it. They sang the next song on the CD as well, and then they turned off the stereo and sang together for hours, until they made it home.

8

LITERATURE

Though Tata would sometimes read epic poetry to me, the main domain whence his bedtime stories came was his childhood. I tolerated the epics but found them distressing—in one of the famous poems, a mother loses all nine of her sons,* which somehow turns out to be noble and honorable. But his childhood stories I loved unconditionally, particularly the wartime stories. My favorite was the one in which he and his brother Teodor found a box of ammo, and when the *čerkezi* came to harass the family, maybe even kill them, they threw the ammo into the fire. The *čerkezi* heard the bullets exploding in the fire, jumped on their horses, and rode toward the ruckus, or away from it. Either way, I loved the cleverness of the plot, and the fact that ammo was involved, for I was at an age when I desired guns

* And her husband, and then she dies too. The poem is, I believe, "*Smrt majke Jugovića*"—"The Death of Mother Jugović."

and played with my friends games articulated around pretend shooting.*

My favorite character was Ovan Janko—a ram named Janko—who had somehow hung around the house untethered and liked to charge at people and knock them over with his powerful horned head. There was a whole cycle of stories centered around Ovan Janko, and night after night I implored my father to tell me one, and then another one. I can't now remember all of those stories, but I do recall that Ovan Janko's main targets were a certain Savka Troglavka and her friend Makivija. The basic template, endlessly exploitable for bedtime story purposes, featured Savka and Makivija on their way to the market in Prnjavor, walking down a dirt road straight into an ambush set up by Janko, who would inevitably charge and force them to hit the dirt. In the most hilarious version, Savka or Makivija (or both) carried a handful of eggs in their bosom to sell them in the market, so that when Janko attacked and they threw themselves down, the eggs were smashed and pasted against their chests. Janko would then loom over them while they kept their heads down, his horns ready to inflict punishment if they moved. Each time they tried to get up, Janko would bump into them again. They wailed—and my father imitated their voices to my great mirth—and called for help, which would sometimes take a long while to arrive, usually in the form of one of my grandparents. It was all Bosnian-peasant slapstick comedy.

I had Ovan Janko well conceptualized before I ever saw an actual ram, which is to say that the first ram I'd ever see was, as it were, an actualization of Janko.† I'm sure Tata made up a few of the stories, but what made them great was not just their slapstick

* We must live as though peace will last for a hundred years, and be ready as though war will start tomorrow.

† This is how storytelling shapes the world.

quality, but also that Janko the guard ram possessed a kind of mythological agency. Neither did it hurt that both Makivija and Savka Troglavka had near-mythological profiles and names: in the stories, they had no husbands, as was required of mature women in the Bosnian peasantry world, nor did they ever do anything other than reliably walk into Janko's ambush on their way to or from the market; I had never encountered the name Makivija outside my father's narratives, while Savka Troglavka not only brandishes an internal rhyme (-avka/-avka) that makes her sound like a slapstick character, but also suggests a quality of three-headedness, as *troglav* means three-headed in Bosnian. And Janko's powers were truly, mythically awesome: after many a neighbor had been brutally charged at, resulting in many a bruised body and smashed egg, my grandfather chained a log to Janko's neck, so that he could not attack people. Janko, however, figured out how to run sideways, developing an ingenious assault strategy whereby he would swing the log to knock the victim over with it, sometimes even wrapping the chain around the legs to pull the victim down.

Many years later, in Canada, at an extended-family dinner, I mockingly expressed admiration for my father's narrative embellishments in the Janko story cycle, particularly the log-swinging detail. Both Tata and Uncle Bogdan strenuously insisted that there was not an iota of exaggeration in any of it. Uncle Bogdan—whom I'd never heard tell a Janko story—described the Janko move exactly as my father had for many years, and dressed me down for doubting the veracity of their common memory. I have now accepted that Ovan Janko was very intelligent, aggressive, and capable of swinging a log on a chain to attack passersby as incontestable truth, indeed as history, even if it is possible that the memory of Janko shared by my father and his siblings was in fact formulated by cyclical retelling.

Tata always had a lot of stories set in his native Vučijak, and he dispensed them well beyond my childhood. In fact, they were reliable tools for regaling friends and family, particularly the cycle featuring Branko and Duja, a couple who lived with their eight kids in the house next to the Hemons and who were, in the grand narrative setup, their perpetual comic foils. In those stories Branko quickly gets enraged and does silly things and is therefore the exact opposite of my calm and kind grandfather, who, nevertheless, would shake a swarm of bees gathered on the tip of a tree branch right on top of Branko innocently holding a hive underneath. Duja, on the other hand, would join Makivija and Savka Troglavka on their journeys to the fabled market, whence she would return with three sweat-soaked lumps of sugar in her bosom, which description would cause roars of laughter among myriad audiences. In the most famous and popular Branko and Duja story, my grandfather hears Duja's wailing and calling for help. He runs over to their yard thinking that someone might be dying and finds Duja on the ground and Branko on top of her, slapping her face and demanding: "Who's the man and who's the woman? Who's the man and who's the woman?" Now, Duja could get out of her dreadful predicament by saying, "You're the man and I'm the woman," thereby confirming the cruel distribution of gender roles taken to be natural among Bosnian peasantry, but in her stubborn paleo-feminism she keeps refusing to conform and wails instead. Branko would've slapped her all day long, maybe even killed her, had not my grandfather, in his deep and calm voice, talked him out of it. When my father told this story, his audience would be in convulsions. Why it was funny, I'll never know. The entertainment value of a story in which a person is repeatedly battered could be reasonably related to common patriarchal cruelty toward women, practiced even by domestic animals like Janko. Now I see it as a symptom of patriarchal pathology, even if the story was usually told in a social situation where battering was unacceptable. The narrative came from a transcended past and was delivered in a new life, marking the traveled distance. Branko and Duja were mythological characters cast in a timeless domain to which the only access was narrative.

I remember meeting the two them in my childhood—they'd stop by my grandparents' to greet us when we visited—and could see none of the characteristics they had in my father's stories: they were just two old peasants with weathered faces and a funny way of speaking, devoid of violence or craziness or any inclination toward extreme actions. I remember them as ancient, tired people: Duja kept her hands in her lap like tired puppies; Branko sat slouching over his crossed legs, sucking on a roll-up cigarette and slurping the gratis slivovitz my grandmother served.

Hence were Branko and Duja different from "Branko and Duja," even if the existence of the real couple provided an extra layer of verisimilitude to the ones in quotation marks. This is not to say that Branko did not really beat Duja—rather, the meaning of that action has one value in reality, where it caused pain and distress and was then absorbed into the dynamic of a particular marriage, space, and time, while it had another value in the mythological world of Tata's childhood in Vučijak, where no one ever was in pain or injured (other than my uncle Teodor) and where all situations and people acquired a degree of abstraction necessary for oral narration. In that mythological space, people have only basic bodies and psychologies—much like Ulysses or Don Quixote, they overcome the obstacles without volatility, mental or physical damage, or any kind of inner transformation. They are the same every time they're narrated; they do not age, or die, or suffer; they keep existing for as long as there is a story to be told. This is one of the ways in which storytelling grounds being in the ever-changing world—it worked for Homer, it works for my father.

"Branko and Duja" also served the purpose of providing contrast against which my family could identify their values and validate their self-perception. While "Branko" beat "Duja," no male Hemon would touch his wife in anger, that particular article of gender ethos established at the beginning of my grandparents' marriage.* While "Branko" would get drunk, my grandfather never did. While "Duja" gossiped and went to the market with Savka and Makivija only so she could catch and release base rumors, my grandmother never did. While "Branko" was known to steal stuff in the village, my grandfather not only never did, but also found ways to get the stolen stuff back from "Branko" without ever accusing him. "Branko and Duja" were the Bosnian natives against which my Ukrainian-speaking family could feel superior, precisely because they were not, or not much. To narrate is to abstract and simplify, to make choices that imply a moral vision of the world—there is always an ethical agenda. Narration as a way of conveying self-evident reality is a recent invention, and false at that, for such "reality" is just as much a consequence of abstraction and simplification as my father's outrageous stories.

This is not to say that Tata would ever accept that "Branko and Duja" were not the exact Branko and Duja he knew and I met more than once—he would not be able to identify any narrative operation other than telling it like it is. He deplores the kind of unreal stories Hollywood is prone to manufacturing. "I'm an engineer," he says. "I like reality." But I believe that the difference between "Branko and Duja" and the actual couple is a matter of distance, physical and metaphorical. It was possible for my father to abstract Branko and Duja only because he had long left the space in which they and their lives were fully real. Storytelling is not only not reporting, but the opposite of it: it is reimagining

* See the chapter "Marriage."

what happened in a different domain of experiential reality, including the past. Furthermore, the "Vučijak" that is the setting for his stories is entirely different from what it was when he left to go to school, or to live in Canada, let alone from what it is now, to which version he has little access. Vučijak truly exists only in his mythology. This is how memory, particularly its nostalgic variation, operates. Nostalgia pins the original place to an inaccessible distant position in an unalterable past, where it can exist beyond time and place, and therefore must be forever narrated.

The earliest recorded rendition of the complete "Vučijak" cycle was at the time of his great migration to Belgrade to go to college. He was at his narrative peak: it was then that he was capable of narrating his dream in installments, a bar I would like to reach one day. But the stories about the home he left must've been contingent upon a significant geographic distance, since he could not return home as frequently as before. Perhaps more important, there was also an uncrossable social, or indeed historical, distance. During his college years, what with his studies of advanced math, his exposure to rock 'n' roll and Mexican songs, and the stimulating complexity of his big-city experience, he migrated from the confines of his parents' nineteenth century peasant life to the cutting edge of the twentieth century urban world. He could never return to his childhood home, except narratively, and some form of nostalgia would thereafter always be present in his storytelling.

When Mama, Kristina, and I went to spend the summer of 1982 in Zaire with Tata, all the Yugoslavs who we met in Kinshasa were fully familiar with the characters from the Vučijak epic cycle. I remember the ambassador, a veteran diplomat born in Slovenia, and his wife, retelling us the "Branko and Duja" story and repeating the punch line "Who's the man, who's the woman?" with laughter. We learned that Tata was telling these stories at the gatherings of the few Yugoslavs in Zaire who had not much to do except tell stories to one another, a field of practice my father soon pretty much monopolized. For them, as for Tata, "Branko and Duja" lived in the remote homeland, populated by familiar people with whom they had totally lost connection—Vučijak represented the land that was to them what Ithaca was for Ulysses.

My father is a great storyteller, and the fact that he was rarely, and in some ways never, at home must have played a role. Movement through space, literally and figuratively, generates stories—narration equals migration squared—which is why many of his other stories are a consequence of his travels around the world. They could be delivered and made sense of only upon his return home.

Back when he went regularly to the Soviet Union, he'd come back with stories upon stories. From one of those trips he returned with a slide projector, which was, like many of the Soviet toys he brought back, Communist gray. He would use it to show us the color slides of people, places, sights, and Russian fairy tales he had come across. He would schedule a show, sometime after dinner and before sleep, turn off the lights, and project the slides on the blank wall in our living room. Each image prompted a story, sometimes anecdote-sized, sometimes dipping into the vast sea of history. There were stories of the charge at the Winter Palace that had started the Revolution; of Lenin mummified in his mausoleum; of Vasilisa Prekrasnaya, who had a little wooden doll and a mean stepmother; of the enormous size and power of Siberian rivers; of Victor Alexandrovich Strobel, who confided in my father about his difficult life as a non-party (*bespartiyniy*) Jew in the USSR, whose many friends left for Israel, etc. The images of princes and horses and firebirds were explained and contextualized with the Russian text at the bottom of the screen. My sister and I could not understand Russian, so he would have to read it to us, embellishing, no doubt, along the way. All these stories were on the same never-ending continuum, full of details I cannot recall right now, as they dissolved in the long-crashed adrenaline high. What we learned was that there was always an enormous elsewhere full of people and that things happened there.

Tata would always go elsewhere and return with stories. After a couple of years in Zaire, he returned with an African cycle he is still exploiting. I remember a time when my various uncles, aunts, cousins, and my grandfather gathered in my grandparents' kitchen to listen to his African stories: about Philip, whom he hired at double the going wage (and probably still low) to cook for him, and the things Philip had made for him; about the talking cockatoo belonging to his friends Mirko and Roza that could imitate a doorbell and curse in the vilest Bosnian; about his trip to the jungles of Katanga, a place none of them had ever heard of; about the amazing Congo River; about the hippos and elephants and other unspeakable creatures; about Le Grand Marche in Kinshasa, where you could purchase marvelous fruits and wiggling worms and dried monkeys; about La Cité, the slum on the outskirts of Kinshasa where Philip lived and would eventually die of malaria. My grandparents didn't even have a TV, while few members of my extended family had ever left the country; none of them had ever met a black person—I am sure, though I honestly don't remember, that my father deployed various available racial and racist stereotypes to conjure up for them the Africa he had seen. Be that as it may, I remember the wonder on their faces as they imagined a place so distant from them it might as well have been on Mars, my aunts gasping in shock, while one or another of my uncles kept spontaneously exclaiming: "You don't say!"

But there is more to Tata's storytelling savvy than his (and our) peregrinate history. While there are great storytellers who can turn a trek to the loo into a gripping tale, there are also those who spontaneously generate a kind of a charged field wherein things happen regardless of their narrative skills and irrespective of their will. I conceived of this theory after spending a day with my father in the summer of 1986. Bad things happened.

We were staying in the countryside for a week, at my grandparents' house, now empty because they had both died. He needed to attend to his apiary, which he kept on the family homestead, and had asked me to come and keep him company. I agreed under two conditions: one, I would be allowed to read without limit, which meant I wouldn't have to do any manual work; two, we would bring our color TV so I could watch the World Cup games taking place in Mexico at the time. So, one afternoon that week, I was happily reading inside the house while he was attending to his bees. The day was hot and humid, so the bees were exceptionally angry and aggressive; I could hear them pinging suicidally against the windowpanes. He ran into the house under the assault of a few particularly enraged bees, wearing a full beekeeper's outift and still getting stung. Breathlessly, he suggested that we go and see my aunt Filjka, who lived fifteen (or fewer) minutes away. I refused because there was an important game* I wanted to watch and Aunt Filjka's TV was black-and-white. We'll take ours, Tata said, and I succumbed to his pressure, as I often did. We made a plan: given that the bees were rabid, he would go and close the hives, take off his outfit in the barn, run over to the car avoiding kamikaze bees, kill all the ones in the car, and honk, whereupon I would run carrying the TV, he'd open the door so I could load the TV and slip in before the bees could, and we'd be good to go. This we did as planned and were thus merrily on our way. My grandparents' house was close to the top of the hill, while my aunt lived a couple of miles down in

* Italy vs. France, I believe. The final score was 0–2.

the valley. Halfway down the hill, my father said, "I forgot to put gas in the car," whereupon—within an instant, as if on cue, *as if in a fucking sitcom*—the engine shut down. We went on rolling down the hill while I was discombobulated by a combination of fury and disbelief. We couldn't simply roll on all the way to my aunt's, for the road leveled off in the midst of a vast, flat field. When the gasless car finally stopped, we looked around and saw nothing moving between us and the horizon, over which dark clouds forebodingly loomed. There was no one near, no one to help us. We were in the Bosnian countryside at the height of the summer, just before a storm. My father, however, is a kind of person who lives to solve problems, an essential and necessary skill for someone who constantly creates them for himself and others. First, he considered our pushing the car to the gas station, which was at least a kilometer or so away, and uphill at that—which, of course, I refused. He then spotted a far-off tractor advancing along the main road and instantly realized that it could tow the car to the gas station. This was what happened: he waved down the tractor and offered the man money for his help, so they hooked it up. As we chugged along in the wake of the tractor, I moped without restraint. Italy vs. France had already started, and I really wanted to see it, and the tractor was in no hurry to get us to the gas station. Then it got worse: once we got there, it turned out that their power was out and we could not refill the gas tank. I was close to tears. Our next desperate move was to walk to my aunt's carrying the heavy TV alternately, looking like common thieves. By the time we made it down the road to my aunt's, I was sweaty, thirsty, hungry, angry, and the game was almost over. I plugged in the TV and turned it on, only to find out that down in the valley the reception was terrible and that instead of the game the TV showed only a ground-pepper blizzard. The whole adventure took two hours or so; in some other family, some other father and son would've reached their desired destination in fifteen minutes or less, but we had to go through a fucking adventure. I was so exhausted I could no longer even be irate. I just sat there accepting the fact that I was but a loose particle in my father's hypercharged narrative field. Meanwhile, he was already contentedly slurping his soup.

Among other dreadful things, war is a universe-sized narrative field because it inescapably and brutally results in migration. After the war in Bosnia and my parents' subsequent displacement, a number of new epic story cycles have been created, all of them rooted, so to misspeak, in removal. These stories are now hashed and rehashed, told and retold, with compulsive regularity, each time a new layer of details added. Meanwhile, I've become the family's prime storyteller, largely because I'm now a professional. I've appropriated many of those stories to tell them elsewhere, some in the form of fiction. This is tolerated, sometimes even appreciated, by my extended family. As for my parents, they're proud, and willingly submit themselves to my interviews and inquiries, knowing full well that sooner or later it will all end up in some published text. Tata called me once and when I picked up asked me what I was doing. I was doing nothing: it was Sunday night. "Well," he said, "why are you not writing something?"

When a few years ago my father was laid off,* he fell into a deep despair. It was typically gray and cold in Hamilton in January, his bees were dormant for the winter, he worried about money, there was nothing to do, no task at all to be completed, which is to say that life appeared temporarily, or even permanently,

* In the spirit of seasonal kindness and generosity, the company he worked for would fire a lot of its workers before Christmas to save money on holiday pay and then rehire in January. Tata was fired and rehired a few times, until one January the company didn't call.

meaningless. In a stroke of filial inspiration, I talked Tata into writing some of his tales. I told him I needed material for my writing, and I wasn't lying. First, he wrote a history of bees in our family, sending me the first part before he finished it all.* He enjoyed writing, though he found it difficult to sit down and stick to it for a long time.† His style is matter-of-fact, sometimes containing explanatory paragraphs of random, baffling details. In writing about the days in 1943 when they became refugees and trekked down to the Vijaka River, he remembered he was carrying a coffee grinder; he was seven at the time—the exactness of the detail is soul-rending. But he does not see his writing as an artistic endeavor at all, and imagination plays no role—he doesn't read novels, or any literary texts. "I am not going to read made-up stuff only because it's nicely written," he told me.

Ever since "The Bees," Tata planned to write a piece called "The Pump," which would be about a well pump near the Hemon house where all the neighbors and animals got their water back when he was a kid. It was not clear to me why that was his most pressing idea, but he kept coming back to it. When I called him to ask questions for this piece (*How many kids did Branko and Duja have? What was Strobel's patronymic?*), he declared that he was about to get to writing it.‡ He also wrote a short piece called "Salt," which was about his father going in the middle of the war to look for salt: Grandpa Ivan was gone for days, passing checkpoints and crossing front lines, and when he finally came back with salt, it was ruined because he carried it in his backpack with the baking soda he got for washing clothes. My father hasn't produced enough

* I used it, occasionally quoting verbatim from his text, for my story "The Bees, Part 1" from *Love and Obstacles.*

† Tell me about it.

‡ He has written "The Pump" and sent it to me. The pump itself plays a minor role: the story, full of harrowing details, is about Uncle Teodor's injury.

writing for a dominant theme to be established, but a prime candidate has already emerged, and it is loss.

There were no domestic animals in the bedtime stories my mother told me. There was a hedgehog—Ježurko Ježić—but he lived in a book she read to me and every child knew. After I learned at the age of five to read on my own and moved on to new pastures with more diverse animals, Mama would sing to me before sleep, and, most often, recite children's poetry. I can always recall the lines Mama recited before bed throughout my childhood:

Điha, điha četiri noge
Sve četiri krute.
Điha, điha, mi idemo
Na daleke pute.

Sedlo mi je od marame
Uzde od kanapa.
A bič mi je od očeva
Prebijena štapa.

The lines were from a poem by Jovan Jovanović Zmaj,* in which a child pretends to be riding a horse, using a scarf for a saddle, a rope for a rein, and the father's broken stick as a whip. The imaginary horse is missing, however, and to this day I don't know what object was supposed to stand in for it.

My mother, in other words, was not a storyteller. The Zmaj poem was not the only one she recited, though the rest of them

* Or, as the kids knew him, Čika-Jova Zmaj.

have vanished inside my unretaining mind.* Mama is a generator of words, not of narratives, and the field in which she conducted and sang was language. The unfortunate English-only reader will never be able to assess the bizarre beauty of words and phrases like:

šandoprc—The kind of uncontrollable temporary madness that often possesses children and adolescents, used with the verb *uhvatiti*—to catch. My sister and I were often caught by *šandoprc*.

kreveljiti se—To make funny faces and/or behave in an unserious, clownish manner. My sister and I liked to do this at the family meal, just because we were kids.

trnđo-mrnđo—A sloppily, carelessly dressed individual, i.e., the high school version of me going out in jeans torn at the knees. Used in a sentence: "You look like a *trnđo-mrnđo*, the world will think you're an orphan."†

trapav—Clumsy. I was always *trapav*, because things would just fall out of my hands and break.

trapađoze—The word originally referred to the ugly winter boots worn by those who worry more about their warm feet than about their looks. The root *trapa-* suggests physical awkwardness and a lumbering appearance, and the word reached its full potential upon my mother's arrival in Canada, where she devised the verb *utrapađoziti se*, which means "to

* For some reason or another I've long been unable to retain any song lyrics or lines from poetry I learned after the age of ten.

† In Bosnian, "the world"—*svijet*—is commonly used to mean "people," implying, to say the least, a particular ethos.

wear hand-me-down Canadian clothes given to refugees and thus to look pathetically ungainly."

pustiti goluba—Literally, "to let the pigeon out," which was a euphemism for a fart, as in, "Who let the pigeon out?" Not so long ago I was in Piazza San Marco in Venice and saw pigeons crowding around tourists, and instantly thought: *A flock of farts is about to envelop the piazza.*

She always deployed the whole range of the Bosnian language,* which, like many languages, has appropriated from the neighbors and conquerors. Speaking Bosnian, she always covers the full range from Turkish to German (Austrian, really) words and back, by way of many Slavic ones in between. One of her favorite jokes is the one about a Bosnian who had never seen a banana. "You know what a *takiša* looks like? Well, banana is not even close." *Takiša* is an obscure word for a variety of pear I learned from her telling the joke (and laughing uproariously) and never in any other context. She likes to use the word *oberlopov*, which combines the German word *ober*† and the quintessential South-Slavic word *lopov* (thief), so that an *oberlopov* is an upper-rank officer of thievery. There was a whole subset of words formed by applying the inflection *-roca*, entirely exclusive to her, and used as diminutives, so that I had to be sure to wipe my *kitoroca* (*kita* = dick) after

* Though she prefers to call the language she uses Serbo-Croatian, as it was the official, federal language of (most of) Yugoslavia, she speaks in a recognizably Bosnian way: her idioms and vocabulary, her accent and tonalities, could not have come from any other place.

† *Ober*: higher, upper; normally used in the context of army ranks, as in *Oberleutnant*, which is to say that the word came with the Austro-Hungarians.

peeing. Feeding the feral cats in Hamilton, she speaks in a language even I have a hard time understanding.

Mama was the one who talked and listened to me when I was a kid, to whom I had to formulate my complicated feelings and ethical conundrums, particularly when I hit the slippery adolescence patch. In the fifth grade, I was a model student who came back home on the last day of school with an armful of citations for my good work. The first parent-teacher conference of the sixth grade, however, had to be interrupted because Mama nearly passed out as the teacher reported all the mischief, property damage, and rule violations I'd commited in the first few weeks of the new school year. With Mama I argued over doing homework, at her I yelled to stop nagging. Even if we had some regrettably spectacular arguments, all this made language the shared field where we could be close—Bosnian was and is indeed my mother tongue—which is to say that in some ways there was never a need for the mediation of stories. Stories work at a distance,* whereas language is immediate and instantly impactful. We were too close, metaphorically and literally, to convert experience into narratives for each other. This was possible because, unlike Tata, she never traveled, never left us to go be somewhere else. Mama was, like language, always there. Tata was, like stories, always elsewhere.

In the fifth grade, I joined the school team competing in something called the League of Young Linguists.† The linguistic situation in Bosnia and Herzegovina was convoluted to the exact same extent that its ethnic situation was complicated, which was why the language was officially standardized in a meeting of linguists in 1960, the result of which was a thick book containing a set of rules and a dictionary we had to study word for word to compete

* Migration is the square root of narration.

† *Liga mladih lingvista*, a competitive after-school activity.

as Young Linguists. I cannot remember if Mama made me go, or she just succumbed to the demands of the teacher, but it was her constant presence in that particular corner of my school life that ensured my committment to being a Young Linguist. In other words, she made me stay in language up to my ears even when I didn't want to. Many years later, when I was in my twenties, I found a file she'd kept containing clips from newspapers and award certificates, providing evidence that my Young Linguists team and/or I were often the champions of the all-Bosnian competition. I'd forgotten how good at it I was, but she kept the record. If language was a field, she was the one whose duty and pleasure were to attend to it and turn it into a garden.

Which is why it's not surprising that not only was Mama the one who taught me to read, but she was (and is) a devout reader herself. While my father never read books unrelated to his work—and even those I never actually saw him read—she was the one who filled up our shelves. Ever since I was little, a bookseller would stop by her office a few times a year, and she would call me from work to consult about what books to get. The earliest purchase was a set of thick hardcover books containing stories and pictures from many Disney classics and then some I'd never heard of. These I read until they fell apart, whereupon I kept reading them. She bought books in bulk: we had a shelf with *The Complete Tolstoy*, and then shelves with the *Ten Great Russian Novels*, and *Ten Great French Novels*, and *Ten Great German Novels*. Off those shelves I picked my Babel, my Proust, my Mann and Rilke for the first time. She also acquired risky books: not only the Solzhenitsyn, whose *The Gulag Archipelago* I remember seeing on our shelves when it was frowned upon (but not necessarily banned) by the Yugoslav Communist Party. I never read it, but I did browse, as an adolescent, Erica Jong's *Fear of Flying*, right at the peak of its scandalous life. Mama bought encyclopedias, coffee-table books, and life manuals, which I flipped through and memorized for no reason other than a voracious hunger for knowledge that the books stimulated. It is from her *The Book for Every Woman*,* which contained sections on knitting, tailoring, cooking, homemaking, health, and reproduction (with illustrations), from which I gleaned early information on what sex was and how it worked. The two-dimensional representation of the genitals and their expected deployment was utterly confounding, while I knew symptoms of sexually transmitted diseases well before I understood how the actual transmission worked. In the sixth grade, before I even held a girl's hand, I discovered some rash on my penis and spent a horrible day worrying how to break to my parents the news that my brain was likely to be consumed by syphilis.

We talked about the books, my mother and I. When, in high school, I defied the language and literature class reading list and refused to read *Anna Karenina*, as I was all about J. D. Salinger and Raymond Chandler, she tried to convince me that Tolstoy's novel was a great one. (She was right.) When a book was too disturbing or hard to get through, she would call it "heavy" or "a psychological drama," which terms could also be used to describe movies. When she didn't understand a book, she would say, "This is some kind of symbolism," which was what she said when she read the first story I ever published. Even now, I bring her stacks of books from my travels, mainly translations into Bosnian, Croatian, or Serbian,† and then we discuss Zadie Smith or W. G. Sebald, or Orhan Pamuk. She never read romance novels, or any kind of pulp literature. When I asked her what made her want to

* *Knjiga za svaku ženu* (Znanje, Zagreb, 1972).

† As everyone who knows one of those automatically knows the other two.

read—a dumb question, I concur—she said: "I don't want my brain to atrophy."

I showed my sister all of these pieces about my parents, for critique, objections, and suggestions. Invariably, she noted that more text is devoted to our father than to our mother, reproducing, she fears, the structures of patriarchy within which our parents came of age, internalizing it. She is right, of course, and I readily concede her point, but the narrative imbalance cannot be eliminated for a couple of reasons: One, our father has always moved in space, as had his family, while our mother's position was fixed and stable. She was always with us, so I have a hard time finding stories to tell that feature her solo adventures. One tends to tell stories about that which is not here. She was always here, as was her language and her ethics, and we didn't absorb those in narrative units, but during constant conversations, including frequent lectures and arguments. To the extent that I can formulate my ethics, it is because of my mother—because she formulated principles and declared them ethically necessary. "Respect your female friends," she taught me, which was why when my male friends started groping them in the eighth grade the girls came to me to ask for help, and I vetoed such behavior with a threat of violence. But I also developed my ethics in conflict with Mama. When I was sixteen, we had a raging fight over freedom of speech and human rights. At the end of that fight, she said, "I taught you nothing," and I retorted, "You taught me to use my own head." So that, as much as I love my father, he is a character in his own stories, which I sometimes get to retell. Whereas my mother is in my head, not as a nuisance that would require psychoanalysis, but as an ethical code, a linguistic system, and a perpetual source of warmth.

9

MARRIAGE

My parents' wedding ceremony took place on November 11, 1962, at the municipal offices in Palilula, Belgrade. Its highlight was the signing of the marriage record before an official whose name or face no one ever remembered, though his bland profile is visible in the picture that captured the moment. My mother wore high heels and a nice dress, and had a bouquet of flowers. Not many people were present, no one from either family, except for Ivan Cacko, a cousin of my father's from a nearby town. He's dead now, as are most who attended the wedding. In fact, it is possible that, other than my parents, there are no more living witnesses. The wedding party took place around the corner from the municipal office, at a friend's modest apartment, where the attendees sang, danced, and broke the sofa because my father and two of his friends, as big and tall as him, dropped onto it simultaneously. Because my parents couldn't afford a hotel, they spent their wedding night at the apartment as well. The following morning, their first married one, my mother woke up, put on a headscarf, rolled up her sleeves, and started wire-scrubbing the hardwood floor where the dancers left dirt marks. To Mama, this was supposed to be a commencement of marital collaboration, the beginning of their making a home together, even if in someone else's space; Tata, however, balked at that particular exercise of marital bliss; she ended up cleaning, he studying. Marriage houses a world of meaningful gestures people interpret as expressions of love, but the meaning is not always self-evident, or shared. My parents understood differently what happened on the first morning of their marriage. It didn't seem too important at the time, but that interpretive crack was the size of a dirt mark, and no less significant for that.

Two weeks later, they went to my grandparents' for the wedding of Tata's youngest sister, Filjka (who died as I wrote this). All of my father's family was there, and they danced in the front yard mud, and sang the Ukrainian wedding songs, and there was a lot of uncomplicated hearty food and homemade slivovitz. No one mentioned my parents' recent marriage, no one congratulated them, not least because theirs was not a church-sanctioned wedding and therefore, as far as the traditional Hemons were concerned, was not sufficiently substantial and legitimate. After the wedding, Mama cleaned the mud off her shoes and went back to Bijeljina, where she had a job. Tata returned to Belgrade to work on his bachelor's thesis.*

A few months later they moved to Sarajevo together and rented a little room with Teta Jozefina and Čika Martin. Mama wanted to clean it with Tata's help before they settled in—this was going to be their first home together and the nesting operation had a self-evident symbolic value. This time, Tata agreed to do it, but then midway through the operation declared, "This is not for me," and balked, again. Thus did the crack become the fundamental

* "The Influence of Atmospheric Pollution on High-Voltage Insulators."

fault in my parents' marriage: a gendered division of labor and duties, whereby Mama was in charge of domestic space, while Tata was operating outside it. She would stay at home, static; he would be out in the world, mobile.

When I sat down not long ago to talk to them about their marriage, Mama contended that at the time Tata was not mature enough for marriage, for a full commitment to having a family. In his own defense he pointed out that he was hardwired not to sit still, never to be settled; curious and ambitious, he was always burning to learn. Mama acknowledged that her expectation of having her partner by her side at all times may have always been unfulfillable, while he regretted that he was not more involved. Neither of them denied that love was demanding, that it created expectations of fulfillment, that it was rooted in promises that could not always be delivered.

Still, when she had a miscarriage in 1963 and needed to go to the hospital, her expectation that he'd be the one to take her there couldn't have been unreasonable. Instead, his work sent him to Doboj to fix a fallen power line. When I was born, he was in Doboj as well, another fallen power line. The theme of his absence from my mother's side at the time of need (objectively correlated in the recurrence of a fallen power line) will prove to be a long-lasting one, repeating itself with stubborn, disheartening regularity. It culminated in 1969, when Tata was in Moscow for six months while Mama was pregnant and then gave birth to my sister.

He'd applied for a fellowship that would send him to study for his Ph.D. in Moscow before Mama got pregnant. It was a hard thing to get, an achievement in itself, and there seemed to be no way to postpone it, so in January 1969 he went and would not return until the summer. My mother spent the couple of months after his departure in a state of high anxiety, worrying about her ability to handle a second child, while the first one (that is, me) still demanded quite a bit of care and attention. She did not sleep well, my father's calls from the Soviet Union were infrequent, the connection was always bad. Teta Jozefina was often by her side, helping her, but Mama still felt alone, as there was no family around. Tata understands now that he should've come home from the USSR for my sister's birth, there was enough money for the ticket. But now, of course, it is too late.

I can recall the night my mother left to give birth to my sister. I remember a few women, including Teta Jozefina, and the din and fuss and distress, and her big belly and her departure. I also remember going to bring her home from the hospital with Duško, Tata's work friend. She'd insisted that she'd take a taxi home, but Tata deployed Duško to pick her up. What made her distraught, then and thereafter, was a sense that at difficult moments in her life she was surrounded by well-meaning strangers, which is to say that she was alone. My mother, my baby sister, and I sat in the backseat of a Fiat 500, unbuckled. I rubbed my sister's face with my finger and was baffled by her dark skin; she seemed like a stranger to me.

It was around that time, Mama says, that something broke in her; she stopped laughing* and her hair started turning white. She struggled to manage my sister and me by herself. It couldn't have been easy. I, for one, was jealous, once attempting to strangle my infant sister and, fortunately, failing. I continued to be demanding of attention. Mama went back to work seventy-seven days after my sister's birth, which was common at that time, and was never enough. The way she looks at it now, generations of Yugoslav women were betrayed by the socialist state, as well as by their husbands.

After Tata returned from the Soviet Union, they spent a whole

* Temporarily, I can attest, and I have witnesses.

night talking. This is, I must say, the only known instance of their having a talk aimed at fixing a problem between them, the kind of heart-to-heart conversation that one imagines necessary for maintaining a modern marriage and therefore often seen on television. She told him everything about the way she'd felt, she told him she wanted him by her side, and asked him to travel less, to help her with the kids, to be her partner, and do things with her, and he promised he would. He probably meant it, but it didn't quite happen. Not long after his return, he needed to go and see his parents and family in the countryside, and then his work and ambition were pulling him away and he traveled again, and before long he was back in Moscow finishing his degree. After that, Mama says, her heart became heavy, and a latent, constant displeasure set in.

Thus was the tone of my parents' marriage irreversibly established in 1969. Fifty years later, they're still married, but Tata's being in Moscow at the time of Kristina's birth is still his original, irredeemable violation of the marriage covenant. As I was growing up, it came up often, never in a blowout fight (my parents never had those), but at a steady pitch of irrevocable resentment, as the background noise to all things said and unsaid.

In the era when my paternal grandparents got married, there was no such thing as dating,* not even with a chaperone. The early contact that led to marriage normally took place in the context of work, so that eager young men would come by the house where there was a marriage-age young woman and volunteer to help with mowing the grass fields for hay, cutting wood, harvesting corn or wheat, slaughtering livestock, etc. In the course of that work, the young woman's family would assess the qualities of the prospective groom—his strengths and abilities, his

* In fact, there is no word for "dating" in Bosnian.

temperament—while the prospective bride, whose wishes would be respected only if deemed reasonable, could conduct her own evaluation of the candidate, exchanging glances, smiles, or whatever other signals might encourage a quality fellow to return and continue the negotiation, and ultimately pop the question to, of course, the father. The purpose of the negotiation was not so much to identify the groom who would provide a reliable supply of love and happiness to the bride and their subsequent progeny. The whole ritualistic, work-related setup was meant to match the couple in terms of their survival-by-way-of-work value—the love, or even happiness, could come later, but the parents had to ensure the survival of their children, and their children's children, and their children's children's. Marriage was not a container for love, nor a vehicle for the pursuit of happiness, but a survival pod that also included a lot of children—the more were produced, the more would survive. Such marriage reproduced patriarchy, of course, while asserting itself as natural and eternal by way of being allegedly approved by God. This is not to say that, even then and there, parents did not hope that their children would exceed them in ways they could not imagine and live better lives—it was just that the children had to survive first.

Soon after my paternal grandparents got married in 1925—my grandfather Ivan was twenty-five, my grandmother Mihaljina nineteen—they had a daughter, my aunt Marija.* One summer day, Ivan was helping his father stack hay, and he kept calling Mihaljina to fetch him some water. She was slow at it, what with a baby in her arms, while Ivan demanded: "Mihaljina, fetch me some water!" By the time she finally brought him some to drink, he had reached the boiling point of his impatience and slapped

* She now lives in Edmonton, Canada, where she has a number of great-grandchildren.

her. His father descended from the top of the stack and smacked him good. "Don't you ever slap a woman with a child in her arms," he told him. The prohibition would not, however, automatically extend to hitting a woman *without* a child in her arms. For there is another story in which Ivan gambled away some money, and Mihaljina objected to his gambling. Miffed, he slapped her; his mother, my great-grandmother Marija, having heard from her house Mihaljina's wailing, walked down the road to find out what had happened. When she did, she ordered my grandfather to kneel before her, whereupon she beat him with a mallet used for grinding poppy seeds.* His filial duty prevented him from getting up or talking back, let alone resisting—he stayed down on his knees and endured as Prababa Marija hit him on the head with the poppy-seed mallet, blood running down his face. Thus did his gambling and wife-beating experiments end. No one in the Hemon family, I'm pretty sure, has gambled or battered women since.

In the world of Bosnian-Ukrainian peasantry, no body could claim full sovereignty. Women did not own their bodies, the family did, and at the top of the family hierarchy was the man, except maybe for his parents for as long as they were strong and alive. But even the man's body was predominantly functional, only as valuable as it was capable of work and procreation. This was the kind of gender politics my father came from, shedding by way of education many of its obsolete practices, while adjusting others to life in a different, modern context.

What would be retained in his outlook, as well as among the people of the socialist, presumably modern Yugoslavia, was a gen-

* I love the arbitrary exactness of this detail, passed down through the generations. Therein lies the difference between story and history.

dered distribution of labor, rooted in its peasant past, where women worked in the home, cooking, washing, taking care of the kids, while men, helped by women and children, toiled in the field, wrangling the livestock, cultivating crops, brewing and drinking alcohol. Some variation and overlapping notwithstanding, the division of labor was taken to be self-evidently natural. Laterally, but crucially, related to that basic division of labor was the concept of motherly sacrifice—mothers deserved respect and worship for their sacrifices, for their extinction of selfhood in the name of the family. The motherhood cult was really enslavement, since in patriarchy, the main—or even only—shape in which women could earn respect and (limited) human value was as mothers.

Though my maternal grandparents' marriage was based on love, in that my grandmother ran off for my grandfather and was subsequently disowned by her rich father, the same division of labor applied. My mother, like so many other women, internalized it by default, as it was culturally enforced even in the socialist Yugoslavia, where nominal gender equality was guaranteed by the people's regime. My mother's generation of women was the first one in the history of the western Balkans to have full access to education and employment. But they were also expected to take care of the house and children, to cook and clean, all the while going to work full-time. The women made a giant step in comparison to their mothers, yet not giant enough to undo and reconfigure the dominant, patriarchal distribution of labor. In my mother's case that often meant sixteen-hour days divided between her work and our household. Unlike her mother, however, my mother was financially autonomous, had her own job and bank account, never asked my father for any money or permission to spend hers. My father never openly claimed special rights based on his male privilege, never dared suggesting that she was supposed to obey him, but even if he had, she would have ignored him or told him to fuck off.* She unflinchingly demanded from him respect for her and other women. If he'd ever laid a hand on her—a truly unimaginable proposition—she, my sister, and I would've been gone in a blink. Nevertheless, she could not undo the structures and systems that made her the one who had to cook the next day's lunch at 11:00 p.m., look for women to watch my toddler sister, launder our clothes, or attend parent-teacher conferences devoted to my misdeeds to such an extent that she once nearly passed out and needed to be given water and sugar to recover.

The tragedy of my mother's generation of women was that the social transformation they were instrumental for did not go far enough, stalled by age-old patriarchal practices and prejudices. The women of socialist Yugoslavia were caught between the old and the new, forced to carry both the old and the new burdens. In return, their sacrifice would, at best, be culturally appreciated as inherent in motherness. Mama rightfully perceived all that as blatant, demeaning hypocrisy. Left to deal with enormous challenges with little support, except of the rhetorical kind, she often talked (and still does) about women having been betrayed by the state and exploited by the men who benefited from it. "Everybody wronged me," she says. Or: "I have always been a victim!"†

* There was a married couple they had known since college who had a dynamic more typical for that time and place: when we went over to their place for coffee, made in a little pot and drunk from a demitasse, the man would never, ever pour coffee into his demitasse, waiting instead for his wife to do it for him, for, he seemed to believe, it was her job to replenish his coffee. In fact, he wouldn't even say anything or look at her to indicate he wanted more—she was supposed to recognize the need and react to it. Something like that was unimaginable in my family.

† *Ja sam uvijek bila žrtva.* In Bosnian, the word *žrtva* means both "sacrifice" and "victim."

My mother's personal and social agency far exceeded anything that the women of the previous generation could even begin to imagine. Yet that amount of agency was not enough for a full liberation. Mama's claiming herself as a perpetual victim was, paradoxically, an expression of that agency, which she practiced by speaking out and confronting verbally the instances of disrespect and inequality. But a claim to victimhood also marked a difficulty in changing outcomes. My mother knew what needed to be done, but was not able to do it, for not only were all the escape exits blocked, but there was no place to go. To my knowledge she never seriously considered leaving Tata by way of divorce, but she often made claims that one day she would not make the meal for the next day and let us fend for ourselves, or that she would just go on a vacation by herself and finally have some rest. She never did it, and when Kristina asked her once why she'd never followed through, she said it was because she was afraid she would cause a catastrophe by destroying the family.

The seeming impossibility of getting out of the oppressive situation set up a resentful, passive-aggressive dynamic in my parents' marriage whereby my father was primarily culpable for my mother's inescapable victimhood. While he tried to pay her back (insufficiently) with empty praises of motherhood, she always took umbrage for his privilege of being able to go anywhere and do whatever he liked. In other words, a distribution of moral responsibility aligned with the division of labor. This caused a lot of friction between my parents, constant arguments always addressing the basic, unjust situation, which would often spill into their children's lives. I was often blamed for masculine selfishness, as was even my sister, who, if she pushed to expand the domain of her sovereignty, would resemble Tata in being stubborn, selfish, and self-absorbed. In our daily life, there was frequent bickering, which never rose (or descended) to any substantial fight, or traumatic conflict, or resolution. I'd go off on Mama and Tata, reprimanding them for the squabbling, and they would say, "This is just the way we talk," remaining deaf to my objection that that was precisely the problem. Angered by the pitiless pitch of constant discord, I used to suggest that divorce might be a good idea for them, partly, to be honest, in the hope that I would thus acquire two sources of money. But they were bound by marriage and children, and never considered, could not even imagine, any alternatives; they could not figure out ways to break up the division of labor.

It's possible that the belief that love is the purpose and the essence of marriage is not unlike the belief that the heel of the bread is its best part, or that the chewy meat around the bone tastes best. It's not hard to see the propagandistic value of the idea that love is fully actualized in wedded bliss and family. It might well be that marriage and its alleged moral necessity have for centuries been but a vessel for biological and social reproduction of oppressive patriarchal structures, even if the lucky couples managed, against the odds, to find and maintain a modicum of love and some sense of shared experience that tempered the hostile world around and the void beyond it. Perhaps love-based marriage is a bourgeois notion, for in the world of poor subsistence peasantry a marriage was primarily a survival device, maybe not the best one, but the only one available, wherein romantic love was a bonus and not an entitlement. People coupled to ensure the extension of life; love might have helped the evolutional aim, but was not necessary for it. This could be why for centuries, and even now in many parts of the world, marriages were arranged, or why, before there could even be any communication between the potential bride and the groom, my grandfather needed to check if the candidate could get the work done. In a social context where a more just distribution of wealth (assuming there is any wealth to distribute) is achieved, the shape of marriage changes so that it can not only accommodate love, but can even afford to be organized around it.

When I was young, the seemingly rare occurrence of affection and intercourse between my parents made me think that there was a shortage of love in their marriage. If my sister and I asked them if they loved each other, Tata would say, "Of course!," which Mama would instantly declare insincere (*Ti, ćale, samo foliraš!*), not much different from the motherhood cult bullshit. When cornered she'd say: "Well, love works differently in marriage." I remember Tata calling Mama *dunjaluk* (an old Bosnian word for "the world"), which she also routinely dismissed as fake. Eventually *dunjaluk* went out of circulation.

In 1982, we spent three days in Ostia, near Rome, on our way to Zaire, because our flight to Kinshasa was canceled. One of those evenings, we took a family stroll on the Lido, and my sister and I saw our parents spontaneously holding hands, which we'd not often seen before. They were not a hand-holding couple; their normal strolling formation was Tata hurrying a few steps ahead of Mama as she tried to keep up.

A few years later, when I was in my mid-twenties and still living with my parents, I once came back home much earlier than usual (which meant well before midnight), and saw that their bedroom door was closed. It was too early for them to sleep, so, without thinking or knocking, I walked in on them: they were in all likelihood having sex, though it was hard to tell, as the duvet was all the way up to their noses. I stood paralyzed at the door, while they, startled, responded to my presence instinctively, with the first thing that came to their respective minds. My father said: "Where have you been until now?" My mother said: "Go get something to eat."

For years, I told that story as a funny one, belonging to the age-old parents-having-sex genre popular among the grown-up children of the world. But it's really a story about my inability—practical and emotional—to see them as anything else other than my parents. For a moment, at least, they were a man and a woman exercising love, but when I walked in, they instantly converted back into being a mother worrying about my nutrition, and a father disciplining me. In some ways, they were never a romantic couple for their children—they were mainly the people who engendered my sister and me, and did everything to ensure and extend our existence. I wanted the fireworks of love, getting instead the works of parenthood and marriage. They were always only parents, and I could comprehend them only as such, never as civilians with lives unrelated to mine. My physical presence automatically turned them into parents, so that I could never see them as a man and a woman together. I've long wondered what they talk about when they're alone, which I'll never find out, as the presence of an observer changes the situation. It might be that the full capacity of their love for each other, and the ways they practice it, will always be obscure to me.

It would be wrong to think that my parents did not progress in their concept of marriage, which was, despite all the residue of oppressive tradition, very different from their parents'. In the social transformation of Yugoslavia, my parents' generation imagined and endorsed a transition from marriage as survival machine to one that conceived of marriage as a domain founded on loving self-actualization—the modern, bourgeois format. But they never made it all the way, remaining caught in between. For the next generation—my sister's and mine—heterosexual marriage became merely but one possible arrangement for human connection, with many equally viable alternatives. Our parents, however, never managed to shed the survivalist dimension.

And the war and displacement did not help at all. If in their previous Yugoslav life my parents strove to practice modern marriage while being unable to abandon the older model, in Canada they reverted to full-on survival mode. They landed in Hamilton in their mid-fifties, with scarce knowledge of English, and no family within a thousand miles, and no one else to help them and support them. In the new land, they improvised to survive. They learned enough English to get jobs; they made enough money to get a home and establish a sovereign domain.

Now they're in their eighties. My mother has malfunctioning kidneys and arthritic knees, while my father has survived prostate cancer. Every morning, after they get up, my father makes tea for them. They drink it while watching a terrible Canadian channel that simultaneously shows broadcasters rambling, entertainment info, a news runner, a live traffic report, and the weather forecast for the day and the week, which is what they really want to see. Then my father leaves the house, sometimes to buy bread and milk for breakfast, sometimes to check in with his bees and make a plan for the day. My mother, in the meantime, starts making breakfast, and then they eat together, likely discussing the logistics of their day. And on they go with their daily operations, choreographed and rehearsed for decades, complete with standard-format bickering. Tata works on his projects in the Barn or the apiary, sometimes running some obscure errand in town; Mama attends to the house chores, including making lunch, which they have together around two. Then they nap, after which they have coffee and bicker a bit more, whereupon they return to their work. In the evening, they doze in front of the TV. If they watch anything together, it's most likely to be a western, or an old movie, in the course of which they both pass out. Their life is highly structured, mainly around daily chores, which are part of everlasting projects.

The operation of this survival machine consists of work, of reliably completing all of their tasks. Their lives, and therefore their marriage, are project-based—indeed, their marriage itself is a project, which they work on and maintain daily. They get up in the morning to work on it, not to pursue the nirvana of ceaseless happiness or the meaning of life. All they ever do is part of the greater endeavor of survival—that is, of life—which binds them in perpetuity. That work is their love, just as their love is what they do.

10

LIFE AND DEATH

There was a moment in my adolescence when I noticed that my parents were highly prone to making pronouncements about the impermanence and shortness of life. They'd regularly deliver annoying statements like: "Life just flies by," or "You blink, and life's over," or "We won't be around for long." A particular place in my annoyed heart was reserved for my mother's "You don't have to worry about me, I'm going to go to the nursing home," and her perennial favorite: "You'll be sorry when I'm dead." I was annoyed because I thought that was the kind of thing old people said, and I didn't want my parents to be old; their aging annoyed me; their implicit impermanence was not something I wanted to contend with while wrestling with the issues pertaining to my adolescent struggles.

But not so long ago I experienced an epiphanic moment of realizing that, at the time I was entering my adolescence, my parents were quite a few years younger than I am now, and nowhere near old.* Perhaps because of my rampant puberty, or because of their working so hard since their childhoods, they appeared to have aged early, certainly mentally, even if not necessarily physically. In any case, to an adolescent nearly all adults are old, but now, as I've uncomfortably entered my mid-fifties, I can fully understand and own the feeling that life just flies by, or a sense that I won't be around long enough to see how my children will live in a world I probably could not understand anyway. My parents' thinking still baffles me, however: they thought they were about to reach the far horizon of their lives while being in their fucking *forties.*

Little did they know that the horizon keeps moving away as it gets closer.

One possible reason for their untimely reckoning is that the previous generations rarely lived into old age. People died young, and life, fundamentally marked by poverty, was too hard to last. Mama's parents died in their early sixties, a not-uncommon age of departure. The age-old cultural practices did not favor the elderly—those who did not turn senile, like Deda Ivan, could perhaps claim wisdom, but only due to the ruthless proximity of death. Even in socialist Yugoslavia, where the quality of living improved all across the board and life expectancy rose dramatically, the elderly were culturally relegated to a kind of holding pen for death, where various forms of humiliation, physical and metaphysical, were common. I remember a joke Mama used to tell about two senile ladies making and drinking coffee together over and over again, because they kept forgetting they'd just had some, until one of them finally had to go home, said goodbye, and, as soon as the door closed, thought: "And she didn't even offer me any

* When I was sixteen, Mama and Tata were forty-three and forty-four, respectively.

coffee!" My mother also remembers the headline in *Oslobođenje*,* "A Very Old Woman, Aged 60, Died in an Accident,"† and is still very troubled by it.

After Sarajevo began attracting a lot of tourists in the eighties, due to its newly acquired Olympic-city status, my mother would marvel at the busloads of sprightly, aged foreign—often U.S.—women (*bakutaneri*) who showed no compunction at all about traveling to the world's remote corners, trekking enthusiastically in shiny white orthopedic sneakers, regardless of heat or cold, clad in bright, optimistic colors, with their hair impeccably done. Mama admired the tourists' mental and physical wherewithal, their refusal to be defeated by biology, their keen interest in new experiences. Around that time, I believe, she started imagining that her retirement would be similar: she hoped that if she retired young she could travel and read, and never again rush and work all the time. She retired a few months before the war started, at the age of fifty-five. Little did she know.

My parents' long-lasting sense that they were approaching the far end of their lives might have had an upside in that they possess a well-formulated philosophy of living and an accompanying ethic. They thought about life long before the grand catastrophe of war and the inescapable disaster of aging. If an unexamined life is not worth living, my parents' lives have been well worth living.

Mama is particularly willing to reflect upon the past. At the age of eighty, she compulsively considers where she has been, what she has done (*gdje sam bila i šta sam radila*), and the ever-haunting possibility that it could have all been different. For the past few

* The main Sarajevo daily, which Mama would always start reading with the obituaries, a very common practice among old people.

† "*Poginula starica od 60 godina.*"

years, her obsessive regret was that she had failed to do enough for others. Her life is incomplete, she says, because she would've liked to have left *something* behind, something charitable and enduring, preferably for some children in need, something human and humane that would be valued and remembered and would make people speak of her and her goodness.

She proudly asserts that she was always a good worker and a good person; she spent her working life in Energoinvest doing something worthwhile; she always cared about others, submitted to her charitable drives, her need to give and share. But she also regrets working too much. She should've taken off five years or so around the time my sister and I were born, she says, in order to spend more time with her children, in order to attend to herself and her needs. She would've felt less anxious, less testy and exhausted. She could've spent more time reading, gone more frequently to the theater or the movies with her friends. But she had worked so hard and invested sixteen years of her life to go to school, while her family had sacrificed so much to enable her to do so. Her generation of Yugoslav women was the first one to have access to education, a chance to rise out of poverty and attempt an escape from patriarchy; moreover, she had a strong, inspiring feeling that Yugoslavia was a country that had a future and needed her help being built. On the way to becoming the hard worker, she'd made commitments; it was hard to take time off. Work was all, work was what made her, a (limited) field wherein she practiced her agency.

One of the insidious traps of old age is an urge to make past decisions based on present knowledge, in a delusion that we could've lived a better life and still be the person who deserved it. But when the future is foreshortened, the past is an endless field. What would her life have been if she had taken a five-year break to wrangle her children? There is no way of knowing, but because of that, the moment when the decision would've been made is constantly revisited.

Be that as it may, she thinks that she and Tata created something substantial together, something that was destroyed by the catastrophe of war, along with the infrastructure that made it possible. When I asked her whether she'd say that her life was good overall, she said: "No, it was not. Because of the war." It struck me then, and broke my heart, how obvious and brutally simple the evil of war is: war takes away lives and never gives them back. It transforms people, unless they're killers, into something they never want to be; it diminishes them, even when it doesn't kill them.

And I remembered, for some reason, a day when Mama came to pick me up after school. I was waiting for her in the schoolyard and I saw her from afar: she'd had her hair done; she was very elegantly dressed, and had makeup on, which she never used to do. I didn't recognize her at first; she was beautiful, but that somehow bewildered me. I told her that I had not recognized her, that I wondered: *Who is this bedecked woman?** She was embarrassed, I recall, as though I had exposed some secret, shameful intention to be someone other than herself. After that she would never put makeup on, and I would feel guilty for many years to come, as though I had foreclosed an avenue that would've led to a different, perhaps better life. I know now I should've never said what I'd said, but I also know that no present knowledge can affect past decisions.

Now Mama believes that if you're eighty years old, you must be sick of something, so it's quite normal to be having health problems—she, for instance, has weak kidneys, arthritic knees, and high blood pressure. She regularly sees doctors, and abides

* *Ko je ova napirlitana?*

by their suggestions halfheartedly, occasionally deciding that she's taking too many pills and arbitrarily skipping medicine. Mama's matter-of-factness, however, can result in passivity: because illness is normal at a certain age, she speaks as though there is no particular need to do anything radical, just get used to the new situation. Even so, I can see shadows of fear flittering on her stoic face as she talks about her high creatinine levels, or about the difficulty of going up and down the stairs while not being able to bend her knees. Part of her stoicism, I suspect, is her desire not to be a burden, and to show that she can take care of herself, as she always could. The other part is that she, like most people, avoids imagining the ultimate catastrophe. Just like she, on the eve of the war, said to me, "They're already shooting less than yesterday," so today she says to me: "I can bend my knees a bit more this week."

In the summer of 2005, Tata was diagnosed with prostate cancer. I remember the day he called to inform me; I remember the sofa I was sitting on; I cried, still gripping the phone, unable to get up, my sweaty skin sticking to the leather; it hadn't occurred to me before, not even during the war, that my parents could die. Tata's initial reaction was fear as well, followed by hypomania, which differed only in degree but not in kind from his normal state of being constantly busy. As a means of managing the new health crisis, he'd spend fourteen hours a day in the Barn or in his apiary, focusing on short-term goals, aiming to finish what was at hand so as not to think beyond it. His bees, as always, offered solace: on top of the soothing continuity of work, he concocted a mix of royal jelly, propolis, honey, and pollen, which he ingested daily, in the belief that the apiary's healing power would defeat the disease. He still underwent radiation therapy, while estrogen pellets were inserted subcutaneously in his belly in order to shrink the prostate. The estrogen made him extremely emotional: for the few months he housed the pellets, he cried every time he said goodbye to me and/or my family, recalling, as I did, how Baba Mihaljina wept saying goodbye to us, because she always expected never to see us again.

But Tata did see us again: the cancer went into remission, and, after a couple of trying years, he returned to his normal operating intensity. It's tempting to conclude that his near-death experience made him more contemplative, but, ever since he landed in Canada, he had suffered from a compulsive need to reexamine his long-made decisions and the life that came out of them. More than once he pondered the alternative life that would've followed if in 1961 he had accepted Herr Bittner's job offer and stayed in Germany. He has also realized that his marriage would have been different if he had come back from Moscow for my sister's birth in 1969. He still torments himself with the thought that in the eighties he should've looked for employment abroad, as he was at the peak of his professional expertise and prestige: he could've gone to France, or to Switzerland, or to some such place. He thinks he should've persisted in trying to acquire his engineering license upon arriving in Canada, and not given up pursuing it so easily, etc. Sometimes he can't get out of the loop of reexamination and reevaluation: he has spent sleepless nights imagining his alternative lives, battling the badgering thought that he had, in some ways, failed, that we could've all somehow avoided the catastrophe if some decision of his had been different. In the morning, he continues to live the only life available. Because no present knowledge can affect past decisions.

When I suggested that such self-punishing analysis might be a symptom of depression, Tata was adamant that he was never in his life depressed. Though I loved him at that moment for his commitment to life—to being as alive as possible—I reminded him of the depressive depths he'd sunk to in Zaire when his mother died, or when his bees in Bosnia were destroyed. It was just sorrow, he said, which was normal in such situations. Yet I also remember the time after he was finally fired from his steel-mill job, and his surviving the cold Canadian winter with nothing to do and with nothing to think about but all the wrong decisions he'd made that brought him to that place. Worried, I'd call him and ask him what he was doing. "Waiting," he'd say. "Waiting for what?" I'd press. "Waiting to die," he'd retort.* These days, Mama says, he sits at the breakfast table recalling his dead friends and family, and, once in a while, lets the tears run. In Bosnian,† the soul can hurt; many of the songs he sings feature a hurt soul.‡ Indeed, the pain might be the only evidence of the soul's existence.

With all that, Tata refuses to complain too much about their life because, he says, they have everything they need: they're pretty healthy, given their age; they have a nice place to live; they have a car; they can pay their bills, although that would be difficult without his honey money. Everything they need for life means everything they need for survival, and just being alive is always a potential source of joy. There are times when he responds to my long-distance inquiry by describing an idyllic scene in which they're dozing in their basement room, the fire is crackling in the

* "Let me talk to Mama," I'd say.

† And many other Slavic languages.

‡ Take the chorus of a song ("Noćas mi srce pati") my father and his brothers sing regularly:

> *My heart suffers tonight,*
> *My soul hurts tonight . . .*

The singer, Silvana Armenulić, who made the song famous, died in a car accident on the road that my mother worked on building as a young woman.

stove, soft Canadian snow is falling outside, and soon they'll have some coffee and sweets, and maybe some family will stop by, and they'll cut up some smoked meat, and sit around and tell stories, remembering nice and funny things from their lives.

Last winter, Tetka Filjka, my father's youngest sister, and Ujak Dimitrije, my mother's youngest brother, died on the same February day. Mama thereby outlived all of her six siblings. As for Tata, only three of his siblings are still alive: there are Bogdan and Štefan, his two younger brothers, and Aunt Marija, the firstborn, ninety-three years old.

It's easy to think of death as a thing unto itself, as a metaphysical unit that is the opposite of life. Life and death, being and nonbeing, appear to be in a binary relation. If you're young, however, or if death is not within your sight,* it's far easier to think that life and death are an either-or proposition: life is the absence of death; death is the absence of life. But death first appears in my parents' lives as the devastation of the human network around them; their family are dying as if struck by an epidemic, their friends are departing at an alarming rate. My parents are bearing witness to an emergence of a wasteland devoid of shared memories and a referential past embodied in concrete, real human beings. Before reaching full nonbeing status, death appears in their world as a depletion of life, as the rise of nothingness, as an encroaching loneliness.

In nearly every phone conversation we have had lately, Tata has asked me, "Do you know who died?" as if the news ought to have reached me independently and I was thus overdue for being shocked by the outrageous injustice of human mortality. I usually

* Though that is only a matter of which way you look. Philip Larkin, in "The Old Fools": "The peak that stays in view wherever we go / For them is rising ground."

don't know the person who died; most often, I've never even heard of the dearly departed. It would not be unfair to say that the person's death doesn't directly affect my parents' lives. What Tata's reports are really about is his growing awareness of the inevitability, about his trepidation due to the fact that death is always a rising tide, and his ankles are already wet.

Once a year, my parents lock up their house in Hamilton and return to Bosnia. They leave in early March and return by the beginning of May, when the garden and apiary work commences. They land in Sarajevo, where they spend most of their time meeting old friends, getting the news on who has died since last year, who might go before their next visit. Then they set out for a little family tour, visiting Bijeljina and Banja Luka and Prnjavor. Occasionally, particularly if there is a university class reunion, they might hop over to Belgrade, to see the few remaining friends. Apart from the first few years of their displacement, when they had little money and the war in Bosnia was still raging, they've been doing this regularly. Each time, they've come back to Hamilton replenished, because they enjoy returning, sharing news, walking everywhere, using their native tongue, and speaking their minds to their full potential. But with each year, the quality of their return visit changes, because each time there are fewer friends, less family; lately, they've been mainly visiting cemeteries. The inescapable biology has changed the landscape of their lives, past and present, just as it has changed their bodies. For a while now, the report I receive upon their return to North America always features Mama's determination that she is done with going to Sarajevo, as they're now too old to travel that far. Her arthritic legs are swollen, which turns a long flight to Europe into torment, and makes climbing the four floors to our apartment in Sarajevo painful and difficult. The time is nigh when they will not be physically able to return home. The moment Bosnia becomes inaccessible to them, the depleted territory of their lives will substantially grow, as they will never again see the few friends and family who still live there. This reduction of the life field is what dying is. It ends when the field is a hole in the ground.

A couple of years ago, Mama and Tata announced that they'd found the place where they'd like to be buried—a cemetery plot in Oakville, Ontario. They asked me to help them financially to purchase the plot, which I refused, mainly because it seemed to me it was too early for them to think about their eternal rest and, more important, and selfishly, it was too early for me to think about it. One of their compelling reasons was that my father's brothers also obtained their plots there, which is to say that his plan is that they should be singing together through eternity, as they always have.

They did buy the damn plot, and without me, and raised a tombstone so as to have their resting place ready for their arrival or, as we would have it, for their departure. They have long completed a will, which they also proudly told me, though I avoided talking about it as well. Obviously, they don't know which one of them is going to be leaving/arriving first. Though Tata is presently hoping (and therefore planning) to live for another ten years, thereby reaching his nineties, he has already established that he wishes to have a religious burial, not because he believes that Jesus died for his sins, or that God and His love are eternal, as he doesn't, but because the presence of a Ukrainian priest at the foot of his grave guarantees a certain amount of poignant singing. For one thing, the Ukrainian choir will inescapably perform "Vichnaya Pamyat" ("Eternal Memory") over his casket; and there will certainly be a church memorial—a *panaheda*—at a later time, which will feature more vocal harmonizing.

Mama, on the other hand, is an ardent atheist and therefore adamantly opposed to any possibility of leaving under the auspices of God and His vocal troops. But because Tata would no doubt like to sing at her farewell, if alive at the time, he's dared to suggest the possibility of a religious ceremony. Mama told him that he should not even think about it; for my part, I threatened him that I'd make a scene if he even tried, and that just attempting to do it would lead to severe consequences. Apart from everything else, I don't want them to spend eternity in Oakville, Ontario, bickering about the last things they did on earth.

My parents always had something to do, and therefore had a goal, and therefore a meaning; there has always been a concrete horizon toward which they moved, obscuring the ultimate, dark one. Their lives have always been project-based. They get up in the morning to work on something that needs to get done; when they have nothing to get done, they will not get up. Life, in other words, is its own project. "Before the war," Tata says, "our life project was to secure some kind of future in which we could live better. But now we're only securing the present." In that present, which I still share with them, if only partially, it took me forever to finish my own project—this book. If life extends for as long as there are projects to be done, ending this book cannot be easy. Moreover, I am too terrified of reaching the point at which I'd have to imagine a world devoid of Petar and Andja Hemon, of the meaning they have put into it, into me. Extending the writing of this book has meant extending the time I need to return all that they have given me—or even to return anything at all. I do not want to know, yet, where the knowledge and love I need in order to be in this world will come from when they're gone. Where will I ever find parents like these?

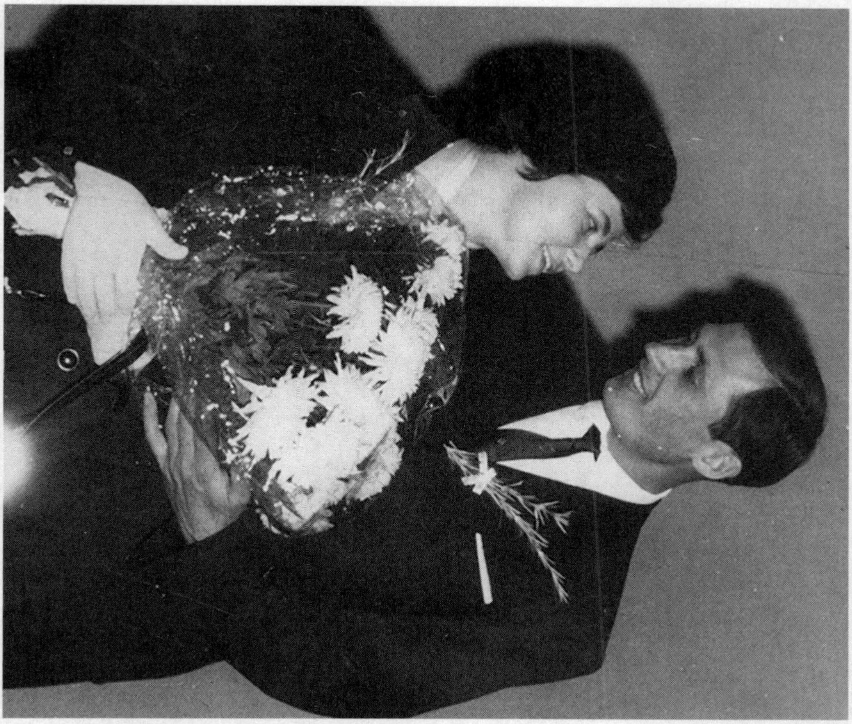

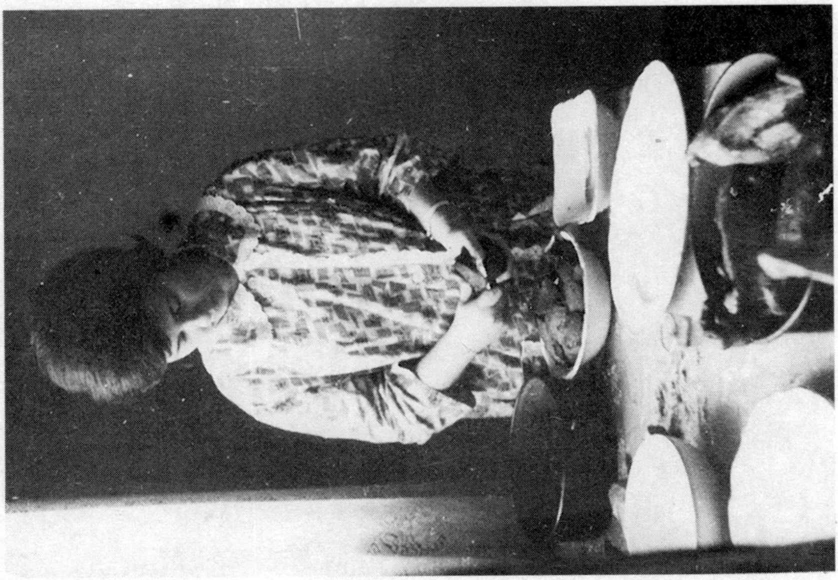

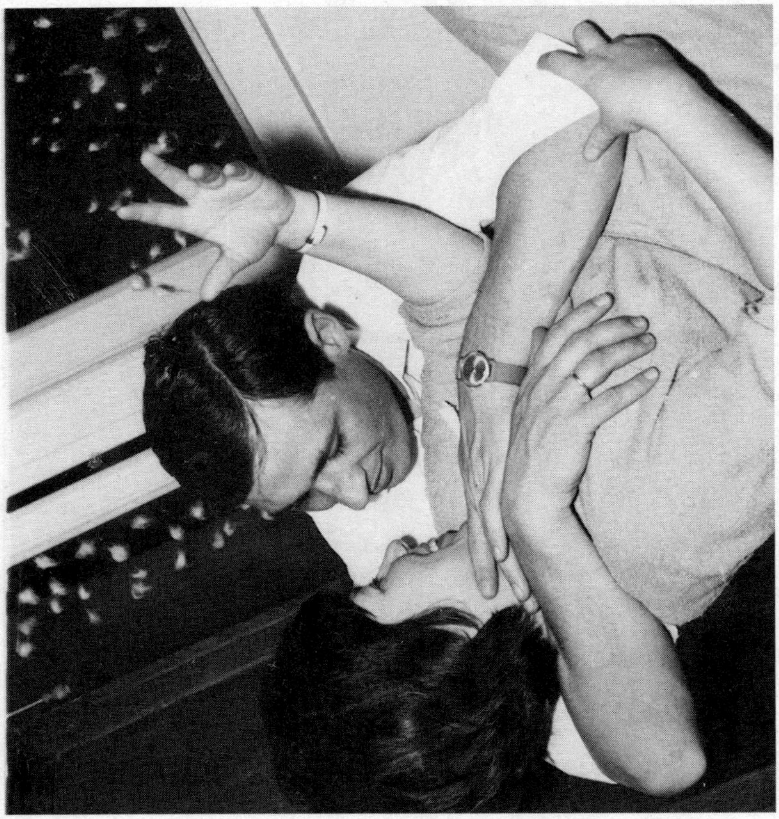

Louvre
2007
Me Jane
Fonda finds serenity in movie biz jungle
COTTAGE

HEMONS
Traditional Ukrainian Folk Songs
Українські Народні Пісні

because the car's engine is in front so it was always going to be flooded. But our Fiat, he said, has the engine in the back, so if we part the water it will not close behind fast enough to flood the engine before we get across. What do you think? he asked me. Should we try? I was no more than six years old, I knew nothing, I had no ability to imagine consequences, nor could I anticipate anything other than what my father told me would happen. Neither did I ask why we had to get to the other side instead of simply returning home; it did not occur to me to question why moving forward was so necessary. Still dreamy, I endorsed the plan to get across. I was not afraid, for I could see the beginning of the road on the other side, the unpaved future ahead. Tata told me to lift my feet up on the seat, and he took off his shoes and socks; he pulled out the plug in the floor so that the Fiat would not float; he put the car in gear and slowly slid into the flood. The water burst through the unplugged floor hole and rose, muddy and cold, climbing up to Tata's ankles. I did not consider the possibility that we could drown after being pushed off the road by the flood's might. The water parted wearily, we just moved through it, as through time, without thought or stopping. After the flood receded a couple days later and we returned home, Tata said, Tell your mother what happened! At first I didn't know what he was referring to, because when you're six there is no time when nothing happens, which is to say that the happening is all there is. Tell me, Mama said, how you survived the flood. I want to hear it too. Tell us. So I told them.

A moving field of water covered the road, reaching the dense woods, extending beyond what we could see. There were a couple of cars stopped ahead of us, the water lapping at their wheels. Tata and I were on the way to my grandparents' for the weekend, while Mama and my baby sister stayed at home. I'd just woken up in the backseat of our Fiat 500, confused as to where we were and why we were there. The road had been unpaved and narrow, with a lot of curves that even in my sleep made me nauseous. One of the cars ahead of us moved into the water, following the invisible road, hoping to reach the other side, where the road reemerged and where there were other stopped cars, facing us like a mirror. Gingerly, the car parted the water reaching its headlights, the eddies connecting and merging in its wake, until it stopped and stood there for a moment before the flood pushed it off the road, toward the dark woods. The driver struggled with the door, creating a wave when he opened it with great difficulty, then stepped out wearily into the current only to watch, helplessly, his car sink. Tata said, That guy made a mistake,

Plato, the wise man of cave shadows, imagined memory as a wax tablet. Freud, of bourgeois accommodation, felt that memories were like familiar objects placed in the rooms of a strange house. One thinker, the name I don't recall, likened remembering to a search through the random assortments of a garbage pile. Another one believed that it was really like reconstructing a dinosaur from a single excavated bone. There are even those who think that memory is a replaceable part of a humongous machine. But I'd pluck the grays from my mother's hair, one at a time, because it gave her much pleasure. With an itch at the root of each gray hair, she suffered, so that my plucking provided relief. One day her hair turned all gray. Nothing to do about it but remember. Remember.

No one will pretend that, in the glance by which we take in a limpid night, the exact number of visible stars is prefigured. I once faced a cold, starry firmament, while lying on the snowbank with Nina. The frost was biting our cheeks and fingers; we wore ski jackets; we could hear nothing because there was no wind, snow muffled everything, and everywhere around us was Jahorina, its dark forest. Thousands of pinprick stars in the sky, right above the firs snow-swollen to twice their size. I don't think I'd ever experienced a more beautiful moment; it was all understood. Yet I tried to impress her by claiming that some of those stars had long exploded and no longer existed, that their light was reaching us only now, afterthoughts and stories from vanished worlds, and that we might not even notice tomorrow if their light was gone for good. Unspeakable numbers of stars had been lost, I said, and we could not even begin to know their true light. Nina knew all that. She is an architect in Trieste now.

It is possible that I received *Heroes* as a present for my birthday; probable, in fact, because I remember receiving it from someone's hands. I remember the hands, the actual movement of giving, even if I don't remember who gave it to me, just as I remember being confused by the record. What confounded me first with *Heroes* was the black-and-white-and-grayness of Bowie's picture on the cover and on the inner sleeve; then the sound, the shrill jangling of the guitars and the sharp gurgling of synthesizer; and the world inside it, which was some version of Berlin, I imagined. I remember *Heroes* because it is possible that the record changed something in me. 'Coz we're lovers, and that is a fact. Yes, we're lovers, and that is that. The riddle does not exist. It's easy to think that I remember only the things that changed me, that a jolt in the neuron network is what allows for retention. If we are to root personality in remembrance, what claim of ownership can be made on the elapsed instants that, because they were quotidian or stale, did not stamp us with a lasting mark? What if I remember what changed me even if I was not—or am not—aware that it was transformative? Heaped up over years, memories lie buried, inaccessible to our avid longing. And there is this possibility: What if I remember only the things that didn't change me so that I can find a way to believe that they changed me, while what really changed me has sunk into the sludge of my actual being, has been so fully incorporated into myself that it is so absorbed and present now it's not even necessary to recall it? This tingle that comes with *Heroes*, with those synthesizers buzzing at the advanced positions of the apocalypse, right at the Wall. If I did indeed get *Heroes* for my birthday, I had little use for it in my pursuit of girls. What you needed for the pursuit was a record with either danceable stuff, which back then meant disco, or slow songs, which meant slow disco—*sentiš*—so that at school dances you could put yourself into a situation in which you were pressing the palms of your hand against a girl's back, plotting how to move them toward the front. Heroic endeavors, no doubt, but to *Heroes* I listened alone, longing for what hadn't happened yet or what could never happen, imagining becoming myself in an unimaginable world. Our duty is, and remains first of all, not to get into confusion about ourselves, but there is nothing without confusion. One self fills immensity, and then there are many, each of them a hero staring at a wall.

It had to have been the summer of 1979, because *The Man-Machine* came out in 1978. I was in Subotica, a town on the Hungarian border, visiting my aunt Jela. My cousin Jasmina, her daughter, was older, so she had a *gramofon*, and a few records: a Paco de Lucía album and Kraftwerk's *The Man-Machine* are the only ones I remember. Jasmina also had a friend, Valentina, whom everyone called Valika. Valika was tall, thin, athletic, and blond, and I'd never seen anyone as gorgeous as she was. I remember being constantly spellbound inside the fragrant cloud she emanated. She smelled of heaven, though I'd guess today that it was probably imported Fa deodorant. I fell in love with Valika after I tripped on a wire that marked the border between sidewalk and park; I fell indeed, face-first, on the grass, and ended up with two identical horizontal lines, like high-water marks, on my shins. Valika helped me get up, worried about me, considered my pain, all of that, fragrantly. Consequently, I'd spend hours listening to Paco de Lucía slap his guitar with Iberian passion and yelp unexpectedly at the staccato of the flamenco heels, in order to gather enough courage to implore Jasmina to call Valika and ask her if she wanted to go outside and hang out in the park. Jasmina had a gaunt motorcycle, and Valika once showed me how to ride it—I wasn't good at it, I was afraid of acceleration and nearly crashed into the wall at the end of the cul-de-sac. Another time, she took me to meet a friend of hers, an older boy, who had a wild motocross bike, and was, when we stopped by his garage, polishing it with fetishistic caresses. He had some kind of a name but I can't remember it; he was ugly as a thief, all the more so because of gossamer hair and oil smudges on his face. One day, Jasmina, Valika, the motocross boy, and I went to the sand dunes outside Subotica, where there was an off-road track. Valika sat on the back of the boy's bike holding on to him, her hands locked at his belly button. I held on to Jasmina, who would, many years later, be killed by a train. But back then, we watched the ugly boy speed up and down the dunes and spring into the air like a startled cat to land on the soft sand without falling. From where I stood, I could see a helmeted Hungarian guard perched on top of a border tower. The ugly boy took Valika out for a ride on the dunes, and she screeched with joy, her fucking hands on his belly button. It was clear, of course, that I stood no chance, that she preferred the boy-machine, that the handsome motorcycle, with colorful flaps and shapely fenders and thick shock absorbers, most generously compensated for the boy's abominable visage. All that was clear to my cousin, but to me it wasn't. After I found a way to tell Valika I loved her—though it is more than likely that no actual words were spoken—she started avoiding me. Jasmina claimed that Valika used me to make the motor boy jealous. I was heartbroken. The rest of my time in Subotica I spent staring out the window at the grass, at the wire that brought us together and left the dashes on my shins. One day, I read a book called *7,000 Days in Siberia*; it took me thirteen hours. I drank a lot, mainly blueberry juice. Throughout all those travails, I listened to *The Man-Machine*, over and over again, which opens with "The Robots." *Ja tvoj sluga. Ja tvoj robot.* I'm your servant. I'm your robot. So too at death the world does not alter but comes to an end.

How does one become the chosen one, how can one recognize that he's unlike anybody else? What can be described can happen too. There once was a boy who made another boy mad and nearly died. When I was in the fifth grade there was a seventh-grader who thought I was exceptional enough to be committedly bullied. The first time I suffered, my class lined up outside the history classroom and he elected me for being smacked around, for twisting my arm, for an unforgiving series of fillips. Day after day, he'd come for me: he was tall, clean, and good-looking, with an acolyte who would always grin in support and adoration of his abuse. Worse than the physical pain, or even the humiliation that came with it, was the arbitrariness of his hatred. I did nothing to him, yet he saw in me someone that could and should be hated, some intolerable quality, something that belonged to me yet I wasn't aware of it. He tormented someone other than myself in me, yet it was my body that hurt and endured and was humiliated. Eventually I complained to my father about the bullying. He explained that he could track down the boy to scold him or threaten him, even slap him, but sooner or later I'd have to return to school on my own to face my tormentor. What should I do? I implored. When he bullies you again, hit him back, my father said. But he will beat me up! I cried. Probably, my father said. Definitely. But next time he'll pick on someone who won't hit back. It never crossed his mind, or mine, to report the problem to a teacher or the principal. What we thought we were dealing with was but the violent, naturally selective way boys interact, a fact of brutal life, so to speak, a matter of things being as they were and had always been. There was no word for bullying in Bosnian, no concept as such. This story is thus inescapably an approximation of what happened, as it features the word "bully," which has no equivalent in the language in which I suffered. What we had no word for we passed over in silence. When the boy selected me for torment again, I kicked him in the shin as hard as I could. He promptly beat me up, but as soon as I completely buckled and was thus defeated, he fell on the floor clutching his shin. He would never touch me again. And I, I turned courageous, became someone who would no longer back down, so that when one Sadik, a famously tough kid—a budding *jalijaš*—came down the path swinging a broom and daring us not to get out of his way (*Koga udarim, toga ne žalim!*), everyone in our bunch scattered but I stood my ground. He hit me with the broom, I immediately punched him in the face. He kicked my ass, of course, but then had to walk around with a black eye everyone knew had come from my fist. Next I stood up to Kemo, who was an eighth-grader several times over, built like a sumo wrestler, and already shaving, and I got smacked down by him too. But Kemo had respect for my intransigence, and the title of Kid with a Heart was bestowed upon me before all the tough boys and bullies who looked up to him, and I was henceforth under his protection. If anyone touches you, he said to me, come and find me. Even the *jalijaš* crew headed by the notorious Pajdak brothers, often loitering around our school and preying on the weak, knew that under Kemo's protection I was inviolable, and would not shake me down for my pocket money or beat me up for pleasure. Once some gormless eighth-grader erroneously supposed he could push me around, so I beckoned Kemo. His very presence paralyzed the foolish boy, who didn't even try to escape. His school uniform was severely misbuttoned, his sleeves streaked with dried snot, his cheek gossamered. Sock him, Kemo told me, sock him as hard as you can, so I socked him, not too softly, and not too hard, just enough to hurt him, to inflict regret for ever talking to me. It was pleasant, socking him, even more so because the boy dared not disobey Kemo's authority, wouldn't even turn his face away from my fist, let alone hit me back. The price of my newly acquired untouchable status, however, was that when my protector summoned me, I had to show up. And when Kemo ordered the lisping Jasmin and me to determine by way of a direct fistfight who was tougher, we had to do what we were told. We had no choice but to go after each other like gladiators, full force, blood running down our chins, hoping all along that Kemo and the Pajdaks, watching bloodthirstily, would eventually interrupt our duel and save us from each other's punches. They enjoyed it for a while and let us end it while we were still even, before one of us got on top of the other, yet not before our faces were banged up and streaked with nose blood. Pretty soon I reached the level of confidence and toughness that entitled me to pick on other kids myself, to slap them around gratuitously. At that point, I would've been a bully myself if the word existed in Bosnian, but without it, I was merely a tough Kid with a Heart. I asked my mother to get me pointy shoes, the kind Kemo always wore, the kind that could snap a shin like kindling wood. I changed the way I walked, the way I talked. I spat a lot, mad-dogged other boys, hoping they'd talk back so I could kick them. I once beat up a boy single-handedly, with one of my fists behind my back, just kept floating around him like a butterfly, stinging like a bee. I liked being a Kid with a Heart, but it could never last, for I had no violent wherewithal. That Kid with a Heart phase of my life ended when I was picked on by an eighth-grader called Zlojutro, a name that translates very nicely as Evilmorning, fitting far too perfectly someone whose gaze was morbidly glacial, who bent kids' arms with aplomb and choked them in a hold so avid that hitting back not only could not deter him, but made him tighten it more enthusiastically. By the time fate led me to Zlojutro, Kemo had finally been done with school and had gone for good so that my only protection was my attitude. When Zlojutro assaulted me, filliping me and twisting my ear just to enjoy my pain, I did hit him back as per protocol, but then he kept coming at me until I picked up a sharp rock and threw it straight into his face from two yards out. It collided with his nose, the rock, cutting its side. I escaped while he was busy stemming the vermillion flow, happy to have defended myself, thereby successfully retaining my don't-fuck-with-me aura. But Zlojutro was not a *jalijaš*, he was special, his violence wasn't a matter of the boyhood practices, but of a deep and profound personal, metaphysical need to cause pain. He pursued me for weeks, thirsting for revenge; for a while I managed to stay out of his evil-morning talons. Once he followed me home across the river, past Hotel Bristol, and then down Vojvode Putnika Street. Before long he was chasing me all the way to my building. I didn't want to run up to my apartment and thus show him where I lived, but I couldn't shake him. He was getting closer, about to grab me from behind, when I saw Čika Mustafa walking down the street, and in order to make Zlojutro think he was my father I called out to him: Tata! Tata! He's chasing me! Zlojutro bought my bluff, turned around, and ran away, just before the bafflement was visible in Čika Mustafa's face, which looked nothing like my father's. Thus I was saved. Yet Zlojutro was always going to catch up with me; he was as inevitable as the sun rising in the morning. One unfortunate day, I was deployed by the physics teacher to wet the board-wiping sponge; in the school hallway I ran into Zlojutro. I still remember the grin of joy on his face upon spotting me alone in the tragically empty hallway, his dream coming true before his very eyes. He put me into a very crafty choke hold that allowed him to bang my head against the wall with exquisite power and exhilaration, while I could do nothing other than scream. It was clear to me he would not stop and he would have likely brained me, had all the teachers and kids not run out of the classrooms to discover who was wailing for dear life and saw him cracking the wall with my melon as if there were no tomorrow. He might have been the first truly evil person I'd ever suffered from; he was there to welcome me to the world. There is always tomorrow, because there is always today. There is always morning, because there is always day.

It was October, we sat on the concrete flower boxes that contained neither flowers nor any kind of plant, and our butts were cold. The tinge of roasted chestnuts and toxic smog made it all romantic and beautiful, so I placed my arm across her shoulder in preparation for a kiss (with a tongue), which would've been our first, my second or maybe even third. Her name was Amela, she was the tallest and the sportiest girl in my class and she had long, waterfall hair and, relatively speaking, substantial breasts, which she unsuccessfully suppressed with oversized sweaters. I dared not think of the possibility of touching her breasts—summoning enough courage for a kiss (with a tongue) was well beyond me. We sat on the concrete boxes, saying nothing, as we both knew that the only possible thing to do next was to press our lips together and go from there. Yet I couldn't. What we cannot speak of we must pass over in silence, so we sat in silence, except that every once in a while she'd say, I have to go home, and I'd say, Five more minutes, whereupon we would sit in silence for an additional five minutes. There is no solution to time. I could come up with no words, no actions. My fingers were still sooty from having peeled roasted chestnuts. Had I touched her I would've left a dark trace on her body. She finally got up—unkissed, untouched—and I walked her home, which took five minutes. I know now it was then that our coupling became improbable, that I lost her, the fact I'd never had her notwithstanding. I often wonder what would've happened if I had kissed her (with a tongue) and thus got upgraded from being her *simpatija* to being her official boyfriend. She could jump-shoot on the basketball court; her ponytail bounced in splendorous slow motion; she could dribble the ball too, get past defenses. She was a winner; she was a star. I couldn't see then that it was all already lost, so I hoped, and I kept hoping, and when she invited me to come over to her house one Sunday when her parents were gone to their weekend house, the hope tumesced like a teenage penis. A field of possible kisses stretched before my mind, and then another virgin landscape beyond it, a vast world where things unimaginable took place, where all-access nakedness would surely have been the norm. For days, I rehearsed in my head that cool pre-kiss head tilt and the subsequent slow-motion advance, past the defense, toward her lips, where, as I'd been advised by my allegedly experienced older cousin, I should insert my nimble tongue and move it around the oral cavity while making manual inroads to at least one of her substantial breasts. The day of my visit to her quarters, I spent time blow-drying my hair until it resembled a helmet and I donned a V-neck sweater without a shirt, or even an undershirt, and I wore clean, tight, somewhat short pants, exposing my white tube socks. I did have doubts when I regarded myself in the mirror; it did occur to me that I might have looked like a prime cretin, but I decided to believe in myself. It was a grave mistake. For when I got to Amela's place, it was instantly clear that I'd fully misunderstood the promise

I'd perceived as implicit in her invitation—her best girlfriend at the time was there, as well as a couple of eighth-graders, not only older than me but confidently and shamelessly adolescent, which is to say they smoked cigarettes and spoke with that brash *jalijaš* braggadocio, using a street code I could not attempt to comprehend, showing no interest whatsoever in me, what I had to say, my claim to Amela. And she was enthralled with one of them, a certain Amir, whose unruly hair bespoke a studied negligence, and who was so full of himself that he could even afford to pretend he had little interest in her and her substantial breasts. He kept cracking jokes that made Amela repeatedly giggle and push her Rapunzel hair behind her ear as if to invite him to whisper into it, whereas I, the boy in tube socks and a V-neck sweater sporting a cretinoid 'do, sat glumly and passively, signaling my despondence with the subtlety of a socialist factory siren on May Day. So devastated and disconsolate was I after that romantic fiasco that I wrote a poem entitled "Is This Death or Rebirth?" ("*Da li je to smrt ili rođenje ponovno?*"). It had four long stanzas, in the first of which the poetic subject dies, just like I had that Sunday at her place while Amir sneered at me, and is subsequently miraculously transferred to a prehistoric afterworld wherein dinosaurs roam and pterodactyls flock in the sky darkened by volcanic eruptions, where he is forced to ask himself and the reader—that is, the pitiless Amela: Is this death or rebirth? The world of an unhappy boy is very different from that of a happy one. I put my poem in an envelope, moistened the flap with my tears, metaphorically speaking, and dropped it in passing into her school uniform pocket. She would never say anything about it; she would never let me get close to her again. What if we live in the unhappened, in the universe of the nevermore? The world, the world is everything that is the case, and life is everything that might have been so.

In the seventh grade Mirza became enamored with Azra, who was a year older than us. This was love, I tell you, but it would've been stalking if a word for it existed in Bosnian. In any case, he'd call her, and when she responded he'd hang up instantly. We found a way to call her at home and record on a cassette tape her voice as she picked up and said, "*'Alo? Ko je to?*"—Hello? Who is it? Mirza would listen to her voice over and over again, *'Alo? Ko je to?* We would follow her from a distance as she strolled with her friends around Grbavica, misinterpreting random glances as communication, as a possibility of her interest in Mirza. If she had for some reason tried to approach us I'm certain we would've run away. I remember her school uniform—blue, neat, clean overall—her laughter, and the way she kept her hands in her uniform pockets, her thumbs sticking out; she was a good student, active in all the after-school sections. Mirza wrote her a letter once, describing his infatuation but not himself, asking her to love him in return even if she couldn't know exactly who he was, and recruited me to slip it under her arm during the long recess, which

I did, very skillfully, as I'd delivered love letters before. Mirza's love was not a process but a state of mind, a mental field endless in precisely the same way his visual field was endless. He wore glasses, yet his life spread as far as he could see. An essential part of writing is accepting the guaranteed absence of its consequences, reconciling with the possibility that the words might vanish in the ubiquitous void, that none of it could ever really matter. But we also believed that the letter might work, we hoped there would be some love reflecting back upon him to complete the circle. We never found out if she'd read it.

The world, the world is everything that is the case, and many birds, and more. Say, the raven Mirza and I saved one bleak December, many and many a year before. On the surface, the bird struggled away from the river flow. We slid to the shore, grabbed the black plume, the ungainly fowl pecked at our hands, desperate to be. Everything that lives wants to continue as itself, to endure evermore. Not men yet, we wished to be good to nameless life, to that which could be, or was. We force-fed the dreaming demon with scraps, with hope that it could return to the Plutonian shores. It would not, nevermore. We left it to shiver in a shoe box, under a chestnut tree, to look up at the croaking in the crown, from below. Up there an unkindness perched, still, and nothing more. There, its loneliness unbroken, the limited whole.

There was a time when I wanted to compose a rock opera, the first and only time; I was twelve. That deaf, dumb, and blind boy sure played a mean pinball. *Tommy* was big in my life, because the movie had been shown at Kino Arena, and I saw the record in Jugoton repeatedly, beckoning. But it was a double album and therefore ambitiously expensive, requiring a lot of embezzlement and saving. Moreover, its high concept was dauntingly serious, so much so that adults talked about it on TV in a late-night program. I wouldn't see the movie until a few years later, when I found it terribly confusing and dark. Now I can confidently say that *Tommy* was one of the unlistenably pretentious albums of the seventies, the exact opposite of rock 'n' roll, and the movie managed to be even worse. But we assumed that that which confused us must have been profound, so time and again we—Marka, Mirza, and I—listened to the album (which we borrowed from someone) and, under its pernicious influence, decided to write a rock opera of our own. I could not play guitar, nor any other instrument very well, or even read music, but somehow it didn't occur to me that the total absence of musical skills could or should prevent me or anyone else from writing a rock opera. Our abilities had no limits, in exactly the same way our life had no end. I'm free, I'm free, and freedom tastes of reality. We got together at my place, because my sister had started playing piano and my parents bought one (piano, not sister), which, of course, I couldn't play, we merely used it to pretend to be tuning our untunable East German guitars. Before we started writing the music, we had to decide what the rock opera would be about, what aspect of human experience it could address, and we couldn't think of anything, couldn't formulate any concerns. Once we managed to make our guitars sound slightly better than sheer cacophony, we had nothing to say, no ideas. Unfortunately, we were neither deaf, nor dumb, nor blind, we were healthy and twelve, and we could interpret nothing; we climbed the ladder and found ourselves in the unclaimed vacuum up there. In the world everything is as it is, and everything happens as it does happen. It was all there, all of it, every day, who were we to complain? We had no thoughts we could sustain, only flashes of considerations and impressions; we could not frame a question, so the answer was impossible, and thus necessarily irrelevant. Hence we sat around the piano, East German acoustic guitars in our hands, striving to conceive of a rock-operatic aria. I can't now remember how we gave up on our thematic pursuit, but eventually a decision was made that we would write the music first, then the libretto. We couldn't think of any music to write either. Nothing to play, nothing to say, with no means to say it, armed only with a desire to be creating something—no path, no walker, no walking. This is what I remember: We came up with two simple chords, labeled *A* and *B*, and I drew two rectangles next to each other—the purpose of which now escapes me—and wrote *A* and *B*, respectively, above them. No Messiah pointed to the door; still, we tried to leave the temple. A and B would have been the opening chords, had we not absconded from the rock opera project in order to play Pong on the TV. Reality is compared to propositions, and not favorably. I would keep the notebook where the opera would've been written, use it for writing some of my early poems, and for years, I remember, I would see the A and B rectangles on its second page, reminding me of all that could've been, all that wasn't because something else was and always would be.

Marka and I, we would sit at the back desk, away from the tedious teacher, whisper, exchange notes, invested in putting together the list of the ten greatest guitar players of all time. We considered the totality of time, even if all time was but a couple of decades, the very age of rock 'n' roll; we deemed guitar greatness to be self-evident. In the back of the classroom, we pursued the absolute and made absolute claims. In the tree crowns outside, black birds flocked. There are plenty of birds that fly under the sun, and most of them, I assure you, are birds, not omens. Jimi Hendrix, Jimmy Page, Steve Howe, Mark Knopfler, David Gilmour, Robert Fripp, Steve Hackett, Bill Nelson, Brian May, and someone else. It's amazing to me that we even knew those men's names; it's even more amazing that we'd heard their music, if only superficially or randomly. Moses and his friend argued over what the coolest commandments were. I couldn't play the guitar at all, and Marka was just beginning to be good at it, but we believed we knew what was what. We had an epistemic system in place, we were ready for what mattered; we built a framework. Growing up is learning to know before you can. Now I know a lot but I don't know how to know, or why. I remember a story about an ecstatic skunk who kept licking a rasp, hungry and convinced that it was the source of the endless flow of blood.

I've walked around for days now with a feeling that there was something I could not remember, a memory I could not retrieve. The memory was present in my mind by way of its absence. I did not want to remember it, I had no reason to recall it, no yearning to fulfill, no pain to address. I didn't know what it was, what it could be, I just wanted to catch and hold that clear bubble forming and then floating on the murky stream of my consciousness, only to burst and be reborn repeatedly, I just wanted to see what was inside it. Nothing has ever been the way it used to be.

It would take me twenty minutes to walk to school. I'd have to cross Vojvode Putnika, go past Hotel Bristol, cross the bridge, and then go past a cluster of bushes and get across another street whose name I cannot remember, but there was a newsstand on the other side where I'd sometimes buy comic books or soccer-player stickers with stolen money. There were a lot of small borders back then. In the fall, the river, brown with the roil, would rise, sometimes reaching the underside of the bridge. The world was independent of my will. In the cascades, swarms of soccer balls would bounce meaninglessly while I longed for one of them, though they could never escape the whirl. Sometimes I'd see birds drowning, and once I saw a dead man, facedown, his armpit hooked onto the bridge pillar. Holding on to the bars of the bridge fence, I leaned far out to see him, nearly falling in. The river rushed around the dead man, who was bloated with the void, impervious to the flow. There is no whole self here anymore, but once, before, I used to hold on to the fence over the rushing river.

I once sprayed a skinny kitten to erase (with poison) the fleas on her spine and her ass. It was orange (the kitten) and it was gone soon, as were all the fleas (it is safe to assume). I found it dead in Baba's pantry (brittle fur), where I sneaked to eat (out of a jar) strawberry preserves. I couldn't undo (no, it can't be done) what I did. The kitten was angry, grinning (stiff) at my guilt: the first creature I have ever killed (but not the last), stretching there, unalive, bloating.

The youngest of the infamous Pajdak brothers was known as Ringo. Why, I don't know. Ringo was not a common name in Bosnia, except in comic books and pulp fiction. Protected by his three older *jalijaš* brothers he was unimpeachable, no one could defy him or disobey him, let alone touch him. Though he was younger than us, he picked on Mirza, for some reason, probably because of the thick glasses, that age-old bully bait. There was, naturally, no need for a reason; the thing with power is that it is best practiced gratuitously.

Why are you looking at me?

I'm not looking at you!

You wanna tell me to fuck off?

No.

So why are you looking at me? etc.

I can't remember what Ringo eventually did to set Mirza on the path of revenge—it was probably just another routine smackdown, or arm-twisting, or *kliker* robbery, maybe he even snapped his glasses—but Mirza devised a revenge plan and executed it perfectly: Ringo would drop his bag somewhere in the schoolyard to play soccer, bully someone, or grope the girls, so Mirza would steal it when he wasn't paying attention. We spent so much time unsupervised, beyond the protection of grown-ups. Our parents worked all day and there was a general belief that the streets were safe, which they were in that no one was ever killed, whereas they were flooded with the perpetually oncoming waves of prepubescent violence. We were at most a generation removed from the cruel life of poverty, from our parents being belted by their parents for discipline, all of which was contingent upon a belief in the pseudo-Darwinistic theory of survival, where becoming a person required learning to suffer unto others and endure. We had to leave the safety of the family nest daily. We walked to school alone, we roamed and played outside unsupervised, showing up at home only for meals and homework and sleep, we were beaten by the Pajdaks of our neighborhoods until we learned, or not, to defend and/or avenge ourselves. So Mirza made an executive decision, as they say nowadays, and stole Ringo's schoolbag. He told me of it, proudly, only after the fact. He even showed me where he hid it in the bushes: a small, cheap faux-leather bag, with buckles and a frayed handle, the color pale green. It was obviously a hand-me-down: just as Ringo had used it to beat Mirza, so had his older brothers swung it at various other victims. For a few days we feared that Ringo would figure out who stole the bag, that someone would tell him, or that he would discover it in the bushes, which was the least likely possibility, and somehow figure we did it, in which case we would be dead, the whole Pajdak gang after us, and they really liked to torture their victims. But besides fear, there was also the thrill, the joy of productive nefariousness, the increased value of our brains—Ringo was stronger, but we were smarter; he had his brothers, we had each other. We spent a lot of time in the bushes. Each kid would have a hiding place—*loga*—to leave precious, stolen stuff, or just to flip through titty magazines and smoke cigarettes. A *loga* was a physical equivalent of our interiority, a place where we would be away from the world, alone and inside ourselves by choice. It's true that we would also come upon condoms there, and bloody cotton pads, sometimes wallets emptied by pickpockets, empty bottles of cheap booze, none of which could fit comfortably into who we, let alone our parents, thought we were. I'd stop by the *loga* every morning. The bag cast light, like a rising sun, from below the horizon toward which we were inexorably moving. Once in a while, I'd look inside it: a dog-eared textbook or two, notebooks brandishing Ringo's inept handwriting, his struggles with math, doodles conveying some kind of kung fu fight, a pencil pouch with a broken zipper, a few blunt pencils. It had rained, and the paper shriveled, the books became swollen, the writing in the notebooks faded, stinking and damp. There is a cold, bright void inside me as I write this random reminiscing, and I'm struggling to keep it away from what I'm saying lest it all become irreversibly meaningless. How can I stay silent, how can I be still? My friend whom I love is turning to clay. By the first frost, I'd imagined Ringo being whupped by one (or all) of his older brothers as he strained to convince them his bag was really stolen. He must have been looking for it, for evidence that it wasn't his fault. At first I relished his imagined suffering, but as I passed by the bag, every day, my vengeful determination—which was in fact not even mine, but Mirza's—weakened, because I knew that Ringo would've been punished by his brutal brothers, and that the teachers were dressing him down and berating him for lying when he said that he had no homework because someone had stolen his bag. Slowly, morning after morning, Ringo kept transforming in my head, against all available evidence, from a mean little *jalijaš*, no doubt destined to turn into one of his brothers who smoked and masturbated and punched kids in the nose so that they could see them bleed, into a boy, not at all unlike me, who was learning how to be in the world, pursuing a way that was his own. Empathy is a terrible thing, blinds you to proper judgment of people and their terrible deeds. Ringo's striving was visible in his *švrakopis* handwriting, in his meager scholastic possession, in the pathetic hand-me-down color, all of it now swelling with autumn rains. And I imagined how unloved he must have felt, the unlove in his brothers tormenting him, gleefully no doubt; I imagined his parents infecting him with violence the way they had the older ones, and how he must have thought that if only he could find the bag, the error would be corrected, the time before the catastrophe could be restored, the time when he'd had the bag, when it had all been okay, the world and all its pieces in their proper places. The day frost covered the dry, decidious bush leaves and whitened the bridge I had to cross to get to school, I stopped by to look at the bag and it was all hoary, even the notebooks inside were crisp with frost, and I picked it up and took it to school, where I would claim I'd just accidentally discovered it, and I gave it to the janitor, or a teacher, I can't remember. I'm not proud of it now. I betrayed my friend and his revenge, and Ringo did grow to be a thug, and nothing was righted then, or now, or ever. As for man, his days are numbered; whatever he might do, it is but wind.

Mirza, my friend, and Slobodan too. We were not studying before school, but chasing each other, from room to room, as boys do. So Slobodan slammed the door with Mirza at his heels, and the pane, glass with relief, didn't stay in place but shattered, and into Mirza's face it flew. Had he not had his glasses, his eyeballs would have been shredded. Blood gushed forth, his nose sliced open, as he stopped at the threshold, unable to move, framed, like a portrait, by the rectangle where the glass had been. Everywhere, there was blood, and shards; witness to the birth of scars on his face, we didn't know what to do, or say.

There once was a boy who caught a mouse. The longest recess of the school day was after the third period, and it lasted twenty minutes, two of which we would use to annihilate a snack—a piece of buttered bread with a slice of decomposing bologna—and the rest to run around. The format for that running was pursuit: the girls chased the boys, and to make them do that, the boys had to bother them in some way, pull their hair, tease them, make them scream and shriek. Once the chase was triggered, we would run around the paved schoolyard like beheaded flies, occasionally skinning knees, breaking arms, or face-planting. No one ever died, everyone always lived. If you liked a girl, you wanted her to chase you. If she liked you, she would. If she liked only you, she would chase you alone. I always wanted Amela to chase me, but her interest in pursuing me was sadly limited. I realized that my friend Saša was her *simpatija* on the day she could not stop chasing him, never catching him—bound by their trajectories, the bodies never met. Had she somehow caught him, however, neither of them would know what to do—the pursuit, like the pursuit of happiness, like any habitual desire, had to be unending, its completion impossible; any form of success would've been dreadfully disorienting. In the world everything is as it is, and everything happens as it does happen, even if it's wrong. Once, and it was after school, on the way home, a few of us—including, most important, Amela—ran into a discombobulated mouse on the street. It was so scared and confused by the vastness of the space around it that it stuck its head into a corner and trembled there in horrible fear. I had an abiding interest in vermin back then, so I instantly recognized the opportunity the terrified mouse offered. I grabbed it by the tail with the intention of dangling it in front of Amela so as to make her scream, not only in fear, but preferably in admiration of my insane courage. She did scream, and then she screamed more, as did I, when the desperate mouse swung up against gravity, like a movie hero, to bite my hand—I dropped it, it escaped, and I saw two teeth dots at the root of my index finger. I'd read about bubonic plague, how Black Death was carried by rodents and wiped out much of the European population in the Middle Ages, and I knew that I could not only die a horrific death, but also infect and thus kill much of Sarajevo. It was therefore essential and urgent to kill the bacteria presently fighting its way into my bloodstream. As a fledgling pyromaniac, I always had a matchbox in my pocket, so I lit a match and burned the wound dots to close the points of entry for lethal germs, then I did it again, my incinerated skin hissing. The pain was excruciating, but Amela sure seemed impressed. It worked, partially—I never contracted bubonic, or any other, plague, and I saved Sarajevo from depopulation; yet Amela kept chasing Saša. For a long time, I had scars, two dots, like eyes, on my left hand, which I'd show to anyone who cared to see. Look, I'd say. Look at what could have been.

When exactly did I become a myself, the first person of the many I would be? I don't remember the enlightenment, but it must've taken place the instant cold water touched my soiled face, poured by my uncle whose name translates as God-given. I remember the coming to, the arrival, the rise out of the darkness into a world of dung, the flash of light, my uncle's eyes, concerned but not scared. That was how I knew I was alive, the water running into my ears, onto my neck. It all lasted as long as it takes a drop of blood on a sword to divide into two parts. One part nothing, the other part me.

Early in the morning, we would have to show up in the schoolyard, line up by class, like soldiers in Roman army centuries. The buses waited across the street, ever faintly stinking of vomit and diesel, the grumpy drivers smoking at the wheel. The field trip—*izlet*—was meant to take us to a place where nature had been previously located, somewhere in the mountains ever looming over the valley where we all lived. The coolest kids—*raja*—sat in the back of the bus, that was where the fun would congregate, where courting would take place by way of cracking jokes, screaming, and teasing your *simpatija*. That's where everything was shared, though everyone always had the same things: a salami sandwich, Jaffa chocolate-and-orange cakes, a Dvojni C juice. The nerds and geeks and bully-able kids sat up in front, close to the teachers. It would take us a while to reach nature, which was usually merely a muddy picnic spot, complete with the garbage left by the previous picnickers. We never explored the nature; it was there but not there, it was and it wasn't. We would just play soccer, hang out, or wander not far from the parking lot to continue doing what we were doing on the bus. Some nerds would venture into the woods, seemingly to collect samples for their botanical collection, but really to be alone, away from teasing and abuse. No one has access to nature; we certainly didn't. People believe that the so-called laws of nature are the explanations of natural phenomena, but for us nature just meant being away from our home in the city; in nature, we'd be sufficiently neglected by the adults to pursue our own projects and desires; it was of interest to us only as a hiding place. As the closest nature was in the mountains, the buses would take curvy downhill roads on the way back, so that, at one point or another, someone would barf, the Jaffa cakes always the most prominent and common ingredient in the vomit. The stink would make others nauseous and there would be a consequent wave of disgorgement. Nevertheless, someone would always sing, particularly the girls who were choir members, in whose attractiveness musicality always played a part. The repertoire was standard, featuring some of the most popular songs at the time, but also the classics. Hey, comrades, are you sad that our parting will soon come? When you're happy, and you want to share that happiness, clap your hands. But, as we descended into Sarajevo and the city became undeniable, everyone would sing "Sarajevo, My Love":

> You were already big, as I was born.
> From Igman with a smile, you sent me a dream.
> The growing boy fell in love with you then,
> Stayed here, rooted in his town.
>
> Wherever I go, I dream of you.
> To you, all roads lead me.
> I wait for your lights

With a certain yearning,
Sarajevo, my love.

You have your songs, and I sing them.
I want to tell you my dreams.
My joys are your happiness.
Sarajevo, my love.

When the winters are over, and May arrives,
The girls are prettier, give them some love.
The dark promenade ripens with sighs:
Some blue eyes, some tender words.

Now the boy is a man, while winter coats the hills,
The park and hair are white, but the snow will go.
The spring and youth will fill
My Sarajevo, my only city.

As we're all tearing up here, let me state the obvious: we did not sing it in English. The memory of what happened on that bus is deposited behind the stained-glass pane of a foreign language. I will restore these verses into the original Bosnian, where it will be more present, but you will not be able to read it. This does not belong to you. But neither does it belong to those who might read it in Bosnian, simply because it all happened a long time ago, to a small number of kids whose later lives were subsequently filled up to the brim with events large and heavy, and some of those kids have grown up to die, some too soon, some too late, no one on time. So here it is, a song about a city in the mountains, possible only in the wrong language, ever unbelonging.

These days, much too often, I despise myself. I can't remember when it started, except that it was a long time ago, and now I don't know how to be without it. That self-contempt works in way articles work in English language—you can live without those minute words but your utterances would be confusing, incomplete, awkwardly bent. When I'm not well, contempt grows into hatred. When bodies of girls in my elementary school class started rounding, boys started gratuitously grabbing round parts. I suppose they thought it was theirs for taking, as no body was ever sovereign in Sarajevo of my childhood. I didn't do it, can't remember why, it's not that I had ethos at age of twelve. Perhaps it was influence of *Book for Every Woman*, but if so, I wasn't aware of it. Perhaps it was my mother teaching me to respect my girl friends, which I didn't really know how to do. Boys in my class at some point started practicing groping—*fatanje*, it was called—as if it were competitive sport, rushing at girls, squeezing their budding breasts, careless about inflicting pain, and then speeding away as they (girls, not breasts) swung at them.

They stood behind girl in line to enter school, grasping her ass to point of pinching. Couple of my girl friends one day asked me to intervene and tell boys to stop, they could stand it no longer; they returned home bruised after school. I had influence among my boy friends: I was good soccer player, I was fourth-tallest boy in class, I had heart. I told boys to stop, threatened some of them, and, for while at least, they stopped. It was good thing to do. But I also had to know what boys thought prize was, what kind of pleasure compelled them to keep doing it. One evening, when I was alone, I spotted random high school girl on street and followed her like hunter into dark passage, and, having made sure nobody was around to witness, I ran past her and touched her ass, not squeezing, just my palm quickly pressed against curve; she was startled more than anything else—I'd leapt from darkness behind her—she yelped and then cursed after me as I sprinted deeper into void of shame. *Srpskohrvatski ili hrvatskosrpski* had no articles. Limits of my language meant limits of my world, but now I live in English, the language of self-contempt.

Because I was a good Young Linguist and won the competition at my class level (seventh grade), I was awarded the prize of spending two summer weeks in the Swallow Colony (Kolonija Lastavica), a camp for kids in Zaostrog, on the Adriatic coast. We bunked in a dorm building overlooking a concrete soccer pitch and basketball court, where in the evenings a band would play covers of terrible songs well known by all. During the day, we lounged on the pebble beach and swam, or played ball on the burning concrete. At night, we danced, twitching incoherently to the rhythms of the terrible songs, or managed the distance between our bodies while moving in circles to the *sentiš* tunes. Sometimes we would huddle in the dark, a starry sky above us, as someone played on the guitar the songs everyone liked to sing and I hated because I listened to "Heroes." Still, it all smelled like resin and the sea and coconut-scented sunscreen. I developed a crush and then fell in love with Emina, who had beautiful eyes, and a smile that made me want to make her laugh all the time, shimmering hair I could lose my hand in, never to find it again. She was, well, developed, so she wore a venerable bra; when I danced with her I pressed closer, and she didn't seem to mind. I followed her like a shadow, intercepted her like destiny. That desire for another body, for the closeness, for another person, experienced as a tightness in the gut, it was ruthless, there all the time, that summer, that year, that universe. I had always been prone to longing for a life as yet unlived, ever crashing upon me in waves of possibility, but Emina was a notch up from that. I was a subject who did not belong to the world I wanted to experience. Therefore I turned on my fragile charm, cracked all the jokes I could think of, described Emina's beauty back to her using myriad linguistic, well-chosen words, told her I would have married her if we'd only been older, at which she laughed, even if I was perfectly sincere. She was the only future I wanted to imagine for those two weeks. She trained me in the craft of kissing, loosened my tongue, suggested that I should be doing something down there—which meant in the bosom area—with a caveat that she didn't mean she actually wanted it to be done, though she did let me practice. She seemed slightly more experienced than I was. Once she pointed at a bottle of shampoo and stated matter-of-factly that it looked like *sluza*; she'd once undressed for an older boy so he could watch her naked and masturbate, whereupon I recalled Lućano. Nonetheless she could not be tainted even by Lućano-like activities, and I kept fawning over her, looking for ways and moments in which we could kiss, and kiss, and taste each other. Her body absorbed the sun during the day; it made me sweat in the evenings. Our last night in the Swallow Colony, we were hanging out in the room she shared with other girls, and then I dared suggest we go to the room I shared with other boys, most of whom were busy courting the girls they were becrushed with, so that we could be alone with each other, Emina and I. I locked the door of my room behind us; there was no one there except for a fourth-grader named Izet, sleeping soundly in the bottom bunk bed with his mouth open. Emina and I went at it on the bed across from Izet—I kissed her mouth (with a tongue), and her ear, and her neck, I undid her bra, touched and then kissed her nipples, her hands moved under my shirt, we pressed our pelvises and ground them against each other in a way that would've resembled intercourse if we had known what we were doing, she touched my hopeful penis through my pants, and I was attacking the button that would've loosened her trousers, when someone banged heavily on the door and demanded that we open it instantly. The voice was adult, belonging to Paja, the headmaster of the Swallow Colony, who shouted claiming that he knew we were in there and that this was not a brothel—the word he used was *kupleraj*, I remember it well. *Nije ovo kupleraj!* Emina and I pulled apart in terror, unable to respond to Paja, who was getting ever more agitated, threatening to break the door down. The moment of standing in the room with no place to escape to, with no solution to the problem of Paja presently banging at the door, the moment of total emptiness and total fullness, when we could not see what would happen because we knew that there was only one thing that could happen—opening the door for Paja to find us there—that moment was endless, until Emina slipped under the cover with Izet, who, drooling and contorted, somehow managed to sleep through it all. I finally moved to unlock the door, Paja burst in, I stepped out of his way as he searched for Emina, shouting at me, What are you doing in here? Where is she? My heart pounded so much, so hard, that I could see the pulsing of the T-shirt on my chest. Paja couldn't find Emina, who had wedged herself between Izet and the wall, and was concealed with a blanket, and he would have left without discovering her, we would have gotten away with it, and would have continued desiring each other across the distances of our lives, if the blanket had covered her painted pinkie toe, the red spot in the murkiness of Izet's bed, which Paja spotted just as he was on his way out and pulled the blanket off to discover her curled-up body and terrified face, her hair mussed up by my passion and her panic and the blanket. Izet finally woke up, wiped the drool off his chin, and looked at what was taking place around him in a blue-eyed bewilderment that would've been appropriate for a dreadful dream. What is this? he asked. What is happening? Get out of here, Paja said to Emina, and she crawled out of bed and left the room, and my life, and this memory. I would never see her again, and wouldn't even have a chance to get her address so I could write her a letter and tell her that I was sorry, that we did nothing wrong, that I loved her and would love her and the memory of her until this very day, that I still thought of her every time I washed my hair, and that I've not so long ago reached the day when there was no hair to wash.

Any mirror can be unfogged by a blow-dryer. Shoes smell bad? Refrigerate them overnight. Before adding sugar, do take a slurp of your coffee, no more need for sweetness afterward. Use newspaper for a streak-free window shine. Beat your morning sickness by sucking on a lemon. Onion and garlic will stop your hair from going gray. Everybody knows white wine takes out a red wine stain, just as a vinegar-soaked cotton ball vanishes a bruise. Flies in the house? They're smitten with bright lights. Clear a room of cigarette smoke by flailing a wet towel around. If you boil water before freezing, it will give you a world of crystal ice. Pillow flattened? Plump it up with sunlight. You can read *The Book* and marvel, for all that is the case is in fine order. Answers are placed into words, no stains or riddles can ever last. My mother and I, we've been there, we asked.

At first, all the girls and some boys had to have a *spomenar*, a padded-cover, fine-paper scrapbook the purpose of which was *spomen*—a memory, in the sense of memento. The *spomenar* owner would ask you—if you had any friends at all—to write and draw something in it for the sake of remembrance, promising not to let time paper over this moment. So you would draw hearts and cute kittens, claim that these days would never be forgotten, write earnest little poems in ostentatious, whorly handwriting, skirting the edges of platonic love. If there is anyone who loves you more, let him turn another page. But there are no more pages left to turn, no one loves you more than I. Or you could be clever and sarcastic, as I routinely was, and mock and mutilate the clichéd verses. If there is anyone who loves you more, let him turn another page. But there are hundreds of pages left, so what is it that anyone can do? Either way, to be asked to write something suggested your relevance, possibly even your being the *spomenar* owner's love interest. The highest love-interest rank one could attain was *simpatija*—a crush, though the translation obscures that the root of the Bosnian word is "sympathy," which, of course, doesn't have the violent, collisional, puritanical implications of the English word. No one was ever crushed by a *simpatija*. In any case, the negotiations that would eventually lead to a mutual bestowal of the title of *simpatija* always included writing in your becrushed's *spomenar*. But as we advanced along the trajectory of pubescence, the *spomenar* became too childishly sentimental and was gradually displaced by the *ispovjednik*, the confessional, which was comparatively devoid of the heart-shaped, badly rhymed clichés. An *ispovjednik* was a simple notebook where at the top of each page a question was asked. Traditionally, your best friends were the ones to be given the *ispovjednik* first, and their responses would stack up under each question. What is your name? When were you born? Your best friend? Favorite band? Favorite book? Favorite movie? Favorite fruit? And then: What do you think of ________? below which you would have to express your opinion of the classmate in question. Some were good friends, some were arrogant (*folira se*), a few were stupid, or had no sense of humor. The pleasure of reading the *ispovjednik* was in comparing the answers, decoding the intricate differences, mapping out the whole social constellation of your class to the smallest detail. There was no a priori order to things. Whenever I'd get an *ispovjednik* to write in, I'd look for my name to see what my classmates thought of me—usually it was a tie between being a good friend and being hopelessly arrogant—but also to detect any signals of random romantic interest. Any kind of elaborate response—say, Sometimes he's nice, at other times he's stubborn and thinks that he's the smartest in the world—would've indicated that more thought was devoted to me than to others. The confirmation of the possible *simpatija* status was to be found in the answers to the questions: Do you have a *simpatija*? Who is it? Many would admit to having a *simpatija*, but would either not name them or provide only the initials, which would often be enough to identify the person. If a full name was written down, it usually meant either a mad, damn-the-torpedoes-of-teasing love, or, rarely, that there already was a fully negotiated relationship. There was thus a time when I was so in love with Amela that I identified her as my true and only *simpatija*, therefore effectively proposing to her, but it didn't help one bit—she remained friendly, but distant. In a perfect world, she would've responded to my public statement by naming me in return as her *simpatija*, which would've practically been a contract between us. Alas, the world is everything that is the case, and Amela's love for me was never the case. Now I understand that the primary purpose of the interrogation in the *ispovjednik* was to extract answers to all those questions in the hope that they would help you identify yourself as a subject. If a question can be asked, there is an answer, and you were the answer. The *ispovjednik* was a subjectivity ledger, a place where the logic and the limits of your world were established. Which was why the whole confessional project depended on a necessary minimum of honesty and sincerity; we expected to read truth—the full truth of ourselves—even if it was encoded, like poetry, in predictable, clichéd ways. And then, as we grew older, as we descended into adolescence, we started lying, because subjects imagine and invent themselves. I have reason to believe that I was the first one to do it, and I did it because sincerity didn't work out for me, because I realized I could not avoid adolescence and whatever was beyond it, which is to say that my feelings were so confusing as to be shameful, embarrassing, and worth concealing under the guise of irony and sneering. At the beginning, my lies were tongue-in-cheek; I'd praise to high heaven someone everyone knew I disliked; in response to, What do you think of Mirza? I'd write, I have no idea who that is. Then I escalated it into making up my favorite bands, favorite books, even favorite fruit; I'd identify my *simpatija* with false initials, or even a false name, thus creating avatars for my obscure fantasies, causing some rewarding jealousy, inventing in the process an alternative self with a different life. This wasn't my original intention, but an accidental discovery. That is what I do now, all day long, all the time; it's like breathing to me. Take this thing you're reading. I could've assembled a different version of it from an alternative set of fragments; I could've been born of different parts; I could've assembled someone else. I could've tried to kill my little sister and then pretend that I didn't know what I was doing because I was a little boy. I could have read a lot of books, including, repeatedly, *The Paul Street Boys* (*Junaci Pavlove Ulice*), which would've led me to organize the boys in my building into a makeshift military unit that would fight a number of battles and wars against other, similar boys. I could've been a boy who listened to ABBA, watched them win the Eurovision contest with "Waterloo" and had a long-lasting crush on Agnetha (the blonde). I could've had a different best friend, named Boris, who left for Belgrade in the sixth grade, and whom I once beat up out of jealousy, and who'd visit his grandmother in the summer, which we'd spend playing chess and listening to the Stranglers. I could've made a different original decision and written all this in Bosnian, my mother tongue, which is both different and the same as *srpskohrvatski ili hrvatskosrpski*, and thereby avoid all the heartbreaking explanations of things that would be—to everyone who exists and existed within that world—entirely self-evident and plain. I could've been a different person, someone who never hurt a fly, who would never hurt a fly. Instead, here we are, Hemon, you and I.

We'd usually leave the coast early to escape the heat, sometimes it would still be dark, but eventually we would witness the yolky sunrise. My sister and I would be in the backseat, unbuckled. Our bodies would still be warm, but also itchy because the sunburns we had earned on the beach matured into dried skin, which would now unpeel in little scrolls. We'd smell of salt and NIVEA cream. Our hair would be longer, drier, like hay; our nails sharper, talon-like; the tips of our fingers desiccated from the sea and the sun, so that everything would feel different to the touch, brittle and more distant. We'd drive through the expanses of blazing Herzegovinian stone, through the valley of the Neretva, the green water, the blue sky, and the sheer white cliffs. Tata, ever impatient, would be tormented by a slow truck ahead, until he'd pass it at a speed beyond the limit, so Mama would object, scold him for the way he drove. They'd bicker for a bit, but everything would eventually be okay. We'd have just spent ten days in Makarska, in a modest hotel (*odmaralište*) owned by Elektroprenos, the company

Tata worked for. He would usually be bored during the vacation, because there would be nothing to do, no projects to invest time and effort in, nothing to complete, nothing to leave behind. Sometimes he'd vanish from the beach in search of something to do, and would not come back before it was time for lunch. Mama would dispatch me to find him, and I'd wander up and down the beach like an orphan, or along the asphalt path where I'd have to walk barefoot and once stepped on a burning cigarette butt; I'd search for him in bars, which he had no interest in, or in places where teenagers hung out, smoking and playing foosball, where he would never go, or at newsstands, where he might browse through the newspapers before buying one. It would never be easy to find him, he'd always be elsewhere, pursuing obscure leads out of vacation ennui. Once I discovered him painting, in his swimming trunks, a fishing boat with a local guy. He had struck up a conversation with the man and then offered to help him, and when I found him his hands were smeared with paint, a blue blot on his chest. Mama would not wander. She'd prefer to read, or sunbathe while watching us pretend to be swimming in the pebbled shallows. My sister would swallow copious amounts of seawater because she opened her mouth wide when she laughed, and the beach made her happy. When Mama got into the water, she'd not play with us, taking her swimming as seriously as she did everything else. She'd swim paddling with her hands, keeping her head above the water lest her carefully puffed-up hair get wet. In the evenings, we'd take a stroll together, have sugar-powdered fried dough (*mekike*) and ice cream from a cone whose top was shaped like a three-leaf clover so that we could get chocolate, vanilla, and banana flavors and keep them separate, moving our tongues from one to another until they became tricolor. All of that would be converted into the past as soon as we headed home, driving up Biokovo Mountain, and then farther, leaving the sea behind and out of sight. And it would become thick distant past after we passed through the Ivan Mountain tunnel and entered Bosnia proper, which would sometimes be smothered by clouds and rain, the sun thoroughly exterminated. My sister and I would be bored for the duration of the drive, and we'd sing. We wouldn't break our boredom, we'd embrace it by singing a song that could last forever, driving our parents crazy. There once was a dog, we'd belt, who made a cook mad, and the cook took a knife, and cut the dog in two, and other dogs came, dug a grave for him, and put up a tombstone, on which it read: There once was a dog who made a cook mad, and the cook took a knife, and cut the dog in two, and other dogs came, dug a grave for him, and put up a tombstone, on which it read: There once was a dog who made a cook mad, and the cook took a knife, and cut the dog in two, and other dogs came, dug a grave for him, and put up a tombstone, on which it read—and so on, ad infinitum, or until we'd arrive home. We can describe the lapse of time only by relying on some other process. In the hallway of our building, which would always be cool because it never saw the sun, I'd inhale the smells of our neighbors' lives: their cooking, their sweat, whatever was used to wash the hallway stairs. At the top of the third-floor staircase leading to our home there would be a stain cascading down the stairs, a consequence of my dropping a bottle of milk when I was five or six. Nearly fifty years later, the stain is still there, I see it every time I return to Sarajevo and stay in the apartment my sister and I grew up in. And when we'd enter the apartment, everything would be exactly as we had left it, except for the pungent scent of our absence. Without us there, there was no life: no one cooked, no one went to the bathroom, no one washed hands, no one drank coffee, no one turned on the lights, no one lived there, and all the windows and doors to the balconies were closed, so that only walls, carpets, furniture, and old magazines and newspapers stacked on the radio or the coffee table exuded existence. I loved that emptiness, because, each and every time, we'd refill it with ourselves. Before we returned there would be nothing, and then, within a moment, there would be everything, because we were there, and there was a here that belonged to us, that was us.

THIS DOES NOT BELONG TO YOU

ALSO BY ALEKSANDAR HEMON

FICTION

The Making of Zombie Wars

Love and Obstacles

The Lazarus Project

Nowhere Man

The Question of Bruno

NONFICTION

The Book of My Lives

THIS DOES NOT BELONG TO YOU

ALEKSANDAR HEMON

HAMISH HAMILTON
an imprint of Penguin Canada, a division of Penguin Random House Canada Limited

Canada • USA • UK • Ireland • Australia • New Zealand • India • South Africa • China

Published in Hamish Hamilton hardcover by Penguin Canada, 2019
Simultaneously published in the United States by MCD, Farrar, Straus and Giroux,
120 Broadway, New York 10271

www.penguinrandomhouse.ca

LIBRARY AND ARCHIVES CANADA CATALOGUING IN PUBLICATION

Title: My parents ; This does not belong to you / Aleksandar Hemon.
Other titles: This does not belong to you
Names: Hemon, Aleksandar, 1964- author. | Hemon, Aleksandar, 1964- My parents. |
Hemon, Aleksandar,
1964- This does not belong to you.
Description: Two separate works. | Title from distinctive title pages.
Identifiers: Canadiana (print) 20190044047 | Canadiana (ebook) 20190044055
| ISBN 9780735238381
(hardcover) | ISBN 9780735238398 (PDF)
Subjects: LCSH: Hemon, Aleksandar, 1964-—Family. | CSH: Bosnian Canadians—
Biography | LCSH: Yugoslav
War, 1991-1995—Refugees—Bosnia and Herzegovina—Biography. | LCSH:
Refugees—Canada—Biography. |
LCSH: Sarajevo (Bosnia and Herzegovina)—History—Siege, 1992-1996. | LCSH:
Sarajevo (Bosnia and
Herzegovina)—Biography. | LCGFT: Biographies.
Classification: LCC FC106.B68 Z6 2019 | DDC 971/.004918390092—dc23

Book design by Abby Kagan
Cover design by Terri Nimmo
Cover images courtesy of the author

Printed and bound in Canada

10 9 8 7 6 5 4 3 2 1

Penguin
Random House
HAMISH HAMILTON CANADA

THIS DOES NOT BELONG TO YOU

Once upon a time, in a land far, far away, on a mountain called Jahorina, there was an old hotel called Šator. It was half an hour from Sarajevo, but a stone's throw away from our family mountain cabin, from what I now refer to as my previous life. The hotel was open only in the winter; when you stood in the snow outside it under a frigid, starry sky it reeked of cafeteria grease, of woodstoves, and of cigarette smoke; you'd hear the thumping from the disco club in the basement. For the rest of the year, the hotel was vacant. One summer, when I was ten, I broke into the hotel bar by cracking its window—it took me an hour—and stole a bottle of blueberry juice. I had no interest in juice, I just wanted to open the window, but once I got in I had to take something to prove that I'd done it. The bartender, who idled in the summer, caught and blackmailed me, asking for money not to tell my parents. There once was a boy who made a man mad. I told him to fuck off. He told my parents. They punished me, but that blueberry juice was the sweetest potion, and I would never have any regrets. The hotel cleaning staff was Baja, a woman of an

indeterminate body shape and age who lingered in and around the hotel, always clad in a blue overcoat, a black scarf on her head, one of its corners covering her jaw to warm it up. She was, like a ghost, impervious to pain. She had an eternal toothache she would not treat, the abscess swelling until it devoured and destroyed her eye. Nobody ever saw her clean anything, though a friend of my parents' who'd stayed at the hotel told us that Baja had once walked into his room without knocking, looked around, and said: "Why don't you clean this up? It's disgusting." Right behind the hotel, there was a peaked boulder where we'd climb when there was nothing else to do, which, in the summer, was most of the time. If we looked from the top toward where we came from, we could see the weekend-house cluster below, hear the buzzing of circular saws, the banging of hammers, the din of aspiration, for everyone was perpetually getting ready for some future in which their active lives would be successfully completed and there'd be nothing but peace, virginal nature, and socialist retirement. The war would cancel the future, but back then, when we were kids, the future was always on its way, its advance currents humming inside everything we knew or cared to know. If we looked in the other direction, wooded vales and ridges, meadows and roads, stretched toward Sarajevo and farther beyond it, onward to the horizon, into which the sun would slot like a coin at the end of the day. We'd stand at the edge of the boulder, pine and fir tips arising from the verdant void beneath our feet, and we'd look, and look, and look—our visual field had no limits, in exactly the same way our life had no end. The garbage from the hotel was dumped right behind it, down the slope at the foot of the boulder. My sister and I didn't find that strange. By the time we emerged from our unconscious childhood, the world seemed fully established, everything as it was, everything happening as it happened, all the points and objects fixed, all the hierarchies and structures natu-

ral and unalterable. We'd descend from the peak to the garbage dump to browse through trash-stuffed plastic bags and rotten food remnants. One day, we found a plethora of plates, saucers, cups, and bowls strewn all over the dump—the hotel had replaced their dishes with new ones. We spent the whole day breaking the old dishes with rocks, against one another. We discussed nothing, devised no plans; it was clear to us what needed to be done, and we just did it. The dishes were nondescript, beige; we shattered them into smithereens, taking a break for lunch, smashing some more in the afternoon. We sustained small cuts, but didn't care, they were the blisters of toil, the stigmata of devotion. Thus we discovered the pleasure of unbridled, unlimited destruction, the endless joy of converting everything into nothing. Now I realize it was one of the happiest days of my childhood, perhaps of my entire life. And when we went back to the dump some time later and found new garbage, new generations of refuse, we knew that underneath it all were our smithereens, that we could keep forging them for as long as we lived, and that we would always remember the day we broke the limited whole.

I fell into a deep ditch where piss and shit from the cowshed drained. This happened in '68, maybe '69, at my grandparents', in the countryside, three hours away from Sarajevo—on the fringes, so to speak, of the known world. I would've been four years old; evidently I thought I could run as freely as I wished to. I had indeed run freely and everywhere until I fell into the ditch and started drowning in excrement. I like to entertain the occasional impatient audiences I encounter at readings and dinner parties by claiming that my oldest memory is of sinking in shit; although the memory is pure Freudian gold, the audiences are not necessarily impressed. They hope for greater secrets, for something that could cast light on a writer's oeuvre, explain the mysteries of creation, establishing a leitmotif spreading throughout the life narrative. But the fact of the matter is that I remember my uncle Bogdan (who must've pulled me out of the shit, and whose name can be translated as "God-given") pouring cold water from a beaten tin cup onto my face. I can presently see his face looming above me in a halo of backlight, the coating of

filth being washed away and running down my cheeks and temples and into my ears, the taste of manure on my lips, the sensation of coolness on my tightening skin as I rise out of the shitty darkness. This cold is what I always recall, the moment I emerged back into the world. The enemies of cold water, they speak without experience.

It has been well established that my father spent the summer of 1961 working somewhere in Germany, whence he brought back home a Grundig reel-to-reel recorder, which we lovingly called the *magnetofon*. This was before I was even a consideration. The reel of time unspooled even without me, however; I don't think that is unjust. Thus the *magnetofon* was there when I was born: gray, the corners snugly rounded; the wide, large buttons and nipple-like protuberances onto which the tapes were to be placed. By way of that *magnetofon* I was recorded speaking when I was two. They asked me, What does a doggie say? And I said, Doggie says av av. What does a horsey say? Doggie says av av. And what does a cow say? Doggie says av av. Okay, but what does a cow say? Doggie says av av. I don't, naturally, remember that particular animal-noise conversation, but I do remember listening to the recording, later in my life, that had me unflappably repeating, Doggie says av av. I seem to have been wisely determined not to venture into any area of uncertainty and stick only to what was already confirmed as known. I also recall the

reels rolling, the Teutonic smell of warm lamps and magnetic tape. However old I was when I listened to it for the first time, the voice came from the obscure past of which I had no conscious recollection. We can describe the lapse of time only by relying on some other process. Whoever was uttering, Doggie says av av, had no organic connection to my listening self, though the voice sounded familiar, if distorted by the weakening of the tape's magnetic charge. The only connection to that kid who had allegedly been myself was the *magnetofon* and the reel of tape I'd thread in to listen, though there was, strictly speaking, no evidence that we were the same person. Anyone could've said, Doggie says av av, any other kid, as it wasn't exactly, you know, a profound thought, an expression of personality, a finished product of a self-fashioned mind. Later, when I was an adolescent, in a fit of deconstructive ambition, I took the Grundig apart. I wanted to understand how it worked, how sounds and the traces of our life were pressed onto the tape, but I failed to achieve that knowledge. I reassembled the *magnetofon*, but there were some extra parts left and I could find no place for them, could not figure out where they'd fit. I reshaped the Grundig to accommodate the new, incomplete me, and it would therefore never work again. What happened to the tapes, I have no idea. The voice of the past me is thus forever lost. All that is available is a memory of my listening to myself, who might not have in fact been myself. The fact remains, however, that Doggie does say av av.

I ran, often. I was chased, often, by other boys who wanted to beat me, sometimes by random adults angry at me, mainly for being a child—grown-ups typically hate all children except their own, now and then even their own. Sometimes I was chased by strangers. Once, I remember, an off-duty postman pursued me, aiming to hurt me, which he did when he caught me, because the world sends out its servants and agents to harm you, they linger out there until such time arrives. There is a pale, unshaven man in a wool coat and brimmed hat across the street looking up this way as we speak, believe me. So I remember myself as a child running toward Kino Arena, along the row of garages; I don't remember who was chasing me. What I do remember was a presence of danger at my heels, and my running as fast as I could, all the while growing aware that I couldn't run any faster. I wanted to accelerate, I willed a greater speed, but the will didn't reach anywhere below my waist and my legs just couldn't. Whoever was chasing me finally caught me and beat me; this was how I learned about my limits, about the existence of limits, about my

finality. My will hit the ceiling of my being like a distraught moth. Beyond the ceiling was who knows what, or just plain nothing, solidified into a sky. The details are sketchy and may have come from another moment in my life: at some other time, I must have also been running toward Kino Arena. I ran along that stretch between my building and the movie theater every day of my boy life—the recollection can't have been that specific, so that when I remember the running, my body doesn't respond. But when I remember the chase and my failed attempt to will acceleration, my body responds—it remembers its inability to transcend itself; it swells with sadness; it hurts. It becomes what it's always been: a slow, dying body, ever unable to restore itself, in recollection, or in any other way. It will eventually run out of itself, out of myself. Kino Arena was shelled in the war, and then it was razed after it. Now it's a gravel parking lot. When I was a boy, I wanted to be a historian.

I used to think that envisioning skeletons was as inappropriate as imagining naked bodies. I'd hide in a corner, crouch behind the dirty-clothes basket, or in the armoire where the winter coats were stored, and I'd envision a skeleton: the ribs, the skull, the hollow eye sockets, the pelvic cage. No flesh involved, just the pale bare bones, the loose joints. My mother would find me cowering in the corner and ask me what I was doing. And I'd look up at her, ashamed, unable to

On a febrile living room sofa I chewed the hem of my blanket soaking it with my sizzling saliva tasted like wool my cheeks burned my toes were grotesquely big throbbing in my high-temperature dream charging Barbarossa knights in heavy armor and their laden horses stumbling through snow slipping on ice I was so cold it may have been winter, a blizzard outside, I'll never know, but I was cold the fever was an adversary to my will wiped it out with its thick swords and horses and swirls of snow this is what fever is being stuck in a body aflame with helplessness and clarity I was all there because I could not get out of it I had no other place to go I remember the fevers of my childhood with salience better than any event I've longed for fevers since delirium is a condition of total presence in the world my mother put honey in marshmallow tea and said, Drink it.

All the grown-ups were huddling around the table in Teta Jozefina's kitchen, half of them smoking, the other half inhaling. There was a little baby in the other room, my sister, I believe, so I couldn't go there either, couldn't get to the bookshelves, to the Bible, *Horse Heaven Hill*, or *The Greatest Spies of World War Two*, because she was sleeping. The hallway was dark and unheated and there was nothing to do, no books, no toys, they smoked in the kitchen and there was nowhere to sit, nothing to do. I drank my blueberry juice, asked for more, they said no. I played with the shoes for a while, lined them up in rows, then mismatched and matched them, scrambled them more, opened the kitchen door, and announced, I'm going home, and they said to me, Go, go, what do we care? They didn't take me seriously, didn't believe me; they thought I was but a little boy, helpless. In the winter of 1970 I was five years old. I put on my shoes and coat, my hat and scarf, my gloves, extended myself on the tips of my toes to unlock the door, and home I went. It was winter, snow on the ground, night all around. A lifelong project, it's been for me, going

home. The streets were desolate, or at least I don't remember seeing anyone outside; strangers were invisible to me. The snowbanks were up to my shoulders, the starry sky above, though those could've been just the lights in the hills. I'd never walked home all by myself from Marin dvor, where Teta Jozefina and Čika Martin lived. But somehow, like a cat, I knew how to return. I followed the streetcar tracks, crossed the street at the technical school, walked along the army barracks' fence. The snow squealed under my feet, I wasn't afraid, I knew where I was going. There were scattershot lit barracks windows, soldiers awake. Though I'd never done it, all I needed to make it home was in place: my world had been established with all the relevant markers, because I was my world, and everything was as it was—I possessed a map of myself, and I knew how to read it. Meanwhile, at Teta Jozefina and Čika Martin's, my parents turned on the lights to look for me all over the apartment and I was nowhere to be found, because I wasn't there. They phoned Tetka Katica, who was staying with us that winter, but I wasn't home either. Where is he? my mother cried. Is he there? I wasn't there, I was here, walking in the snow along a narrow path, the soldiers beyond the lights greasing their rifles, keeping their eyes on me.

We'd drive back home on a Sunday afternoon in early September, the experience of my time in the countryside ebbing already, the cherry stains on my hands fading like misremembered jokes. The last stretch of the road, before Sarajevo opened like a palm of a hand, went through the Bosna River Valley. The sun would already be tucked in beyond the hills, a blue sky turned gray, the river fading into black, the cars would have their headlights on, ready for the onslaught of darkness. Summertime shuddered, quietly awaiting its end. We would see the rash of feeble fires on the slopes where the peasants scorched the summer grass and dry bushes. That smell of burning in the Bosna Valley is the smell of coming back home at the summer's end, a few days before school started, before my birthday, before the rains, before everything stopped being what it was. The smell of home, however, was different: when we walked into our apartment, it would have the fragrance of our absence, of silence and cleanliness, of no one being there. I'd always be the first to inspect the apartment as if to see if something had changed,

if somehow the order of things as we'd left them was altered, if something other than our life had taken place in that space, if someone had slept in my bed, touched my toys, read my books. But nothing, of course, would ever be different: when we were not there, nobody was there, and I always found comfort in that. Home is a place where there is a void when you're not there; home is what your body fills out. Nowadays we live elsewhere and otherwise, but there is still nobody in our place when we are not there. When I visit, that's where I stay. When I'm there, I'm not here. Here, there, wherever I may be, I'm always absent somewhere. Home is the fragrant nothing where I am not.

The woman had a retractable jaw; whenever I passed her she'd smile first, then let her denture slide out, only to suck it back in and laugh, exposing her artificial teeth. The first time she did it I thought it was a bad dream, so I screamed, if to no avail. I was there because Teta Štefica, who was my baby sister's nanny, would drag us to her place after her dumb son had called again because he needed to be fed or given money, or maybe was just bored and needy. She lived in a damp old building that smelled of crumbling mortar, mice, and pickled cabbage; to get to her apartment we had to pass through the courtyard where the woman with the jaw was hanging up her clothes to dry. Somehow, she would always be there, this woman, like a mythological creature sentenced by the gods to commit the same act throughout eternity. Perhaps the gods forced her to terrorize me too; she'd expel her teeth halfway out whenever she saw me, suck them back in as I wailed; it delighted her, the whole exercise, my fear. My sister was a toothless baby, so she didn't care, but the whole display was extremely troubling to me. Never should a clothes-hanging woman

be able to disarticulate her face just like that. Objects—people too—make up the substance of the world, which is why they cannot be composite. What, I worried, if she could take her head off and roll it down the stairs like a ball? What if she could rip my arms and legs off, stack them like firewood? What if what I thought I was—me—was but an assemblage of parts, of minds, of *mes*? What if there was no whole self? What if the woman with the jaw articulated herself only to scare me and then fully disarticulated herself after I was gone? Could it be that the world, including the people in it, arranges itself for my gaze, for the audience, making all the present situations seamless and sufficient? I didn't actually think about it back then—I was six—but fear has history, grows inside you until it finds its place and settles close to the fire like a blind dog. The clothes the woman hanged, they smelled of the detergent called Radion, smelled wet and clean, as though they'd never been dirty, and they never would be.

Teta Štefica enjoyed murder and death. She would slurp coffee with Lućano's mother and exchange stories like the one about the woman whose son slit her throat so thoroughly that, when she was found, her head was hanging on a strip of neck skin. Teta Štefica claimed she knew this woman; she lived in the same reality as the mother and the son who decapitated her, but she was not troubled by it at all. She was never worried that something like that could happen to her; indeed, there was a certain joy in her delivery of the morbid stories; she seemed amazed and delighted that such things could take place in this world, that there was darkness others could not see, that she could report from it. She would dip a sugar cube into her coffee and put it in her mouth, and while it was still dissolving, the sweetness spreading all over her taste buds, she would tell her friend (and, therefore, me) about a passenger on a fast train who stuck his head out the window to see if the next stop was coming up, but it turned out that what was coming up was a telephone pole that took his head off. After a while I developed a suspicion that she might be

exaggerating. But I also knew that if she could imagine it, it could happen. If a question can be formulated, there can be an answer. She told me once about the baby that was left alone in the kitchen where there was a bunch of green onions on the counter, and inside the plume of one of those onions there was a snake. Snakes are attracted to milk, as everyone knows, so this snake crawled out of the green-onion plume and across the room and into the crib and then into the baby through its baby mouth because it smelled of milk. I believe she said that the baby had died. I don't know what happened to the snake. This story affected me, because green onions and babies were part of my experiential domain, of my reality. If my mother brought green onions from the market, I'd sit there and closely monitor the plumes, too afraid to check them for snakes, but brave enough to keep watch over my baby sister. Never again in my life—including the present depletion—have I looked at green onions without considering a snake lodged inside one of its plumes. For the world to exist there have to be objects, and inside those objects there has to be nothing, and inside that nothing there must be memories, and inside those memories there are snakes.

There was once a man called Robert Shields who between 1972 and 1997 chronicled his life every five minutes. He slept for two hours at a time, so he could write down his dreams. He left samples of his nose hair for future study. To his mind, there was nothing about him unworthy of being recorded. At 7:00 a.m. on July 23, 1993, he noted: "I cleaned out the tub and scraped my feet with my fingernails to remove layers of dead skin." At 7:05 a.m.: "Passed a large, firm stool, and a pint of urine. Used five sheets of paper." He wanted everything to be *not* forgotten, and to that end produced 37.5 million words that filled ninety-four large boxes, which cannot be opened until 2047. He was a former minister and a high school English teacher. God didn't reveal Himself to him in the world, but in his writing. Reverend Shields wrote as if his every action, his every word had meaning, and then there was meaning indeed. The recording of life was his life; he willed and wrote its meaning. What was unwritten down did not occur; the writing erased that which was not written of. Forgetting was—and is—inescapable, yet there is no

way of knowing what was forgotten, what took place in the empty space between his increments of writing. What could not be recollected never happened and was hence passed over in silence. Only that which was written down was the case. The world was independent of his will, but writing it was not. Death was the blankness after the period.

Everybody and their cousin, and Robert Shields, has written about memories, or memoirs, or remembering. What is there to say? Why insist? Why insist that memory is mystery, or story, or history? Why not just let it go, theoretically or practically? Just let it go. Any and all of life's present situations are seamless and sufficient. So much time and energy and money and living cells are wasted on remembering this and that and the past. Not to mention that the most learned of us are on the point of discovering that we know too little. Perhaps it's just fear: if I remember simply because the mind dies before the body, then remembering, like writing, staves off death, then it's the last wall of defense against death's advances. If I remember, I know not only that I have lived but also that I'm alive. Death takes place when you can't recall the moment that precedes the present moment. What were we just talking about? Time passes in sentences.

Now that I'm past fifty, now that I'm evidently but a slapped-together sum of conscious feelings and judgments and misconceptions, nothing but a self addicted to its belief in itself, it appears I remember only the things I'd already remembered before. There are no more newly discovered memories, the repertoire is presently, eternally, woefully limited, and I'm looping through it. If it's true that memories solidify into stories after the first recollection, then what I remember now are the stories of memories that might have been the memories of stories. Now that I'm the majority owner of a piece of the true life system, of myself and of its many parts thought and spun together, I'm all out of memories, drowning in stories. Before the word, there was nothing, except me, whom I can't remember, except as a character, a unity that doesn't hold together. I, as I write this, am only a certainty that seeks out the words that are most apt to compel your attention. And who are you? Who might you be? Why are you pale like the face on a severed head?

There are no random memories. They would appear random if they were ever out of sequence. But there is always a sequence; some story line, some sentence, some occurrence can always be discovered and aligned. I used to walk the streets of Sarajevo, looking for something to look at. Everything would be known to me: a dark November evening; the nose tip cold; the smog-coated buildings; the rattling of streetcars; the lights and the roar from the Grbavica Stadium; girls' hair redolent of shampoo and their parents' cigarettes; the murky river flowing irreversibly; the chestnut-roasting fires, the soot on the fingers; the murky headlights creeping toward the red-eye streetlight; mats of dead leaves under the chestnut trees. I perceived it all, but what I perceived was always part of my Sarajevo sequence, of my story there: I was born, I lived, I imagined futures, I longed to accrue meaning, I was there. I couldn't see then how the sequence would turn out: I left Sarajevo, I live elsewhere, and now I remember it, randomly pining for that which cannot be retrieved or even uttered. Crows cawing in murders. The sequence will end when I end, but it will never reverse its course.

The head was still connected to my neck nearly touched the hot radiator under the balcony window   I was half sitting up on the sofa, not drinking the marshmallow tea my mother made for me   my palms and soles coated with sweat   she had rubbed lard into my chest wrapped a slivovitz-soaked rag around my throat   I smelled like my grandparents' larder   my nose was bleeding but she put such effort into forestalling my fever that I kept swallowing my blood lest she think that it wasn't working   it wasn't working at all   my stomach filled with blood so I retched coughed coughed it up and it all came out like water from the mouth of a bronze fountain frog at the train station splashing the sofa the coffee table the floor the blanket the other end of me   there was a brief and delirious sense of accomplishment as I'd never before vomited blood and so much of it   my mother rushed back to me and saw blood running down my chin and chest she was distraught even panicked worst nightmare dying child   it's okay I wanted to say it's just blood just blood I swallowed I'm not dying as if I would've

known I couldn't say what I wanted to say instead of words blood was coming out of my mouth she was going crazy by now and I bleeding was in pain because I could not explain I wasn't in pain I remember it all with such perspicuity that I can taste the blood on my tongue right now as if I'd just licked a rasp it tastes like liver like love like a lucid moment of dying.

There once was a boy who saw a dead man. In my mind there exists my Sarajevo neighborhood from the time before it was leveled to build high-rises and supermarkets and a hotel. In my recollection, I move from my building, cross the grass patch, onward past the stacks of marble slabs leaning against the back wall of a tombstone workshop, then a newsagent kiosk where I'd buy soccer-player stickers and chewing gum and comic books with the change I stole from my mother's wallet or my piggy bank, over which loomed a cherry plum tree we would sometimes climb to pick unripe sour plums (*rezdelije*), then along a series of storefronts, which included a cobbler, a sweetshop, where my favorite was something I never knew a name for but was pink-coated and rum-flavored and contained nuts, and then a produce store, part of which was under a green awning that leaked when it rained and you had to step into a puddle to walk in and say, Good day! Beyond, there was a building whose street-facing wall had a glass box where movie posters and showtimes for Kino Arena were posted. All of that would be demolished before I was out of elementary

school. I don't know anyone who remembers that landscape. I don't know anyone who cares what was there before, because there was never a time without a time before, that's how time works, time keeps everything from taking place at once, welcome to this world. Our life has no end in just the way in which our visual field has no limits. But one childhood morning, I was regarding the poster in the box when I saw a man in a worn fishbone coat, the sleeves short enough to expose his hairy wrists, tottering forth in a way suggesting he was drunk. He was unclean, pale, and unshaven, the kind of man I knew to stay away from. I remember that he smelled, but don't remember the smell itself. He stumbled and nearly fell into me and I either propped him up or just showed my concern and confusion. Whatever may be the case, his coat was unbuttoned and I could see a stabbing mark on his front: a wet circle of dark blood. The position of the wound has traveled in my memory's domain between his abdomen and his chest, crossing from the left to the right and back, though it has lately settled on his left side, just under the ribs, where the spleen is, where the stab would've likely been mortal. I don't remember talking to him, or his saying anything to me. The wound was there only for my gaze, for me, yet it wasn't mine, it belonged not to me but to this man. His face has metamorphosed too: presently it expresses fear and nausea. It's reasonable to assume that those were my feelings at the time—the face I see would therefore be mine. Or, it might still be mine, since what I most commonly feel these days is a throttling mix of fear and nausea. But the man never said a word, never acknowledged the wound, never showed in any way that he knew it was there, that death was a possibility. What he could not say, he passed over in silence, and then he moved on and tottered forth and away. I never saw him again. He must have died. He might have well died as soon as he was out of my sight, out of my life. Death is not an event in life, but every wound is.

The movie poster I was regarding was for *The Sound of Music*: Julie Andrews was wearing an apron, twirling in a field of flowers, the Alps rising behind her, the bluest possible skies looming above the mountains, the swirling-font title in Bosnian: *Moje pjesme, moji snovi.* What does it mean, you ask yourself, what does it *mean*?

I don't remember pain. I remember the moments when I'm sure I must've felt pain: twisting my ankle running down the stairs as my sister chased me because I had read her diary in which she confessed her crush on one Edo; sitting in a dentist's chair as the dentist bore toward the sensitive nerve in the depths of my tooth; breaking my arm playing soccer; sticking pins under the skin of my palms and kneeling on corn kernels; my mother beating me with a ladle; my father with a belt; one bully or another slamming my head against a concrete wall. But I cannot recollect the hurt, the body rearranged by pain, the inability to get out of it, its being everywhere and everything. It's probably better that way; it's good. Still, where did the pain go? Where did it vanish? Will it come back, or is it always new, ever in the present? There are indeed things that cannot be put into words. They just make themselves manifest. They are what is mystical.

Why revisit memories? Why the word "revisit"? When did I visit my memories for the first time? Where were they staying so I had to visit them? You visit distant family or strangers, someone who lives elsewhere, foreigners visit tourist attractions, people visit graves of their loved ones, UFOs visit the Earth. I used to have a toy police car, took it out to play with my friends in the park. My car would chase other boys' cars, as we'd witnessed on TV, where the police often pursued criminals. But a proper police car would always flip or get into an accident, get smashed, so that my friend Vuja slammed my car several times against a wall, then smashed it against the concrete, then banged on it with a rock, until it was all broken up, all the plastic little windows shattered, the doors sticking out at sharp angles like origami; it was destroyed, a police car only in abstract, the criminals escaped yet again. And then, Vuja insisted, we had to bury it, because it was now trash; he dug a hole, put my car into it, and covered it with soil, like a corpse. Memories are somewhere in my body; they hurt. Is think-

ing of a memory remembering? Is retrieving a memory thinking? You forget that your neurons wither away like tendons. You lose your memories because you're normally in the process of dying. Once you're gone, they're all gone, tendons too. I went back home, I remember; Mama asked me, Where is your police car? I said it was dead and buried in the park, and she said, Go find it. I went back to look for it. All of my friends were gone home to have dinner or a bath. It was getting dark. I couldn't even find the hole, let alone my police car. I was already over it; it was only because I had to look for it that I wanted to find it. And I never found it; it was just swallowed by the earth, disappeared into nothingness, as such things go. It hurt. Mama thought that Vuja undug and stole my toy car, but that made no sense to me—it was destroyed, it no longer existed as such, what could he do with it? Could he have fixed it? Restored it to its original shape? Suppose there is an afterlife. Would you remember this life in the afterlife? Would your thoughts turn into afterthoughts? Would you reminisce and long for your old body, for all the wounds and desires, for the bangs and pains, for the gray hairs your child used to pluck to ease the itch? Or would all your memories as well as your capacity to remember be entirely wiped out and you'd be but a clean-slate soul with nothing to recall, nothing to recall it with, imprisoned in bliss and orgasmic emptiness, a spiritual shell of your self? You wouldn't know that you used to be yourself, plus the body. What would I do without myself in the afterlife? I'd be lonely. I'd miss the taste of strawberries, of water, I'd miss the hurt. My police car.

The toys my father brought from Russia: a Soviet-gray racing car whose wheels fell off in no time; the electric train set with a little gray station, including no passengers, which I had to glue together from small bits; a grayish rocket that could be pumped full with water, then launched when the pressure was high enough, flying straight up, then crashing somewhere beyond the limits of my sight; the bazooka that ejected plastic balls, and that my mother broke against my hip in a fit of fury; the telegraph system featuring copper wires I spread all over our apartment, then sent simple Morse code messages (SOS) to the other end, where there was always nobody waiting. Toys are not meant to last; only the unplayed-with toys live a long life. All those I loved perished, the rest are I don't know where. My oldest toy memory is of the Lego blocks my father brought from some capitalist country where they made gratuitously colorful toys. I kept trying to build a house with the blocks, but could never build a roof, didn't know how to turn the walls into a home.

What is not carried out does not exist. The linkage of events in a temporal succession does not refer to an absolute order. What I remember best was taking the never-finished house apart, the unbuilding, the pleasure of disarticulation.

My father brought back from the Soviet Union a slide projector, a gray boxy thing with a powerful bulb that always smelled like burnt dust. He also brought rolls of slides featuring classic Russian fairy tales. He'd thread in a fairy tale and then turn a little knob to scroll, image after image being projected on the wall in our living room. An image is a fact, but the colors, oh, the colors! There is a particular shade to the green that appeared in those Russian fairy tales, on a dress of Vasilisa Perekrasnaya, or in the woods where some prince was lost. The splendorous wide headdress—there must be a beautiful Russian word for something like that—framing her face, not unlike a halo, or a tiara. I had a crush on Vasilisa Perekrasnaya, but that burgeoning desire could not be separated from the greenness, or from the smell of the bulb and the gray projector. Vasilisa's mother gave her a magic doll. At first my father would read the fairy-tale text from the bottom of the image, and then, when he learned it all by heart, as did I, he simply told us what happened. At some point, he must have started adding things, maybe even

editing out the parts he found boring. Somehow, at some undetermined time, I either lost interest in the never-changing Vasilisa, in all those silly tales, or he stopped setting up the projections, or both. The end of home projections may have been related to my being able to go to Kino Arena by myself. Images are facts, unless they're strung together. The first film I saw all by myself was *Battle of Neretva*, where a choir of refugees at some point sings: *Zbogom dome, ja ti odo'*. Farewell, home, I'm leaving you now.

Mornings. Whenever it was that I woke up, the radio would already be on because my mother always woke up before me. A children's program: songs, excited little radio plays, reporters visiting schools to talk to new students, more songs. A commercial would extol the value of saving for the future:

Štedi danas, štedi sutra
kod Privredne banke,
pa ćeš i ti imati
lopticu i sanke.

My mother would stir sugar into egg yolk and mix it vigorously. This was my usual breakfast. Outside, it would be dark, sometimes it would snow, sometimes nothing. I have forgotten so much, but not the song from the commercial:

Save today, save tomorrow,
with the Economy Bank,

and you too will have
a little ball and a sled.

The lamp radio was always warm. It was an object with an interiority, there was light inside. Tomorrow was moot, the future didn't extend beyond that day's evening, when I'd be back from school, when everything would be the same, including the darkness outside. Why save for the future when the present is everlasting? I remember my mother's arm moving, as she stirred the yolk and sugar, like a locomotive elbow.

Every summer we would go to the coast for a vacation. We would get up early to avoid the heat, just washing our faces with cold water, skipping breakfast. Which meant that as soon as we got out of Sarajevo, my sister and I were clamoring for food. On the sinuous road, Mama would open the golden lunch box, which always contained boiled eggs, a green pepper, a sausage, a piece of bread, and a small kitchen knife to cut it all up. Sometimes, rarely, sandwiches would have been made. For years, on the sickeningly winding roads to the coast, we ate out of that golden box, sprinkling crumbles of bread and yolk onto the backseat. The food from that box always had a special taste—slightly bitter, tart, yet complete—and even more so if it matured inside the box for a night, refrigerated. Sometimes I'd vomit out all that food before we even got to Mostar, but there would always be more in that box. We could never eat it all, because something had to be kept for the arrival at our final destination, for who could ever know if there would be anything to sustain us where we were going. Or it could be that the box had some mythological

property that made its abundance infinite. Once, we saw a road accident, two cars crashed directly into each other, and we watched the drivers who stopped to help tear the back door off to rip a dead child out of the backseat. I was eating a piece of green pepper at the time. Dangling little legs, rolled-down socks. Boiled egg.

My grandfather lost his left eye when the cow he was milking swung her head and gouged it out with her horn. I remember waking up in the morning and seeing Deda on the sofa with a piece of gauze over the eye hole, the bloodstain representing the shape of what was no longer there, would be gone forever. The cow had a name: Ružava. As for my grandfather, he then went completely blind, then completely senile. For the last few years of his life, he didn't know where he was, what was around him, what that space was called by others, other than home. He lived inside the darkness, which he somehow took to be Ukraine, where he'd been born and then left at the age of twelve, and in that darkness occasional memories would sparkle and perish. Once he collected his pillow and blanket and crawled into a closet to curl up, thinking he was returning home. He fully felt the world as a limited whole, even if it was as small as the closet, even if he forgot my name, or who I was, or who he was. Sometimes he'd snap out of his

oblivion to cry, Why did you leave me in the middle of this forest? He must not have even noticed when he died. But we did, because after he died he was no longer there at all; just, where he used to be, a void.

At the end of the day, I was supposed to go back to Tetka Marija's, but I wanted to stay, and when Slavica, Tetka Marija's daughter, asked me for the last time if I wanted to go with her, I said I wasn't going to go, so she went home. I could go back to playing in my grandparents' front yard, and backyard, and garden, and barn, but after Slavica left, the value of that freedom was unexpectedly diminished. Somehow everything became more inert, devoid of warmth, unresponsive to my intents and desires, perhaps because the day was ending, the shapes turning softer and blurrier, everything becoming something other than itself, all of it darker. My grandfather had chicken blindness, so he could see nothing at dusk, after the sun vanished. It was only later, after dinner, after my grandparents and Tetka Katica, who was visiting them, went to bed, that I looked outside and saw nothing but a distant sparkle of a lantern-lit window on the next hill over, and consequently recognized how vast the field of loneliness around me was, how far it stretched, how immense the darkness surrounding us, and how long the night might turn

out to be, and I started crying, remorseful that I hadn't gone with Slavica, because if I had I would've now been sleeping elsewhere, with her, and she would've told me a story, or sung a song, and I wouldn't have been so alone, I would've fallen asleep next to her warm body. And so I wept; I was my world and I could see no end to its emptiness. I must've woken up Tetka Katica, for I remember eventually curling up against her, sobbing. She scratched my back, very slowly, singing a Ukrainian lullaby I could not comprehend, in a high-pitched grandmotherly voice (she was my grandfather's sister) that slipped into susurrus and then into silence. Except it wasn't silence: I could hear her breathing, and my grandfather snoring in the next room, and an occasional lowing of the cows in the shed, and the crackling in the walls that randomly fractured the night silence. Her hand and blunt nails layered love onto my skin, and nothing could be not said. In the morning, once again, everything was as it had been the morning before.

Tetak Nikola was Tetka Marija's husband; they lived a couple of hills over from my grandparents. Once Tetak Nikola had caught me washing a puppy in a chicken-feeding trough with the cut-off end of a cucumber that looked like a little green French beret, but looked to me at the time like a round soap bar. Once he'd pressed the cold flat side of a knife to the place where a bee had stung me, and I stopped crying. When he got lung cancer, he relied for a cure on a mixture of medicinal alcohol and chicory and drank it daily. It didn't help at all. One summer afternoon, I was in Tetka Nataljka's front yard when we heard the church bells and she stopped in her tracks, somehow knowing that the ringing meant Tetak Nikola had died. This was the first death in my life I would be aware of. I remember thinking at that moment that a door had just opened and death had walked right in. But I was also aware that my thought on death was a deep, grown-up thought, that the setup for its occurrence was perfect: the sun going down in flames behind the echoing hills, my age just right for contemplating nonexistence from a safe

distance, from two hills away. Later I learned that Tetak Nikola had died as he was straining himself over a chamber pot. Once he'd gone on his horse-drawn carriage to Dragalovci to pick something up at the train station, and I hung on to the carriage, out of his sight, until it was too late for him to turn back and return me to my grandparents'. It took forever to get to the train station, but he let me hold the whip, and the reins too. His horse was blind in one eye, but still had both blinders.

It's an established historical fact no one remembers, let alone cares about, other than maybe those who have devoted their minds and lives to the sport of Ping-Pong, that the 1973 World Table Tennis Championships were held in Sarajevo. The world is all that is the case, that once upon a time was the case. Before the competition—of which I remember nothing—took place, they'd torn down the slummy edifices I'd pass on my way to school and built Hotel Bristol. I'd never seen anything like it: its glass doors were self-opening. I'd step on the mat, and the door would slide open. I'd step off, and the door would close. On the mat, open. Off the mat, closed. Open. Closed. More than once, I was late for school, because I couldn't leave the goddamn door alone until a receptionist chased me away. The most sublime act is to set another before you. I never got enough courage to venture deeper into the hotel, though I once charged in through the self-opening door, showed my middle finger to the receptionist, and charged right out. Later, there would be big buses parked outside the hotel, as big as spaceships, buses that

came from some foreign land full of table-tennising foreigners, marked with big foreign words in bright foreign colors. Everything that happened in us was in itself something else that we didn't know. We would stand at a distance and just watch the buses, and thus saw the drivers turning a latch to close the door from the outside when they wanted to go to the hotel for a drink or rest. Soon we knew where to find the latch and turn it: there would be hydraulic hissing and the wings of the bus gate would part. We never went in, but neither did we bother closing the door. For all I know, it might still be open.

I once spent three days in a coal shack reading old comic books. I was eight or so; we were visiting my uncle Bogdan in Bijeljina. In World War Two, he fought for freedom with Tito's partisans and received a bullet in his lungs. He had six kids, all of them older than me, my favorite his daughter Ljilja. His oldest son was already in college; before he left he'd stored away stacks of his old comic books, tied them with a rope like ancient manuscripts. They lay in the shack untouched, until I discovered and untied them to spend hours perched on a pile of coal, reading, my parents occasionally ordering me to come out and spend time with living human beings. And I'd come out, pouting, and be with the living human beings until they forgot about me, whereupon I'd sneak back into the coal shack to read more. Fortunately, it rained a bit, so they couldn't force me to come out and play. I don't remember any light in there. I recall reading in complete darkness, as if with X-ray eyes. The eternal life belongs to those who live in the present. The only comic I clearly remember took place in medieval Croatia, at the time of Matija Gubec,

the martyred leader of a peasant uprising, who was crowned with a red-hot crown, and then quartered. The main hero, a young man, fought for freedom in his own special way: he prowled at night, scaring the feudal oppressors, dressed in a bodysuit that made him look like a living skeleton. I didn't know it then, but it's clear to me now that the exhilarating pleasure of reading in the coal shack was related to the darkness that surrounded me. I licked my coal-flavored fingers to turn, slowly, the pages. Death is not an event in life, yet it was reading over my shoulder. I could hear the living call my name, but did not respond.

My cousin Ljilja lived with us while in college; she came to Sarajevo to study Russian language and literature. She'd sometimes spontaneously recite Yesenin's poems in Russian, or quote Gorky: "Man—how proud that sounds!" She sang around the house all the time, her favorite a song called "Ryabinushka"—to this day I don't know what a *ryabinushka* is. We would record music from the radio on the Grundig *magnetofon* and then play it back. She sang along with the recording in a clean, airy, high voice, and had an infectious, generous laugh that made me want to amuse her all the time—the thing that invariably made her double over was my impersonation of Jerry Lewis, of his funny walk, say, or the way he ran in circles flapping his arms when happy. Sometimes I did Louis de Funès, a thousand faces a minute. But she also told me scary stories. One winter night, when my parents were away somewhere, my little sister must've been asleep, and there was a blizzard outside, and the world was remote, Ljilja told me about her neighbors in Bijeljina who had once been visited by a creature that was as small

as a child, but had a very old, wrinkled face and long gray hair; the creature woke up the neighbor family and when they screamed, it ran up the coal shack waterspout; the father of the house pursued it and managed to grab its hair; it produced a horrible inhuman scream, and he recoiled and let go; the following day, he died. And there was another story about a pregnant neighbor who dreamt that someone was beating her belly with a shovel handle, and woke up in pain and lost her child. And there was a story about our great-grandfather Živko. He was a mean, arrogant man, well-off enough to spend days drinking and gambling. After one winter night of debauchery, he was returning home on his horse-drawn sleigh when he ran across a couple of terrifying giants. He knew that if he stopped they would destroy him, so he stood up on his sleigh, whipped the horses, and rushed straight at the giants, who had no choice but to step aside and let him through. Many years later, Ljilja left Bijeljina with her ten-month-old son to be a refugee in France. Now she lives near Marseille, and her hair is gray. But where are the giants? Where is the little creature? Where are we? I spend nights worrying about these things.

I'd lock myself in the bathroom and create mixtures of nail polish, aftershave, shampoo, hand cream, and baby powder. I'd light the concoction to see if it'd explode, burn, or at least produce fumes. Or I'd bunch up newspapers and set them on fire in the tub and pour the hopefully explosive mix onto it. Nothing would happen except for the flakes of incinerated paper floating up to the ceiling to get stuck there like dark clouds. There were no fire alarms in our apartment; we lived happily in a firetrap, protected only by common sense, which I frequently suspended to pursue lines of dangerous knowledge. I sought the perfect mix of ingredients, the exact proportions, assuming that the perfection would become evident in the flames or the explosion; it took me a long while to discover that shampoo doesn't burn, or that hand cream is chemically inert. And it wasn't just bathroom alchemy I was interested in. I also stuck nails in sockets and bare copper wires in electric heaters, daring our home, our life, the universe, to either kill me, hurt me, or allow me, at the very least, to discover what could happen. Nothing ever happened, but I didn't

care. You go where the inquiry takes you, you follow the path of knowledge. A new possibility cannot be discovered later. I stuck pins and needles under the skin on my palms, knelt on corn kernels until my knees were bruised and tears crept down my cheeks. I devised recipes for a dish that had never been cooked before, requiring ingredients that could not be found, and I'd prepare it for no one, sometimes starting an oil fire in a pan, and no one would eat it; it was like I was performing a black mass, like looking for a gate into an unknowable world. Later, I searched my parents' closets because I didn't know what their true lives were like, who they really were, other than being the people who made me and raised me. I came up with names and shapes for things that didn't exist until they existed. The world is made of strangers, of odd parts and simple objects that strive to be in a space, to be gathered into a whole, like words, like sentences.

Here we have to enter a linguistic field where we're likely to get lost: while the English word "marble" is a fine one for a glass ball with which children play, the value of *kliker* is far greater to someone like me, whoever we may be. For one thing, the Bosnian word comes from the German *Klicker*, which must be referring to the sound of the glass balls colliding. I happen to find that beautiful: I hear that sound right now. The migration that eventually brought a *kliker* to me started with the Austro-Hungarian occupation force that entered Bosnia in 1878. This is how history works: everything begins far away and long ago, with armies moving, women weeping, children orphaned, burning cities scalding the skies; everything ends in my body, with my writing about it. But the vocabulary I recall being deployed during the *kliker* games I played is hard to source, resembling no particular foreign language, having no other application in Bosnian, working only while playing with *kliker*s, meaningless otherwise:

roša—The hole in the ground where you wanted to put your *kliker* so as to have power to eliminate others.

ponte—Used when demanding of the other players that they throw their *kliker* toward the *roša*, where yours is sitting, empowered, waiting to eliminate them.

hopa—The last player who throws his *kliker* toward the *roša* at the beginning of each game.

predhopa—The player before the last one to throw.

slipci—Dropping two *kliker*s together to resolve a situation in which two *kliker*s find themselves in the *roša*, though that has to be agreed upon before the game.

There is more, but the list is beginning to look pathetic in its oblique nostalgia. I have reasons to believe that this particular vocabulary only made sense within my neighborhood in Sarajevo, that it would have been entirely foreign beyond it. The game is now forgotten, as is the vocabulary, as we all will be and must. I haven't played the game in decades, nor have I seen children playing, in Sarajevo or anywhere else, at least not since before the war. Here and there, I run into people who might be able to recall and recite the vocabulary, as I am, like an ancient poem in a lost language. The word *kliker* is still around, but at present it has no value, because its referent world is obsolete and therefore obscure. What we cannot speak about we must pass over in silence. Yet I remember being close to the ground, focused on my *kliker*, inside which there were many-colored petals, lost in a universe of grass and twigs, intoxicated with the smell and texture of the dirt, its softness perfect for the rolling movement among shards of glass resembling diamonds and pebbles, among determined earthworms dying in the dry soil, and here and there

a trail of ants advancing toward some horizon apparent only to them. It all used to make sense, all of it, which I cannot retrieve now. My friends, some of whom are now dead, followed their own orbit around the *roša*, as if none of them had any other place to go, as if none of them could ever end.

We lived close to the old Sarajevo train station. Steam trains, choo-choo trains, dark gray coal dust coating our clothes hanging out to dry on the balcony. I'd sneak into the station, hop over the rails, and, small enough to do so, crawl under a standing train to pull a handle that released a white (actually, grayish) nimbus of steam. Incredibly, I didn't get burned or crushed by the wheels. It's also possible that I only imagine reemerging from that steam cloud like a boy Aphrodite. Because the Sarajevo station was a dead-end one (yeah, I know), the locomotives had to turn around to pull the train to whatever destination was next. There was therefore a kind of merry-go-round onto which a locomotive would be driven and then revolved to face and move in the opposite direction. The kids from my building would crowd the rails on the empty merry-go-round and a few would push it and we would ride on it, and it would catch speed and we would get dizzy—spinning on it was my first experience of revolution. One day, one of the boys got his foot caught between the rails and the wall and it was crushed.

He'd limp because of it for years, and we would follow him around and mock his off gait, chanting:

Kljukljo kljukljavac
Nabijem te na kurac.

No translation could convey the casual, ruthless meanness of the chant. But what goes around comes around. When he recovered after a while, he'd kick our asses with that same foot. We didn't fear hurt or death. We lived in a world without horizons, just a vast, spinning, ever-expanding space of being. The cloud-covered peak I couldn't even see back then is now rising ground.

There were flies everywhere. There was life on my grandparents' homestead and land wherever you looked, because they had chickens and pigs and cows, and there was shit everywhere, you were always liable to step into it, it would squeeze like toothpaste between your toes, cake your nails, wounds, and scratches, and there were legions of creatures that lived off the refuse of that life, and there were fields and woods and something lived there too, and there was a fetid pond where frogs hatched, we called it a *kalabanja*—a Ukrainian word that had no application or meaning outside my grandparents' domain, outside my family. In all directions, in every hole and corner and in the trees and the grass something was growing, living, dying, rotting, disintegrating, exuding smells. Life was endless in the exact way in which our visual field was endless. Therefore flies were everywhere. They tormented the cows, attacked the hens, dove onto the fresh shit; they bounced off the windowpanes, descended upon my breakfast, drowned in my milk, landed on my nose or knee and rubbed their little legs gleefully while I strived to catch them with a quick

forehand. I was good at it, unless these country flies were just stupid, and I'd catch and kill a lot of them, rip their legs and wings off, put them in a shoeshine can to hear them buzzing in delicious despair, wrap them in newspaper and incinerate them. Once I made a hook from wire and attached it to the end of a thin rope that I tied to a stick. This contraption I used to catch frogs. I'd stick a fly on the wire hook and wave the bait over the *kalabanja*, and the dumb frogs would leap up after the fly. I filled up a cauldron with water and deposited my prey there, the little brown yellow-spotted frogs trying to climb up the slick walls. And then we'd kill them, my sister and I, always looking for new ways and tools to do so: we killed them by throwing them against the wall, and tossing them to each other to smack them with a stick like a baseball; we smashed them with a hammer. There was so much life everywhere, nothing could ever end it; our killing was life, we lived it. My grandparents killed animals all the time: chickens were decapitated, cute lambs' throats cut, pigs carved into pieces, but all that was somehow for the purposes of the continuation of the whole project of life. Death was not a solution to the problem of life, because life was not a problem at all. Now I don't think that. I don't kill anymore, and, though I can make sound ethical claims and establish legitimate reasons for not doing it, I know it's mostly because now I know I shall die and thus I'm afraid. Now I know that the amount of life available is fixed and horribly small, that we could soon run out of it, and I'm running out of it. When my grandparents' dog got old, Tetka Marija's new husband took him to the woods and killed him with an ax blow to the head, smashed his skull just like that, left him there for the flies to feast on.

Only that which is difficult or impossible to remember is worth remembering. Only that which is hard or impossible to say is worth saying. On top of a fire we built from grass and sticks, we put upside down a large cracked pot, the kind used for boiling clothes on the woodstove. When the bottom started glowing with heat, we'd put a snail on it, its foot sizzling as it died in that instant. What I remember best, to the last crack, is that pot: gray, with small ears and a curled rim, its enamel peeling, the crack in its bottom spreading with heat. He who defines personal identity—that is to say, me—as the private possession of some depository of memories is mistaken. Fine. But how have I become who I am now, whoever I may be, which I did not will? Is there anyone else, anywhere, who has the same memories? I remember the fucking sizzle, I can hear it now. The fire too, the burning of the unsayable.

They tore down the old train station, they ripped out the rails, they dismantled the locomotive merry-go-round and whatever else could be dismantled, and after it was all gone, they built a street, and high-rises, and a parking lot, across from which there were stacked shipping containers. I don't know who they may have been, but that's what they did, and that's what happened. There was also a stretch of dirt depression left behind, and it collected water and became a large, shallow puddle. The puddle was littered with debris: bricks, rusted pieces of metal and wood, tires and paint cans. Frogs bred in the puddle, and we played in it, got our feet wet, jumped from one brick island to another, and fell into the muck and water. In the spring it stank, in the summer too; we would hunt for tadpoles, collect them in jars to kill them. In the winter the puddle would freeze, and we would skate on the soles of our boots, tripping over the bricks sticking out. Somehow, it took a while for the water to entirely evaporate. The puddle appeared in our domain and lasted

for a while, leaving no trace when it vanished. No one remembers it, other than me. I'm the only one who can recall the puddle. If I forget, it will vanish again, and it will never have existed. A memory, like a picture, is a model of reality.

Our windows looked out at a railroad factory, named after a liberation war hero, a certain Vaso Miskin, who used to toil there before the war, and who, like many a Communist who went underground to fight the Nazis and Ustashe, had a nom de guerre—Crni, which means Black. The factory was centered around a tall smokestack, and there was also, somewhat inexplicably, a conical bunker with a lightning rod on the top that looked like a concrete mud-and-straw beehive. What was inside it I'll never know. After the train station was destroyed, part of the detritus field was cleared and flattened for the storage of shipping containers made in the factory. They were bright red and empty, and emitted a throat-burning chemical smell, which the adults claimed was poisonous. But nothing could stop us from going there; like the black obelisk in *2001: A Space Odyssey*, the presence of the containers transformed our world. They were stacked on top of each other two at a time, so that the spaces between them were organized into a grid of little alleys. Retching, we walked those alleys, as though exploring a newly created city.

We climbed on top of the containers; we figured out the way to open them and then banged their walls to experience being inside the thunderous echoes and vibrations. Soon the older kids and some sinister grown-ups discovered the space too. They'd gamble and smoke in an open container, they'd make out or even fully fuck inside them. Sometimes the grown-ups let us watch their card games until a guy with a lot of tattoos acquired in Zenica Prison, his time served marked on his forearm, decided we were bad luck and told us to get lost. Sometimes we would find slimy rubber balloons in the containers or the alleys between them, and once we saw a couple coming out of the container city and it was obvious they'd just fucked—they were sweaty, glistening with fuckness, their walk coming from their groins, they didn't look at each other because what had connected them was fully spent. The boy vanished from my mind. The girl's name was Biljana, her hair was curly, and that's all I know about her. I think that was the first time I conceived of a notion, and was therefore scared by it, that people could fuck even if they were not parents. We called the containers *kontejneri*, the word obviously coming from English, but so dissimilar to any Bosnian word that it meant nothing to us. It only referred to those red things stinking of poison inside which the young ones fucked and the guy who had been in Zenica Prison gambled. The containers contained nothing, so to speak, except for what we put in them. Yet all of those possibilities were already contained in their nature. Vaso Miskin Crni—Black—was caught by the Ustashe in 1941 and tortured for two months straight, not giving out any names.

I believe that the first verses I ever wrote were in English. The thing was called "If You Know Her Name," and was fundamentally influenced by rock lyrics—it wasn't a poem, because I planned to add music to it, as soon as I learned to play guitar. It was written down in the notebook calendar where I pasted articles from music magazines, folded to fit, and clippings with the translated lyrics of popular foreign tunes. Initially, I wanted to use the notebook as a journal, file an entry every day of my life, except that a couple of days into the project I realized that my life wasn't particularly interesting, and that the ballpoint pen was spitting ink onto the page. The four poorly rhyming stanzas were tucked in somewhere between "Sympathy for the Devil" ("Please let me introduce myself, I'm a man of wealth and taste") and "A Hard Rain's a-Gonna Fall" ("Oh, where have you been, my blue-eyed son?"), and opened with the immortal line: "If you know her name, tell her I love her." It went on to implore the obscure you to intervene with the her but only if the initial condition of knowing the name was met. The I didn't quite know her

name, or who she was—and neither did I—so that was a bit of a problem. She was, you know, out there somewhere, an imaginable potentiality in an unimaginable world, and in English too. The text was a love statement, but only theoretically, since I had a number of crushes going but no commitment to any of them, nor any emotional or intellectual capacity to declare love to anyone, let alone a girl. I don't think I've ever shown the would-be song to anybody. So you only have my word that it existed: I said let there be word and there were words. Please allow me to introduce myself.

We would take a train to Pazarić, then march up the mountain for a long time. I remember no details of that march, however, except that I was panting and sweating, probably because of the altitude, maybe apprehension. We might have carried our rucksacks, but we didn't carry our skis, yet they would arrive in the Šavnici mountain lodge with our suitcases; outside our purview, someone took care of the things, made the world run. I wasn't a good skier then—I was ten—and I hated mountaineering, which was either walking uphill or walking downhill, neither enjoyable, and I was often cold. In short, I dreaded going to the lodge, but my parents and their friends unanimously decided to send their children away to the Bjelašnica Mountains for the winter break. They had plans for us, the grown-ups, they had hopes of exposing us to the varieties of the world to make us better people. The plan would fail terribly in the long run, not because of us or our parents, but because the world is the totality of facts and not of things, let alone intentions. Still, there I was, cold, up on the goddamn mountain. The children

of my parents' friends were all a bit older and thoroughly ignored me as soon we were out of our parents' sight. I shared a room with seven other boys; as the youngest among them, I was given the worst bed—an upper bunk right by a drafty window with an intricate handiwork of ice on its pane. The oldest boy—a tall eighth-grader—was the room leader. I don't remember his name, but I remember his pubescent reek and square jaw and nocturnal noises, which disgusted me and would inspire even more disgusting experiments on my part. He didn't like me, and neither did the other boys, who quickly figured out the advantages of and rewards for their proximity and obedience to the leader. I was at the bottom of the hierarchy, which wasn't my natural position—in my normal life, in my school, at the foot of the mountain, so to speak, I wasn't trampled upon. The mountain was a different setup; in this high-altitude winter camp there were none of my school or street friends, nobody who liked my jokes, who knew I was smart and cared about what I had to say, who had a crush on me. My roommates soon bullied me, teased me, made fun of the way I skied, of my uncouth wooden skis, of my laced ski boots and peasant-knitted wool mittens. The room leader's job was to make sure it was all clean and neat, so he gave me orders to straighten up the beds or sweep the floor, which I defiantly ignored. When I wasn't forced to ski, I spent time reading, which was self-evidently weird to them, and catching flies, which was even weirder. The flies would hibernate in suspended animation when the lodge was unheated, but they would awake after it warmed up and get all excited as though God had suddenly granted them eternal summer. Supine in my bed, I'd watch the flies bump against the windowpane, buzzing as if cutting through it with a minuscule circular saw, but unable to get out, unaware that they would die if they did. I'd scoop them off the pane with a lightning forehand, one or two at a time—my personal record

was seven—then imprison them in a screw-top jar, wherein they would hopelessly continue to run their tiny saws. What was this biological desire for freedom? There are no grounds for believing that the simplest eventuality will in fact be realized. These flies were slow because they were coming out of hibernation, returning from their afterlife, so to speak. Sometimes I'd pour water over them and drown them all. As flies to wanton boys, so they were to me, I killed them for my sport. That winter, in the two endless weeks in the Šavnici mountain lodge, I caught dozens of revived flies, practically every fly that ever made the mistake of entering my room and pressing its saw against my window. My nickname became Flycatcher (Muholovac), and it could never be interpreted as flattering: my roommates readily and frequently deployed it for debasing me in front of others, for mocking me before the girls. I'd considered my fellow girl mountaineers on our way up the mountain, and kept a hope burning I could spend some time alone with at least one of them, talking. Earning the title of Flycatcher extinguished the feeblest of flames, yet it also provided liberation from the chains of hope; now I could just keep doing what I did, what I liked to do, what needed to be done. The more flies I caught, the more my roommates despised me, not only because flycatching was disgusting, but also because they hated the efficacy of my defiance. I'd neither cry because of their bullying nor strive to be their friend. I just killed the fucking flies and read, devouring chocolate rum bars on which I spent all my money at the cafeteria. It drove those boys crazy that they couldn't touch me, that my resurrected flies and me were beyond their mortal powers; it pissed them off so much that one day they planted an icicle in my bed, which I discovered when I lay down on it. It took me a moment to process the sensory information—a sharp cold against my coccyx—as my roommates giggled, proud of their deed. I jumped off the bunk, shoved aside the boy who zealously stepped in front

of me, went straight to the room where the grown-up counselors were getting tipsy on rum-laced tea, and reported the egregious act. I was angry then, as I am now, not so much because they bullied me or insulted me, but because they didn't know me, couldn't see the real me, could never hear what I had to say. They thought I was stupid and weak because they didn't know what was inside me—back then a warm ocean, now this vast frozen sea—and they didn't care. The world of a happy man is a different one from that of the unhappy man. One of the grown-up counselors, whose face I can presently picture, but whose name has always been unknown to me, summoned the boys to a makeshift interrogation. He demanded the facts of the case from them; he asked them questions. They stared at the floor, occasionally glancing with hatred at me, who faced them all alone; the room leader unwillingly confirmed that an icicle had indeed been planted in the plaintiff's bunk, while insisting he'd known nothing about it. The counselor then dressed down the boys for betraying their fellow mountaineer, thereby betraying the very spirit of the mountain, where everyone should stand for one another and help them in difficulty and adversity. He said, He is—and he pointed his finger at me—your comrade! They had to look at me and what they saw was the opposite of comrade. They didn't dare show how much they hated me, but I knew. I wasn't their comrade, nor would I ever be—they were all rank idiots, committed bullies and masturbators, whereas I was the Flycatcher—but I savored their being humiliated, relished the fact that I was now under higher protection. I might have smirked at them triumphantly. It's also possible that the counselor spotted that smirk, because, after he dismissed them, he kept me for an addendum to his lecture on the mountain ethos and mutual loyalty. You're a snitch, he told me in conclusion. A snitch. But he was wrong. I was nothing but a wanton boy, Flycatcher was my name, and I was going to live forever.

There once was a boy who made a man mad. I came home from school, dropped my bag, and went out to find my friends, my *raja*. But it took me a while to track them down, by which time the teams of seekers and hiders had already been organized and were presently running off to play, past Čika Mustafa's door, into the basement. I managed to catch Vampir, who dismissed my pleas to join them—I was late, nothing could be done—and disappeared into the basement darkness. I stood there untethered and furious about being left out, for I could join neither hiders nor seekers. What would you have done? I ask you. Furiously, I kicked and banged at the hallway door, whereupon someone smacked me from behind, startling me, then continued to rain blows on me as I turned to recognize a neighbor, a man with a wool beige coat and a fedora, a proper, old-fashioned gentleman, who went on to twist my ear and scold me for damaging common property, for being a hooligan, a savage. This does not belong to you, he kept saying. This does not belong to you. This is one of my longest-lasting memories: this does not belong to you.

I see the hallway, I see the front door and its wire-reinforced glass pane, and I see Čika Mustafa's unopening door downstairs, and then the man, with a nose knot and wide face, like badly baked bread, the lapels of his coat, the underside of his hat rim. I never forgot any of it, it was never not available to me or to my recollection. But because I've remembered it so often, I can also replay it as a film scene, complete with a close-up of my red ear and the gentleman's enraged face, and the overhead shot of my cowering to protect myself from the blows. There are, in other words, two versions: memory and imagery. What can be shown cannot be said, which is to say that the versions are mutually exclusive. Still, what is at the core of the recollection, what still hurts me, whatever the shape, is that I couldn't explain to the man what I was doing. It was obvious that this did not belong to me, it was clear I was distraught by being left out, but I could explain none of it. I see a close-up of his distorted hateful face as we speak, right now; I could not explain. For his part, he could not see or care that I was but a child; what he saw was some kind of an enemy to his absolutist ethos; he wouldn't even listen to me; the blows rained; the pain flooded me. This does not belong to you. I could produce no useful words. I could say nothing. It never occurred to me that he shouldn't have beaten a child so severely even if I was actually kicking the door to damage it. It never occurred to me that this belonged to me. I do remember the smell of the hallway: roasted peppers, sauerkraut, generic cigarette smoke; basement dampness; his cologne; my tears; the pain. There are hours in which I'm ashamed of it all; to be sure, there are likewise hours in which I'm ashamed of this shame.

A mob of boys led by Dule advanced down the street in a V formation, like geese. Dule would've been a high schooler had he not dropped out; he was tall, lanky, and stinking of sweat, missing many of his front teeth, wearing pointy shoes, his shirt unbuttoned to the navel, all of which signified that he was tough, a *jalijaš*. The boy mob was on a retributive mission: some of them had been smacked around by an older kid, not from our street, who had cornered them behind Kino Arena; he shook them down for money so that he could go see Bruce Lee in *Enter the Dragon*. This happened centuries ago, during the Kung Fu Era. The shaken boys had hurried to fetch Dule, whose duty, by virtue of being older and toothlessly ruthless, was to protect the little *raja*, the kids from his street, who, as part of the tacit code, would pay their tribute by fetching for him cigarettes or titty magazines. So, there was the advancing Dule unevenly grinning, followed by the excited bloodthirsty boys. The adolescent kid who shook down my *raja* loitered behind the movie theater with a couple of sidekicks, assuming a pose of confidence and

cockiness, much too precocious and unwise. I watched it all from the wall above the street, as if from the bleachers. This is what I remember better than anything: as the kid was mouthing off with his cocky attitude, which would've been enough for us to accept defeat and retreat, Dule just walked up and kicked him in the head with such speed and force that the boy's nose instantly exploded, blood splashing on the pavement before he even hit the ground. Within a moment, the kid was moaning in shock and terror, shrimping up to protect his stomach. Dule kicked him in the head one more time, just to show that he could beat him for as long as he wished, even kill him if he wanted to, then wiped specks of blood off his *jalijaš* shoes, and walked away. He was not mad, he said nothing, for he needed no words to produce a clear meaning. I could see his incisors, like goalposts. The sidekicks vanished like a thought; we watched, horrified and triumphant, because this meant that the kid and his *raja* would never again dare come close to us, let alone bully us—our standing in the hood had just significantly and irreversibly improved. The kid got up and tottered away, leaving a trail of nose blood and a single canvas tennis shoe behind, while we taunted him. The whole thing lasted but a few moments. The brutality was exhilarating, the exactness of the violence awesome, the exquisite skill inspiring, the release of tension so pleasing, the victory so sweet. None of us in the little *raja* could ever simply walk up to another kid and annihilate him without hesitation or mercy; watching Dule do it, we learned that to win a fight you have to be willing to destroy your opponent totally, that you must never consider his body, worry about his pain. Do not start a fight unless you can destroy the opponent; do not start a war unless you're willing to commit genocide. But I was not—am not—willing to destroy others; it is arguably my greatest shortcoming. From my high position, despite everything, I felt sorry for the kid. I witnessed

his blood, his terror, and, worst of all, his dirty tennis shoe. He was going home without that shoe. His parents would ask him, Where is your shoe? and send him out to look for it, and he would know where it was, but he would keep away from it, and would wander instead around his 'hood, crying, his face swollen with contusion, breathing heavily through his broken nose, imagining ways of revenge, knowing all along that it could never take place, that he was comprehensively and forever defeated, that he was nothing but a plain, cowardly bully and not a destroyer, he wasn't strong or fast or ruthless enough to be one, and he'd go back home and tell his parents that he couldn't find his shoe and his father would whip him with a belt, or slam his face against the cupboard, make him go barefoot to school, blood dripping onto his chest. After a while, the wounds would heal, the pain would fade, and he'd find himself destroying some other kid, perhaps even me. This is the way of the world. So many of these pieces I start out by saying, or thinking, I don't remember, I can't recall, and then I proceed to retrieve what happened long ago. The domain of memory is surrounded by a universe of oblivion, humming just outside of what I know. Every time I recall, I take off my shoes, dip my toes into that darkness, cold as the snow melting in the spring, until I can feel nothing.

If you keep at it, if you keep speaking, things might start making sense—the general, and largely false, principle of human life, language, and literature. Marka, Branko, Mirza, and I were members of our elementary school's linguistic team, which competed in the League of Young Linguists. We were good at language, knew the rules and exceptions and doublets and palatalization and assimilations and dialect differences and the intricacies of the accent system in Serbo-Croatian or Croat-Serbian, in *srpskohrvatski ili hrvatskosrpski*, which was the full and official name of the language of our childhood. On the days of competition we would take tests featuring tricky linguistic problems and questions that would be scored; we'd thus accumulate points, and if the sum of our points was greater than what other school teams achieved, we won; which we did, often. We were steadily the best school team in Bosnia and Herzegovina. The teacher who ran our team was an exceptionally tall woman, with a spinster hair bun and a huge scar across her throat, as if someone had tried to slit it at some point in her past, which was, naturally, entirely possi-

ble in the land in which we were born and were learning to live in. She was known as Doka, the hard consonants in her name perfectly matching her angular sternness. After regular school hours, we would have Young Linguists study classes, which sometimes consisted of Doka reading aloud the lists of palatalization exceptions or going through doublets: *prijevoj/prevoj*; *prijevod/prevod*. Like the two youths in a fairy tale, like their two horses and their flowers, each double was a one. Between my fifth and eighth grades, the period during which I was a Young Linguist, I repeatedly tried to escape the linguistic team, because I wanted to play soccer, or just to listen to music and do nothing until there was something fun to do. I didn't want to compete, or to know the linguistic rules better than what was enough to get by in the world where language disguises thought and where I never had to know why or how I was saying what I was saying, grunting, or mumbling, and could still be perfectly understood. But through no effort of my own I was too good a Young Linguist to be released, as were my friends, and we couldn't get out of the perpetual competition. Over time, the recondite language we absorbed acquired a schoolroom smell of waxed floors and sharpened pencils, of the thick dictionary; it had distant corners, loaded with rules and exceptions, all the words separated from their meaning by the facts of their morphology or random inflectional deviancy. The way Doka pronounced the words in her sharp, cutthroat voice turned them into objects unto themselves. There must be objects, if the world is to have an unalterable form. My body felt the weight of those words, and sometimes, fatigued, I'd have a hard time staying awake as Doka read the doublet lists, or revisited morphological rules and palatalization exceptions, and my eyelids would drop and her voice would relocate itself to some distant point deep in the void, and a dream would commence wherein I'd be lost in one way or another, but

then she'd raise her voice or call my name and I'd wake up and look at her, at her bun and slit throat, and I wouldn't comprehend who she was, or what language she was speaking, nor could I recall who I was, why I was there, and she'd look at me icily and it would take me a moment to remember what it was that I was doing there, what the question or the purpose of it all was. Language contained dreams, but it also dropped the rope for me to climb out of oblivion. *Prijevod* and *prevod*, I'd say, both are correct.

I don't even know how to explain this, because I've forgotten so much about it that it barely exists in my mind, except for the fact that there was a time when a young man approached Mirza and me and spun out all kinds of stories in which he was good friends with the players and the coach of the best handball club (Borac Banja Luka) in Bosnia and Yugoslavia. He claimed he used to be a professional handball player, and that he'd quit for some reason, and he kept talking about all those players as if they were his teammates and buddies, and he told us locker room anecdotes and provided plausible details from important games. We were mesmerized, but not so much with the stories as such, which were interesting only if you cared about handball, which we didn't, as with the arbitrariness of his claims—why would anyone come up with something like that unless it was true?—which converted the improbable into the plausible. What convinced us the young man was telling the truth was not the verisimilitude of his presentation but its unflinching totality—he created for us, before us, a world unto itself. Obviously, an

imagined world, however different it may be from the real one, must have something—anything—in common with it. What he told us was a world in which everything was the same as in ours, except for his position in it. He was close to the center of that world, and the fact that he chose a handball club was so arbitrary as to be indisputable. I remember very few details about the young man, other than his face, the peninsula of hair on his forehead, and a cheap scarf he wore. I recall that he became, by way of some ploy or subterfuge, the coach of our class basketball team for a game against another class, and that we believed he knew what he was doing even when he put Zoka, our best shooter and by far the shortest guy, to guard Miro, their center, the tallest boy in the school, nearly twice as big as Zoka. I remember believing that it was a brilliant plan, even if they were crushing us, even if Miro repeatedly received balls thrown over Zoka's head and laid them up with no hindrance whatsoever. It was only in retrospect, days after we lost that game, that I realized the young man was full of shit and had no clue at all. Yet I was full of respect and admiration for his claim to authority, because of his commitment to the ruse and his confidence in its feasibility. He acted in his plot, and we watched him and believed him, because why not? He believed in himself, and we had nothing else to believe in. When he approached us, on the street, in the evening, Mirza and I were just wandering around Grbavica, looking for things to do, pondering the unattainability of girls, or discussing Pink Floyd, or practicing Jerry Lewis moves. Next thing you know, we were privy to the heroes of Borac (which means Fighter), to the best handball players in Yugoslavia and the world, and he knew them all, their little idiosyncrasies, their ambitions and faults, and we could recognize ourselves in their struggle to outdo themselves in an inhospitable world. He knew something we didn't, even if he entirely

made it all up. Only days after the game, in which Miro seemed to have scored all of the points, did I realize that one would always go as far as possible before abandoning the pleasing path of internal logic, thereby making it easier to draw correct inferences from a false proposition. I never fully remembered the young man because he never fully existed except, as it were, as a proposition, and yet I never forgot him, never forgot how I willed his truth, how convinced I was that the secret plan of the shortest boy defending against the tallest one would work, how hungry I was for victory, how much I wanted to be like him.

The only girl who ever talked to me at the mountaineering lodge was Silvija. She was one of the oldest, and the best skier among them all. On the slopes, she was amazing, she went downhill at incredible speed, but when off the skis, she was an albatross, awkward, always sitting uncomfortably because she dealt with too much muscle in her thighs and hips—or so I remember, because why else would she have talked to me? I was known as Flycatcher at the time. Yet she talked to me. I didn't know what to talk about, so, in trying to explain why I turned out so blatantly weird, thereby bragging about it, I told her that I once saw a suicide jump off the top of the building across the street and hit a horizontal antenna sticking out of someone's window, so that pieces of his brain stayed on the antenna grid. Why I made that up on the spot, I do not know, but I did; language and lies came to me as easily as stealing. I thought I could claim that witnessing a suicide gave me access to knowledge not available to others. I explained and justified my weirdness by establishing that I saw and knew things others didn't; it made me

belong to a different world. Death is not an event in life, but I imagined it clumsily within my life to make it seem cool, to rub my thighs with Silvija. It occurred neither to me nor to Silvija that the suicide's head would've broken off the antenna rather than going through it as through a sieve and leaving but remnants, like memories, on the hollow antenna ribs. It's also possible that she saw right through me, saw that Flycatcher was just a lonely wanton boy, so desperate for attention that he was sacrificing suicides without compunction, making up gruesome details just to stay close to her and bask in the thick-thigh warmth of her downhill-skier body, hoping she might appreciate the narrative confidence, the arbitrary exactness of the detail, the poetic instinct, the brains. We sat in silence for a while, facing an ice-patched window against which a solitary, bedazzled fly kept bouncing. Why would he do something like that? was what she asked, but nothing more than that. I have no idea, I said. I cannot begin to imagine.

It was many and many a year ago, the first poem I ever wrote, on a toilet paper sheet folded in the middle: socialist asswipes came in stacks of pages sturdy enough to survive a pen, flush the words into the future. I was hiding in the bathroom, because poetry, like pooping, like imagining skeletons, is shame-bound. There was destruction in it, and objects too: bulldozers, a lonely gray flower, concrete. I had concerns about the future. I made claims about the world, I found things to say. From the other side, my mother called: Still in there? Are you alive? You've been inside a long time. Yes, I said. Leave me alone.

I always stole money: from my mother's wallet, from my father's pockets, from my piggy bank. At first I'd excavate coins through the piggy bank slot with a butter knife, but later I found a way to make the bottom fall out. The piggy bank was not pig-shaped at all; in other words, it was but a bank, which is a problem only in English. I never had enough patience to conceive of a future in which I would buy a ball with the money I saved, let alone a sled. Instead, I'd use the embezzled change to purchase soccer-player stickers, marbles, or chocolate, and, later, records and cigarettes. I wanted everything right now, not later, because eternal life belongs to those who live in the present. When I was a teenager, I'd argue with my mother and she'd say, What do you want? You have everything. And I'd say, I don't have a future! I'd threaten suicide. I wrote poetry, and my mother would sometimes secretly read it, worrying about the darkness in it. There is no such thing as a passage of time, I wrote in one of those poems, and therefore it cannot be saved.

There is, in the pantry, a square of chocolate, as I speak. It's been there for a while. I should rise to go and get it, right now. Suppose I don't. What would it be? A tree crashing in an endless forest? The sound of one finger snapping? A dream I wept in and cannot recall? There, where vermin advance up the underworld walls, chocolate waiting for me, sweet and somewhat bitter, to be, or not, what it could be. When my father returned from abroad, he brought thick tablets of chocolate with foreign hazelnuts, and sometimes with rice. We wanted it, all of it, to devour it, now. He implored us to wait, to stretch the joy through time. We were voracious children, he had to succumb. Don't get used to chocolate, he'd tell us. Don't get used to what is here, now, for only that which could be becomes what is good.

There was a time when my body itched a lot. I could not sleep, that's how much I scratched myself, tossing, writhing, scraping skin off my shins. My mother took me to the doctor, who determined I was allergic to synthetic materials, but even after I started wearing only cotton the itch continued, I kept leaving red furrows on my pale surface. Then the doctor determined that I had scabies, that families of mites had burrowed under my skin and crawled along little tunnels and grew and laid eggs, generations maturing and dying inside me. Every night I had to be washed and coated in a milky substance that smelled like rotten petroleum. After a while, the scabies was gone, all the mites were dead, all of their children as well, or so they told me. When I have an itch that doesn't stop, I remember that time—the milky petroleum smell, my furrowed belly, my mother constantly washing and ironing all of my new cotton clothes, and the mites: small, hungry, desperate to stay alive. I also used to imagine that the universe and the Milky Way and the Sun and the Earth and the humans on it all existed on some

incomprehensibly great living human body, tucked inside, say, the crease valley between the knuckles or in some dead-end tunnel in the ear, or in the butt canyon, and that one day an enormous object, the pinkie nail or one of the large fingers, would come down and crush us all without even knowing. Every time I touched myself, I thought, God revealed Himself in some world.

In my father's suit pockets I found a fifty-kopeck coin he'd brought from Leningrad. I found a condom, Ris No Risk. A pencil with a *matryoshka*-shaped eraser. Flat packs of nylon stockings in my mother's drawer. A box of Biberon baby food on the upper shelf of the cupboard, full of dried maggots, which died of hunger after they ate all the powder and did not live long enough to devour one another. My sister and mother standing in the parental bedroom doorframe as an earthquake swings light fixtures and the walls groan. The petunias flourishing in the balcony boxes, until I crushed them with a soccer ball. A barrel of pickled cabbage in the balcony corner. The flat zinc boxes squeezed between the ribs of the radiator, filled with water to humidify the air in the winter. My mother speaking in a high-pitched voice of friendship into the mouthpiece of the black Bakelite phone. These belong to me. The terrible infection of memories, they don't go away, they float around the bloodstream like loose bacteria until they recognize the presence of others somewhere in the system and then, and then they all turn virulent at the same time and here is the sickness.

Lućano lived in a basement apartment, just across the hall from Dule. Teta Štefica liked to rehash rumors of gruesome murders over coffee at Lućano's mother's, so she'd bring us along. She'd never let us eat anything there, because, she said, the food could be poisoned. Sometimes Lućano would be present too, slurping coffee from a demitasse, glancing at me from below, sucking on his cigarette, the tip of his upper lip creeping up the filter like a leech. His hair was receding even though he was in his late teens. Not so long ago, I realized Putin reminded me of him; they must have come from the same unquestionably Slavic genetic cesspool, Lućano's faux-Italian name notwithstanding. One day, Lućano recruited a bunch of neighborhood boys, including me, to jump the fence and sneak into the construction site across the street from our building. He wanted to show us something, he said. We were nine-year-olds, didn't know any better, and were inclined to obey the older neighborhood boys because they provided protection from roaming bullies, including themselves. What Lućano wanted to show us was his dick, and he did

so by pretending to be explaining to us how dicks worked. He pulled his *kurac* out, got it hard, and stroked it—uncircumcised, thick-veined—thereby introducing us to the age-old craft of jerking off. The Bosnian word for jerking off is *drkanje*, an ugly cluster of consonants perfectly matching Lućano's rapid dick-tugging. He instructed us to try it, so some of my friends dug out their penises from the depths of their prepubescent shorts and imitated Lućano's moves. I didn't do it, I was disgusted. Lućano clearly enjoyed the boys hopelessly milking their tiny dicks, his nipple lip trembling with delectation. A picture is a fact. Still panting, Lućano then introduced to us the idea of *kurton*—the condom—which, he told us, collected the sperm. For what, he didn't say. Situations can be shown, but not given names. He used the word *sluza*—slime—for sperm, and then his dick spurted it as he came. I never told anything to anybody, never discussed what happened on the construction site with any of my friends, let alone my parents. The English language doesn't have any words like *kurac*, *drkanje*, *kurton*, *sluza*, but I could seek no protection in it, as I couldn't speak it then. The limits of my language were the limits of my world; Lućano was enfranchised in it, and I was not. The troubling knowledge he imparted was indelible, absorbed by my body, despite my body, which I recognized could enact it in some terrible future, thus completing the abasement. I didn't know what to do. If it ever came to that, then I could no longer be a boy, and I wanted to be like Jerry Lewis, the man who never grew up. I wanted to seek ways of being that required no shame, just a body that loved itself, untouchable.

First, there was the goofy body: the knock-knees, the monkey-long arms, the jutted jaw, the crossed eyes, the whining and the nasal voices, the rag-doll flopping on the floor. I wanted to be as funny as Jerry Lewis. I'd watch the movies, roar with laughter, then replicate the sketches and pantomimes and facial convolutions for the sole audience of my cousin Ljilja, who would be giddy with mirth. Occasionally Mirza and I would choreograph and practice the routines before performing them in the kitchen, where the area near the stove and sink served as a stage. We would even improvise, sing ridiculous made-up songs, often in made-up English, slip on imaginary banana peels, bend our faces into grimaces of hilarious pain and confusion. Ljilja's shrieks were heaven. The golden standard, the level of silliness we strived to reach, the funniest scene ever, was the one from *The Disorderly Orderly*, where Jerry—our friend—wheels Mrs. Fuzzibee around as she describes her many symptoms with unrelenting hypochondriac relish. Jerry has trouble with his exaggerated empathetic identification: whatever symptoms and health disasters Mrs. Fuzz-

ibee describes, he feels them in all their intensity, which can be seen in the twitching of his face, in the intricate contortions of his rubber body. He takes her suffering far more seriously than she does, because he cannot help but imagine every bit of it: her perforated gallbladder drip-drip-dripping bile into her stomach, where it mixes with acid; her leg broken in four places, her shinbone sticking out; her kidneys, the weakest of anyone's in the hospital. He turns his discomfort into ballet, his awkwardness into art, his idiotic boyishness into hysterical charm. He is a silly ten-year-old boy in a very hairy body, he has aged without growing up, his innocence preserved in his sexlessness, in his total inability to desire other bodies, though he can feel them, feel their pain inside his own. He spends a lot of time in his movies imagining being someone else, pretending to be a conductor, or a chairman of the board, a mambo dancer, and he always performs this imaginary self when no one is looking, at a safe distance from the dull and judging adults, who wear suits but have no imagination and can no longer remember that the body was once a star about to turn into a supernova, that whatever they perceived could be other than what it was. I'd look at myself in the mirror, disregard the incipient pimples to recognize the physical similarities, to identify Jerry Lewis–ness in me, to map that firmament before it exploded. I wanted to be Jerry Lewis because I was Jerry Lewis. After the *drkanje* incident, not only did I avoid Lućano, staying away from any space where he might materialize, but I was also disgusted with the very idea of sex, with the possibility that there would be hair growing in the nooks of my body, that my penis would become a *kurac* and produce *sluza*. My body didn't belong to the world; rather, it was the limit of the world. I found *kurton*s—Ris No Risk, imported from Czechoslovakia, whose sweet, slimy smell I can still recall—in my father's suit pockets and was tormented by the knowledge that my parents did what Lućano talked

about, and in the very same bed where my insomnia frequently placed me. I'd rip open each *kurton* package, unroll the lubricated rubber, and flush it down the toilet, but it wouldn't sink, and I kept flushing it and flushing it, the bobbing balloon refusing to submit. Mirza's legs got hairy before mine; in the sofa in his living room we found magazines featuring pictures of naked women, therefore as distant and mysterious as black holes; we read the sex advice columns and I grew ever more confused. He said to me, You'll like it one day soon, you'll see. But I thought that there was no one greater than Jerry Lewis, that one could use one's body for something better than generating *sluza*. One could, say, make a goofy face, do the knee-knock walk only to flop on the floor and make Ljilja screech with joy. I thought that there was no a priori order of things, that I could stay someone other than myself, other than my incipient *kurac* and hairy legs, that I could continue being Jerry Lewis. He is still alive, you know.

And now, the first love. Her name was Suzana; she transferred to my class in the sixth grade. All the boys were hitting on her; all the girls were jealous. I longed for her from afar, from two desks away. She wasn't particularly interested in any of us, just kept looking beautiful without effort or intent, untouched by our desire or will. Naturally, this was punishable. A boy named Almir came up with a story in which he was walking late at night down the street where Suzana lived when he saw light in her window. He went up to her apartment, found the door ajar, and sneaked in. What he saw shocked him: Suzana was in the company of older boys, she was smoking, and she was kissing one of them. They were liberally using their tongues. Suzana's nocturnal actions predictably appalled the rejected boys and the jealous girls, so a few of them founded the Society for Struggle Against Suzana. This is a true story, but then they all are. Every day, I walked back home from school with a boy named Slobodan and he provided an audience for which I refuted Almir's accusations point by logical point:

1. Why would Almir have walked down the street late at night?
   1.1. Does he not have parents?
   1.2. Would his parents not have discovered he was not in bed?
2. Why would he go up to Suzana's apartment unless he had malicious intent?
   2.1. If his intent was malicious, he must have been looking only for what would confirm his supposition.
   2.2. Why was he so sure that there would be something to bear witness to?
3. Why would the front door be ajar?
   3.1. Where were her parents?
   3.2. Even if they left, would they not have locked the door behind themselves?
4. There is nothing inherently immoral in having older boys over.
   4.1. Smoking is bad, but hardly a mortal sin.
   4.2. Ditto kissing with tongues.

Conclusion: If a proposition is true, the state of affairs exists. If it is not true, it does not exist. Almir was a liar. Suzana was innocent.

Thus I convinced Slobodan that we needed to found the Society for Struggle Against the Society for Struggle Against Suzana. I coated it all in principles, soaked it in the necessity of truth and honesty, so as not to admit that I had a painful crush on her, as if he couldn't tell, that in the darkness of my parents' bedroom—a temporary relocation, because I couldn't sleep—I cried and sang, Yesterday, all my troubles seemed so far away, that I was experimenting, as they say, with poetry while envisioning being with

her. The struggle ended too soon, however, before Suzana noticed my logical heroism. It didn't take long for her to become friends with all the girls, dating none of the boys. She never responded to my pinings, which lasted until they stopped. My first love ended as all of the subsequent ones would—in mutual indifference. But there was a time, it was June, when I strolled by the Miljacka with her and her never-leaving-us-alone girlfriend who wore thick glasses. I was so awkwardly ecstatic that I descended all the way to the riverbank to pick a poppy for her. This wasn't what boys did for girls at that age, at that time, in that city, in that unkind universe. This I remember: the poppy had no smell, yet she smelled it when I handed it to her. What if I'd given her a fragrant rose? What was it that she inhaled? There are, indeed, things that cannot be put into words. The struggle never ends. Why she had to go, I don't know.

It was a delightfully bright early-summer morning. The last patches of fog crept up Trebević to dissipate in the sun. The sky beyond Sedam šuma was endlessly blue. I was barefoot on the balcony, watching morning-shift kids on their way to school, wearing the required blue jackets, girls with pigtails, boys' hair nicely combed, holding their parents' hands or not. And the parents: mothers clutching their boxy purses, fathers their briefcases, undercaffeinated pace, some smoking. Cigarette in hand, a woman unlocked the door of the transportation company office on the bottom floor of the building across the street. The company's name, Špedicija, and its circular symbol were displayed large in the window. I could soon see the woman distributing coffee from a *džezva* into a couple of demitasses, offering one to a man sitting across the desk from her. They smoked, slurping coffee simultaneously, an act of shared intimacy necessary before any transaction. I picked up a rock from a balcony flower pot and hurled it full force toward Špedicija and it smacked against the bull's-eye of its symbol and the window cracked. It was a perfect

throw—I'll never have a better one. I slipped back inside, moved to my parents' bedroom to surreptitiously watch the woman and the man run out onto the street to examine the crack and then look around for the culprit. They couldn't see me. The man ran up and down the street a bit, in a choreography of enraged helplessness, until they both looked up, first toward me—except they couldn't see me—and then higher up, toward the sky, as if that might be where the culprit was. They never figured out who did it; they kept looking toward the heavens until they gave up. The crack remained; they never bothered to replace the window. Whenever I considered the crack, resembling a spindly spider, its torso marked by the point of impact and a cluster of concentric circles around it, I'd think, I did this. This belongs to me. And I'd think, Nobody knows I did this. Many years later, during the siege, the building across the street was subject to a rocket attack, in the course of which all of its windows, including Špedicija's, were blown out. The freedom of the will is in the impossibility of knowing actions that still lie in the future.

It occurred to me just yesterday that I'd been wrong about everything, entirely wrong from the very beginning, though I can't tell what the actual beginning might have been, and of what. It's not that all my individual decisions were wrong, or that the sum of the wrong ones exceeded the sum of the good ones. What I realized was that the very first step was wrong and so were all the subsequent ones—indeed, all the consequent ones. At some indeterminate moment deeply buried in my nebulous past, I deemed a false proposition as true and made the incorrect decision. I cannot remember what it was, I cannot identify the moment when it all went wrong. It's reasonable to assume it was related or relevant to how I conceptualized the world or my life, that at some moment I thought, This is this, and that is that, and this is how I'm going to be and do things, and I made a commitment to that decision, and it was a fundamental mistake. Which is to say that the prime moment could've been any moment, even when the proposition and the decision seemed correct, any mo-

ment when I believed that this belonged to me, that there was a connection between the will and the world. All of the decisions I used to consider right are now profoundly suspicious. My confidence, now irreversibly expired, was rooted for far too long in my being oblivious to the fact that the original proposition was catastrophically erroneous. This is why I now appreciate all those obviously wrong decisions, all of those instances that are now devoid of the insidious ambiguity of indisputable correctness. All that happens and is the case is accidental, and I should've known it at the beginning, from the beginning, at any moment thereafter. There was the time my mother dressed me up for a visit to Teta Jozefina, and sent me out to wait in the hallway at the entrance to our building while she was getting ready, fluffing up and spraying her hair or whatnot. I waited for her, boredom bubbling up, and then I decided to lean over the railing as far as I could while holding on to the bars, just to see if I could balance and seesaw my body in that position. I hadn't anticipated gravity, however; I could not see that I would just flip over, so that was exactly what happened: I flipped over my head and found myself hanging three meters above the basement floor, my wrists twisted, my fingers slipping, too weak to hold on to the bars, the void yawning below me. I cried for help—Čika Mustafa's door was right there and I hoped he was home—and I wailed in panic. I was fully aware at that time, and at any time thereafter, that I shouldn't have tried to balance my body on the railing, that the decision was self-evidently and totally wrong. Because it was so, it can't have been based on the obscure, unimpeachable prime proposition wherein I conceptualized the world entirely incorrectly, and therefore determined the wrong direction for my life. The decision to lean over the railing was so obviously and instantly wrong that it cannot have been the original incorrect one, as that one must've seemed

correct at the time. I fell, I tore my pants, I bloodied my knees—the fall was what it was and nothing else. There was only pain, a proposition that always has sense, that has greater value than all the others. My mother heard me wail and ran down from the third floor to find me hurt and broken just outside Čika Mustafa's door. He wasn't home.

Mirza had a portable record player—a *gramofon*—that was smaller than an LP. Its lid was the speaker, and it sounded like a transistor radio, like a transmission from a distant planet where minute creatures sang through their monstrously tiny noses. Everything was smaller back then, including sounds and voices. Nevertheless, we would plot ways to buy records. I'd keep the change after being deployed to fetch bread and milk from the supermarket, or I'd steal money from my piggy bank, or I'd honestly pilfer my mother's wallet while she was innocently afternoon-napping. For Mirza, funding record-shopping required sacrifice: in the morning, before going to work, his parents would leave the exact amount for purchasing one loaf of bread, one liter of milk, and four individual containers of yogurt, one per family member; he'd forgo his yogurt and keep the money. Whenever either of us bought a record, we listened to it together. My first 45 was Osibisa's "Sunshine Day." Everybody do what you're doing, smile will bring a sunshine day. My first LP was by 5000 Volts, because we'd heard "Doctor Kiss Kiss,"

their big hit, on the radio. Mama, I'm Doctor Kiss Kiss. I'm gonna weave my lovin' spell on you. Time and again we waited for the woman singing to reach the five-thousand-volt moment when—right after the line, You'll sow the seed and hope some little girl will play your game—she screamed. We were confused and titillated by the lyric because (a) we didn't know English all that well; (b) seed? game?; (c) would they really talk about it that way? Things were what they were, or not, it wasn't easy for us to tell. The scream was enough, though, to keep us coming back to the record, it just drove us crazy, we'd never heard anything like that. Our parents and teachers had screamed at us, and there were horror-movie screams, and we ourselves had screamed in pain, but this was something else. We knew nothing, just pursued leads into the world, where, for some reason, Doctor Kiss Kiss sowed seed and women screamed. A gramophone record, the musical idea, the written notes, and the sound waves, all stood to one another in the same internal relation of depicting that holds between language and the world. Later, Mirza saved enough yogurt money to invest it in *The Dark Side of the Moon*. Now, that was a long way from 5000 Volts, what with its sequenced synthesizer sounds and clocks ticking, bells ringing, lunatics laughing, the woman in "The Great Gig in the Sky" even wailing on the verge of a scream. Of course, we didn't understand what it was about, what claims the lyrics made, when there were lyrics at all. We speculated and hoped the album was rooted in some kind of spectacularly disturbed mental state—which, of course, we liked, as there is nothing boys value more than insanity—but we understood nothing. Still, like two youths in a fairy tale, we were totally present in what we couldn't understand, precisely because we couldn't understand it. Look around yourself, hear what you can. What is it? Where are we? It is not how things are in the world that is mystical, but that it exists. Never again would I

hear music with such troubling clarity. One not only wants to understand, but also quite as certainly not to understand. I understand too much now, meanings are locked, it empties me. And then we went to the third-floor music section of Sarajka, the big, brand-new department store, and I talked Mirza into buying the first album by the Clash, miraculously released in socialist Yugoslavia. This sequence of memories has its own temporal organization: 5000 Volts → Pink Floyd → the Clash, which is to say that I cannot exactly date any of those purchases—it all happened sometime between 1974 and 1977. I do know that Mirza got mad at me for the recommendation. He didn't like the Clash, the only track he enjoyed was "Police and Thieves." The record was deformed by heat or neglect and undulated on Mirza's *gramofon*, the sound wavering. Police and thieves in the street, oh yeah, scaring the nation with their guns and ammunition. I liked it fine, even if I was confused. I'm so bored with the USA. But what can I do? I'd never been in America, but it was incomprehensible to me how anyone could be bored with the USA, the land of bottomless, murderous entertainment the glimpses of which I caught on TV in the shape of *Kojak* and *McCloud*. It was then, I know now, that our friendship started to come apart—Mirza loyally followed the Pink Floyd trajectory, I went beyond the Clash horizon, and soon XTC was my favorite band, and later I ended up listening to all kinds of scraping. Little by little Mirza and I had less and less to talk about, stopped listening to music together, and by high school were mere acquaintances. I trust he is still alive and well. First you accumulate not understanding, then information, then knowledge, then—rarely—understanding, then your mind dies, then you die. I fought the law, and the law won.

We called it going to town, and it was a big operation. I'd have to cross a big street by myself, get on the tramway by myself, pay for the fare by myself. It was a journey, crossing borders, traversing a different space to get to where I would be out of place. To know home, you have to leave it; to love it, it has to be beyond your reach. When I disembarked at Skenderija, there would be *grad* where there were stores, and cafés, and people worked, a different sort of feral kid loose on the streets, and I'd walk to the Sarajka, an ugly-blue department store, browse the record selection on the second floor, which meant looking at the records from across the counter, as the clerks let no one near those shelves. If I followed Titova Street and walked up Vaso Miskin Street toward Baščaršija, at the very border where the Austro-Hungarian part of town ended and the Turkish part began, there was the Jugoton record store. Sometimes I'd stop at some other, lesser stores along the way to see if by chance they had something I was interested in, but I'd never get anything before reaching Jugoton, the terminal stop, where I bought most of

my records. The store was around a corner from a pretty mosque, down the street from the Egipat sweetshop, across from the Komision, where you could sometimes find expensive imported denim and near which contraband guys (*šverceri*) peddled tube socks and Levi's jeans, and, also, *Never Mind the Bollocks, Here's the Sex Pistols.* A record in hand, I'd continue into Čaršija, where I'd have *ćevapčići*, and then have halvah or ice cream at Egipat, or a piece of cake at Ramis, and wash it down with *boza*, a fermented corn drink. Then I'd take the streetcar back home. I'd go to town after school and be home before my parents returned from work, and the ritualistic journey would be completed by my getting the record out of the sleeve and putting it on my *gramofon* to listen to it, reading the liner notes or the lyrics, my fingers still greasy from the Baščaršija food. I'd be different after every journey, with every record. I accumulated more myselves with each trip; each record promised something I could not imagine yet. I once bought *Modern Music*, an album by Be Bop Deluxe, which was pretty obscure then, as it still is. I was longing for a life unlived, which I also lived. If we take eternity to mean not infinite temporal duration but timelessness, then eternal life belongs to those who live in the present. Will you receive these programs deep within your soul?

These days, I find it strange that when I sleep and have to pee, my dream gets stuck in a kind of loop, unable to get beyond a certain point, keeps bumping into an invisible obstacle. Say I'm about to go through a door, in my dream, but I keep returning to the bottom of the stairs that lead to the door; or I'm about to ask a question the answer to which will take me elsewhere, to a different space, to a world that holds a vague promise of a better way of being, but I cannot formulate the question, cannot find the words, cannot speak—and it's this cycle of helplessness (trying, almost succeeding, returning to the starting position, trying, almost succeeding, etc.) that wakes me up. Somehow, while dreaming, I understand that nothing will be solved until I urinate, and my subconscious is in direct communication with my bladder. I suspect that the body in need refuses to participate in indulgent dream creation, it blocks the fanciful narrative until the urgent need is addressed. Could it then be that the same thing happens in my memory, that the mind can come close to retrieving a bone buried deep in the sand of oblivion, but then

the body blocks the expedition, because it needs something, some kind of relief or cleansing? So that when I try to remember the smell of Suzana and I come close, when I assemble the whole sequence of her strolling gracefully as I clamber up the riverbank with an odorless poppy, when I almost reach her and come close to her skinny neck and her summer dress, just as my nostrils expand ready to inhale, the body—this fucking dying body—blocks the retrieval of her smell. But what does it need really, the body? What does it want, except to live, to live on? I never know, it never tells me exactly when I'm awake. If I could please it by living forever, maybe it would let me remember everything. The solution to the problem of life, to the problem of forgetting, remembering.

And then there was a time when I was an insomniac. I'd wake up in the middle of the night and not be able to fall back asleep and would slide into worrying about how I'd get through the day with so little sleep, and the worry would keep me up, and then I'd go and sneak into my parents' bedroom and wedge myself between them, listening to the hum of their bodies. I was never afraid of anything, merely worried about everything, and I'd toss and turn, keeping my mother awake while my father snored. By the time I'd start dreaming, she'd be unable to sleep and would get up, startling me out of my dream. My father would sleep through all that, entirely oblivious to my presence and the related crisis in his bed. But my mother would be exhausted the following day, so she demanded that I stay in my room even if I couldn't sleep, and I promised I would, but the nightly insomniac despair would overwhelm me again so much that I'd get up anyway and prowl around the house, hoping to wake my mother up. The empty bathroom, the growling of the radiators, the rattle of the glass pane on the living room

door, the grumbling of the water heater, the smell in the kitchen of whatever Mama had prepared for the following day, and the night-city lights pouring through my parents' bedroom windows onto the mounds of their bodies under the covers. I'd stand in the doorway watching them, waiting for my mother to stir, to notice my waking shadow. If only, I would think, day never came, I'd have nothing to worry about. If the night is endless, insomnia is no problem. She took me to a child psychologist. I sat outside in the waiting area, while she went into the psychologist's office to talk about me and my sleeplessness. The other kid waiting seemed a little unhinged to me, blinking rapidly, his parents too. When it was my turn, the child psychologist observed me as I fitted triangles and circles into holes, matched stupid pictures, asked me questions. Questions. Answers. I told her that I liked to listen to 5000 Volts and Pink Floyd. She'd never heard of 5000 Volts, her son listened to Pink Floyd. She prescribed some kind of vitamin cocktail I had to drink before sleep, pink it was, with a punishing medicinal taste. I started sleeping in my bed, because I hated drinking that potion, which may have been, only later would I understand, the child psychologist's intention all along. But I missed the night and the shadows and noises, longed to insert myself into the warmth between my parents. I, as I write this, am only a certainty that seeks out the words that are most apt to compel your attention, but back then I was just my parents' boy. The dream of an endless night.

In the kitchen, a lamp radio, with a Donald Duck sticker, and the round speakers behind a jute canvas. In the toilet, on the pipe connecting the flusher to the bowl, a water-stain silhouette of a caveman Lenin who had not cut his hair and beard since the Revolution. In my room, dried snot pasted against the underside of my bed when I was too lazy to fetch a handkerchief. In my parents' bedroom, their wedding picture: my mother wears heels, my father looks dapper, hanging between them what looks like a large moon, but is in fact a circle featuring, like a coin, Tito's profile in relief. A samovar, wilted flowers, dust in the carpet in the living room, where we'd come to be and love. If the world is to have an unalterable form, there must be objects, and rooms.

I was once in the car with my father as he was recollecting the time Tetka Juljka had been married off to a cruel Ukrainian man who lived in Leicester, England. This had happened in the fifties, before I was born. My father recalled how his sister had left home only with the picture of her future husband, whom she'd never met, and the meager money he'd sent, five pounds sterling, and a small suitcase of clothes donated to her in sacrifice by her sisters, and the weight of sorrow in her soul. She would never come back home, only visit it. He who defines personal identity as the private possession of some depository of memories is mistaken. When the time to leave arrived, she cried all the way to the Dragalovci train station; most of the family went along to see her off, her sisters and brothers, my father included, and they all waved at the back of the steam train that would take her away, to Leicester, England, where she would never learn English and would be miserable for the rest of her life, returning to Bosnia to see her family only twice. The first time she came, I was a toddler, and I can only recall the pictures of me and her—she

was dressed like the Queen, with a pillbox hat and a boxy purse. The second time she came was in the eighties, when my sister and I were teenagers, and we checked her earlobes to see if they looked like everyone else's in our family, and they did, she was indeed one of us. But the story of her departure and returns is not what I recall, it is what I tell; the story had been born and lived outside that moment in the car with my father. What I remember is his face, his sunglasses, the tremolo of his voice, the sprigs of hair sprouting from his clean-shavenness. The story I'm telling here is what I imagined while my father was remembering, while I was looking at his face, while a tear rolled down from under his sunglasses. I remember that tear, although, to tell the truth, the tear may have rolled at some other time, only for me to add it to the scene I'm recollecting here. What I also remember, and what could also have been edited into the memory of my father's recollection of the Tetka Juljka story, is his asking, How is it that I can recall something that happened forty years ago and I can't recall what I did yesterday? It's a reasonable, if difficult, question. I had no answer to it, whenever it may have been asked. But now I can say: I do remember what I did yesterday. What I did yesterday was remember what happened forty years before.

Please imagine, then, for the sake of argument, that there is in our souls a block of wax, in one case larger, in another smaller, in one case purer, in another more impure and harder, in some cases softer. Please assume, furthermore, the wax might come from a hive my father cared for, avoiding harm while suicidal bee patrols went up his arm. He would kill them, yet the stings stayed, his forearm soon itching to the point of pain. Let us, then, say this is the gift of Memory, the mother of the Muses, and that whenever we wish to remember anything we think or see in our own minds, we hold this wax under the perceptions and thoughts, imprint them upon it. Let us, also, assert that Tata would brush the bees off the frame weighted with honey he would thereafter extract from the wax. I would drip that honey on my daily bread. Sticky fingers, viscous life, all that. Whatever is imprinted we remember and know as long as its image lasts, but whatever is rubbed out or cannot be imprinted we forget and do not know. My father learned from his father, who was once stung by two hundred bees. It was summer, apples

rounding on the trees. He lived to die oblivious to where, who, he was. If the exercise of the will does alter the world, it alters only its limits, none of the facts. The world of a happy man is different from that of the unhappy one. It must wax and wane as a whole. I know that the day before Tata's grandfather departed, his son carried him to his hives. Apples falling, he listened to the droning, saw the bees return from the flowered fields, home. He cried, then was in a coffin, dead. Above his head, wax candles, melting.

Here's a confession: for many years—as a child, as an adolescent, as a young man—I'd pick my nose while reading on my bed and then stick the snot to its underside. Laziness, obviously, played a crucial role; I had no handkerchief, I didn't feel like getting up, and I had to get rid of the snot while being reluctant to flick it into the void of my room. At least once, I crawled under the bed, probably to dust the floor, and saw those tiny stalactites of snot, some of them no doubt from years before, and I was proud of my achievement. For if my task as a human being is to leave traces in this world, to mark it as my domain, I had the snot stuck right there, to the underside of my dream vessel. Form is the possibility of structure. A technology exists now that could extract my genetic code from my snot and reconstruct me from a DNA scratch whenever I'm dead and vanished, though I can't think of a reason to do something like that. The bed is gone, as are the stalactites, as is the boy who found pleasure and trust in sticking to what is close, to what is home.

There was cowboy fiction, and science fiction, and romance fiction, and crime fiction, except the word "fiction" does not exist in Bosnian. Whatever could be described at all could be other than it is. We called all that fiction *pisani romani*, which translates as written novels, as distinct from *crtani romani*, translating as drawn novels. Pulp fiction was sold at newsstands, and it was lesser than comic books because there were no pictures. Whatever we could see could be other than it was. In the summer, I read science and crime fiction; sometimes I was consumed by cowboy adventures. I even read romance novels. Someone in my *raja* would steal money and buy a written novel, then pass it around, until it was missing pages, torn in neglect, the remaining ones spotted with grease stains, as we all read while eating. The paper tore easily, it smelled like soured shit. The pulp of written novels was good for starting fires, it burned fast. Sometimes we rolled tobacco in it, smoked the story fragments. A cowboy rode into a small Western town where everyone knew that the cattle rancher was the only boss because his evil son could kill

and rape with impunity. A detective defied a crime syndicate, and the police, and the powerful rich man, and would repeatedly lay shapely babes while wisecracking. A fetching lady looked into the mirror before meeting the handsome tycoon and was happy with what she saw: her seductive green eyes, her shapely body in a tight dress, her ripe lips. When all the computers in the universe were connected, the scientists asked the system, "Is there God?" and the system replied, "Now there is." The pleasure was always in the excessive familiarity of the absurd plots, which therefore required to be devoured. The faster you went through the novel, the less you cared about the nonsense—not a bad recipe for a bearable life. I'd read them in less than an hour. There was a series of novels whose main hero was Lun, *kralj ponoći*—Lun, the King of Midnight. Those could easily be read in half an hour.

Lun i eksodus—Lun and the Exodus
Lun i družina sudnjeg dana—Lun and the Judgment Day Crew
Lun i kradljivci prošlosti—Lun and the Robbers of the Past
Lun leti u pakao—Lun Flies to Hell

Lun was an orphan raised and educated by a sinister organization that wanted to create a perfect criminal. But when he discovered that the same organization killed his father, he dedicated his life to fighting crime all over the globe. Lun spoke many languages. Lun was an expert in technology and science, capable of constructing unimaginable contraptions. Lun was a master of disguise, hypnosis, and martial arts. He was uncatchable, unkillable, and therefore immortal. The subject did not belong to the world; rather, he was the limit of the world. I don't remember any of the plots because I read that shit like there was no tomorrow.

The one plot I remember featured Lun being defeated and outwitted by a mysterious stranger, who at the crucial moment stripped off, like a costume, his entire body, out of which Lun himself hatched and proceeded to defeat, once again, all of his enemies. *Lunova tajna misija. Lun's Secret Mission.* I found the plot twist to be insane, but could never stop thinking about it. Where in the world is a metaphysical subject to be found? Lun, the greatest spy and the loneliest man of all time, he could be inside someone else, be someone else, while being himself, invisible, secret. Who was it, then, that lived inside me? And when was he going to hatch out? Who would want to read about it? I, the King of Midnight. I and the Exodus. I and the Judgment Day Crew. I and the Robbers of the Past. I Fly to Hell.

My mother bought books. She bought shelf-fillers, and the collected works of Erich Maria Remarque in ten volumes, which, for some reason, every middle-class family in Sarajevo owned and which no one ever read beyond the first volume, *All Quiet on the Western Front*; and thick Disney books that contained the retellings with pictures (a picture is a model of reality) of the usual tales—my favorite, *The Sword in the Stone*; and an encyclopedia of the world, which I'd flip through in disregard of the alphabetical order and collect the succinct information on, say, the Eiffel Tower (the tower is 324 meters tall, the tallest structure in Paris); and military histories of World War Two, which I devoured, featuring battlefield maps where the black arrows represented the Germans, and the red arrows the Soviets, and they would rush at each other in an abstract landscape devoid of people and death (in a picture objects have the elements of the picture corresponding to them); and paperbacks of *One Hundred Years of Solitude*, *The Joke*, and *Fear of Flying*, which I wasn't allowed to read but flipped through

anyway and couldn't grasp. She also had *The Book for Every Woman*, which contained—oh, I don't know—tips and advice on good ways of being a woman. I read it all: recipes, crocheting patterns, household solutions (Have flies in your house? They are attracted to bright lights, etc.), and a section on sex and reproduction, where I discovered a lot of curious images and explanations. There was a side-view projection of a dangling penis and testicles, and, more important, a lily-shaped top view of the female reproductive apparatus: vagina, womb, ovaries. As far as I remember, clitoris wasn't part of that representation. I could not picture the whole structure fitting into an actual body, the angles confused me. For the longest time I thought that the vagina was perpendicular to the spine, a kind of a socket somewhere below the belly button where—I'd heard—a penis would be inserted, for which it would have to be—it stood to reason—perfectly horizontal. My early erections caused great distress, because my penis rose at an angle, and I could not imagine how it could be plugged into the socket the way nature and *The Book for Every Woman* intended. I worried that I'd have to hang a weight on my penis to make it grow horizontally, although there was no pressing need, as I was yet to reach a point where I would dare to declare to a girl that I liked her, beyond which horizon the next mountain I would have to climb was touching her hand. The wild and unexplored regions of genitalia were several steep mountain chains ahead of me. *The Book for Every Woman* only cursorily mentioned masturbation, the troubling joys of which I read about in a teenage music-and-sports magazine called *Zdravo!* (*Hello!*), where a letter from a young male reader, no doubt fabricated by the perverse editors, asked about the potential perils of self-abuse. The answer explained in detail how it worked—we picture facts to ourselves, so it was practically a manual—and suggested there was nothing particularly wrong with it, which

was heartening to me, as the whole endeavor of genital pleasure had been sullied by Lućano's *kurac.* But there was a small note of caution in the music-and-sports magazine: since semen is basically protein, ejaculation could lead to dizziness due to protein shortage or something, and those new to it—that is, those like me—had been known to pass out upon reaching, you know, the peak. I was eleven, maybe twelve, and I instantly applied myself to protein production; there was confusing pleasure, there was dizziness, but I did not pass out. What I ejaculated looked much like Lućano's *sluza*, except it was semen. *The Book for Every Woman* featured a rendition of egg fertilization where semen, consisting of spermatozoids—spitting images of the puddle tadpoles—played a role. It was all terribly daunting—I had a body I didn't know how to think about, let alone how to talk about—but I knew that what could be described could happen too. What was also described in *The Book for Every Woman* were sexually transmitted diseases. I read about gonorrhea (painful urination; yellow or green discharge), and about crabs (itching; nits in the pubic hair), and about syphilis (sores, rash). Syphilis scared me most, not least because I'd watched a Czechoslovakian movie in which the main character was a promiscuous-cum-rapacious officer of the Austro-Hungarian Army who contracted syphilis, which eventually led to his nose falling off, and also dementia. I remember him tottering around noseless, going crazy, rotting inside and out. So that when I discovered a sore on my penis, accompanied by a rash on my limbs, I consulted *The Book for Every Woman* as per standard procedure, and became convinced I'd contracted syphilis. My trepidation wasn't at all diminished by the fact that I couldn't begin to imagine ways in which I could've been infected in a life absolutely devoid of sexual experiences. I hid in the bathroom, my tears soaking the paragraphs on STDs in *The Book* as I struggled to imagine a way to break the

news to my parents: their firstborn son was destined to a syphilictic life of rot and dementia without ever having even held a girl's hand. I looked for salvation, or at least a remedy in *The Book*, which suggested antibiotics, except that they worked only if taken immediately after the infection, and I had no idea how long I'd been infected. Moreover, antibiotics were certainly not going to alleviate the humiliation and stigma that came with being an STD survivor, the best-case scenario. When mixed with vinegar and water, honey can remove worms and parasites in your body, I discovered in the course of desperately browsing *The Book*, but there was no mention of how to cure syphilis. Eventually, as there are things that cannot be put into words, I had to make my rash manifest to my mother. She took me to a doctor. It turned out it wasn't syphilis at all; the doctor told me I ought to wash myself more often, now that I was entering puberty. Thereafter I pursued sexual knowledge in the pages of *Zdravo!* (*Hello!*), while *The Book* provided mainly household advice. A flattened pillow? Put it in the sun for thirty minutes. The sun will plump it up.